The Rudd Government

Australian Commonwealth Administration 2007–2010

The Rudd Government

Australian Commonwealth Administration 2007–2010

Edited by Chris Aulich and Mark Evans

THE AUSTRALIAN NATIONAL UNIVERSITY

E PRESS

ANZSOG Institute for
Governance
at the University of Canberra

ANU E PRESS

ANZSOG Institute for
Governance
at the University of Canberra

Published by ANU E Press
The Australian National University
Canberra ACT 0200, Australia
Email: anuepress@anu.edu.au
This title is also available online at: http://epress.anu.edu.au/rudd_citation.html

National Library of Australia Cataloguing-in-Publication entry

Title: The Rudd government : Australian Commonwealth administration
             2007 - 2010 / edited by Chris Aulich and Mark Evans.

ISBN: 9781921862069 (pbk.) 9781921862076 (eBook)

Notes: Includes bibliographical references.

Subjects: Rudd, Kevin, 1957---Political and social views.
             Australian Labor Party.
             Public administration--Australia.
             Australia--Politics and government--2001-

Other Authors/Contributors:
             Aulich, Chris, 1947-
             Evans, Mark Dr.

Dewey Number: 324.29407

Cover design by ANU E Press

Illustrations by David Pope, The Canberra Times

Printed by Griffin Press

Funding for this monograph series has been provided by the Australia and New
Zealand School of Government Research Program.

Contents

Part IV. Rudd as Prime Minister

Acknowledgments

This tenth volume in the Australian Commonwealth Administration series has been one of the most difficult to assemble, primarily because the period of review has seen major oscillations and change in the fortunes of many key figures and key issues. The book was initiated in early 2009 when the Rudd government dominated both the political landscape and the opinion polls, and was completed for publication shortly after the 2010 election when Rudd had been replaced as Prime Minister and Labor had narrowly been returned to form a minority government.

We are well aware that the contributing authors have had to make frequent adjustments to their contributions and to their line of argument to capture the turbulence of the period; in fact, our first working title was *Rudd's First Government*! The editors are grateful for their flexibility and their resilience and also for their capacity to deliver a manuscript so soon after the election result. Our thanks go to them and to the staff in the many public agencies who have provided data to support their research.

We are especially grateful to two colleagues from the ANZSOG Institute for Governance at the University of Canberra who have lent their very different expertise as 'consultant' editors: Professor Roger Wettenhall and Professorial Fellow Bill Burmester. Roger has contributed to all 10 volumes in the series and brings prodigious academic expertise and experience to the task. As a recently retired senior public servant, Bill has typically offered a complementary and valued perspective to that of our academic colleagues. We also wish to acknowledge the contributions of Helen Ayres and Anna Price to Chapter 9.

We wish to express our thanks to Jan Borrie for her exceptionally thorough copyediting and to John Butcher from The Australian National University for his oversight of the publication arrangements with ANU E Press. Finally, we are pleased that award-winning cartoonist David Pope from *The Canberra Times* has offered his cartoons to illustrate each chapter. David has a growing reputation as a fearless cartoonist and the selection in this volume gives an excellent insight to his talent.

This volume is the first e-publication in the series and we invite readers to take the opportunity to download individual chapters and, even, the entire volume. We want our work to be accessible intellectually and hope that this publishing venture will make it accessible physically as well.

Chris Aulich
Mark Evans
ANZSOG Institute for Governance, University of Canberra
November 2010

Contributors

Geoff Anderson is a senior lecturer in the Department of Politics and Public Policy at the Flinders University of South Australia.

Chris Aulich is a Professor at the ANZSOG Institute for Governance, University of Canberra.

Andrew Carr is a PhD student at the University of Canberra.

Richard Denniss is the Executive Director of the Australia Institute.

Harry Evans was Clerk of the Senate from 1988 to 2009.

Mark Evans is Director of the ANZSOG Institute for Governance at the University of Canberra.

Paul Fawcett is a lecturer, Department of Government and International Relations, University of Sydney.

Anne Garnett is a senior lecturer in economics at Murdoch University and a Research Fellow at the Centre for Labour Market Research.

John Halligan is Professor of Public Administration at the University of Canberra.

Janet Hunt is a Fellow in the Centre for Aboriginal Economic Policy Research, Research School of Social Sciences, The Australian National University.

Carole Kayrooz is Deputy Vice-Chancellor (Education) at the University of Canberra.

Phil Lewis is Director of the Centre for Labour Market Research and Professor of Economics at the University of Canberra.

Chris Lewis is a Research Fellow at the Centre for Policy Innovation, Research School of Social Science, The Australian National University.

Andrew Macintosh is Associate Director, ANU Centre for Climate Law and Policy.

David Marsh is a Professor in the School of Sociology, Research School of Social Science, The Australian National University.

Stephen Parker is Vice-Chancellor at the University of Canberra.

Andrew Parkin is the Deputy Vice-Chancellor (Academic) and a Professor in the Department of Politics and Public Policy, Flinders University, South Australia.

Chris Roberts is an Assistant Professor in the Faculty of Business and Government, University of Canberra.

Will Sanders is Senior Fellow and Deputy Director at the Centre for Aboriginal Economic Policy Research, Research School of Social Science, The Australian National University.

Gwynneth Singleton is an Adjunct Associate Professor at the University of Canberra.

John Wanna holds the Sir John Bunting Chair of Public Administration, School of Politics and International Relations, The Australian National University, and is Professor in Public Policy at Griffith University.

Roger Wettenhall is Emeritus Professor in Public Administration at the University of Canberra and a Visiting Professor at the university's ANZSOG Institute for Governance.

Deb Wilkinson is a Research Associate, ANU Centre for Climate Law and Policy.

Part I. Introduction

1. It was the best of times; it was the worst of times

CHRIS AULICH

Charles Dickens began *A Tale of Two Cities* with the wonderfully evocative line that is the title of this chapter. It might well have described the fortunes of both major political parties in the period under review: the Commonwealth administration under Kevin Rudd from November 2007 until July 2010, when Rudd lost both the leadership of the Labor Party and the prime ministership.

In this period Rudd's approval ratings—extraordinarily high in the early days of his government—dropped to below 40 per cent by May 2010 (see Table 1.1), when one million voters turned away from Labor shortly after the government announced that it would not proceed with its emissions trading scheme (ETS) (Stuart 2010:267). From 27 per cent preferring Tony Abbott as prime minister in March 2010 to 41 per cent just four months later (Figure 7.3), the political landscape was volatile. A government with two prime ministers in three years and an opposition with three leaders during the same period, it will be recognised as one of the most turbulent periods in modern Australian political history. As Dickens might have said of the period: 'it was the age of foolishness, it was the epoch of belief…it was the spring of hope, it was the winter of despair' (Dickens 1859:3).

Having managed to respond very positively to the global financial crisis (GFC), Labor, in its spring of hope, saw a historic apology to the 'Stolen Generations', a full agenda for reforming intergovernmental relations and a succession of other policy initiatives covering a huge range of proposed government activity. Even after the demise of Kevin Rudd himself, this hope was again ignited by the appointment of Australia's first woman Prime Minister, Julia Gillard. Yet the period was also Labor's winter of despair, culminating in the failure of its first-term government to be re-elected in its own right, with Gillard forced to accept the support of a number of Greens and independents to form her minority government. The Coalition, too, suffered its own winter with a turnover of leaders and disastrous poll results in the first two years of the Rudd ascendency.

Table 1.1 Newspoll data, November 2007 – August 2010

Date	Intended primary vote	Two party preferred (ALP – Coalition)	Approval as prime minister	Who would make the better prime minister (ALP – Coalition)
Election 2007	43	53 – 47	63 (Rudd)	47 – 44 (Howard)
15–17 February 2008	46	57 – 43	68	70 – 9 (Nelson)
2–4 May 2008	47	57 – 43	68	72 – 9
8–10 August 2008	47	57 – 43	58	68 – 12
21–23 November 2008	42	55 – 45	67	63 – 21 (Turnbull)
6–8 February 2009	48	58 – 42	63	62 – 20
15–17 May 2009	46	56 – 44	58	58 – 24
21–23 August 2009	44	55 – 45	61	66 – 19
13–15 November 2009	43	56 – 44	56	63 – 22
12–14 February 2009	39	53 – 47	50	55 – 27 (Abbott)
14–16 May 2010	37	50 – 50	39	49 – 33
6–8 August 2010	38	51 – 49	43 (Gillard)	49 – 34

Source: <www.newspoll.com.au/cgi-bin/polling/display_poll_data.pl>

The Coalition's period of hope began, however, with the steady emergence of Tony Abbott as a genuine alternative prime minister—coming tantalisingly close to victory in 2010.[1] Nevertheless, the current period threatens to be Abbott's winter as he learns to deal with a substantively new role for an opposition leader facing a minority government, and he confronts potential challenges from the ever-present Malcolm Turnbull should he falter in grasping the complexities of this new role. While the period after the election presented a thrilling climax to the period under review, we leave its analysis to the authors of the next book in this series. In this volume, we concentrate primarily on the Rudd prime ministership.

We left the ninth book in the Commonwealth Administration series[2] with a quote from Mungo MacCallum to illustrate the momentum and the level of excitement that had accompanied the incoming Rudd government in November 2007 (Aulich and Wettenhall 2008:1). This excitement was to reach stratospheric heights with the apology to the Stolen Generations and the Australia 2020 Summit. Two years later, however, Rudd's slide was as dramatic as his rise and was accompanied by a series of policy failures and a succession of problems that hampered Labor implementing those policies, which had promised the Australian people a period of significant and potentially visionary change.

---

1   At no stage, however, was Abbott able to match either Rudd or Gillard in the polls for preferred prime minister.

2   For a full list of the volumes in this series, see Appendix 1.1.

This book traces that journey through the same approach taken in the past few books in this series. The book is divided into four parts: the first provides an overview of the period, beginning with John Wanna's chapter outlining the Rudd program and identifying his many agendas. After discussing the bases of the Rudd election program, Wanna describes the agendas initiated by Labor and the crafting by Rudd of a program based on the 'great battle of ideas'. The list is exhaustive, as Wanna highlights the many issues that emerged as 'first-order' ones. Wanna then explains the demise of Rudd, providing an argument that is developed in almost all of the chapters to follow. His conclusion that Rudd will 'undoubtedly go down as a prime minister who promised much, but who actually achieved relatively little' becomes a dominant theme throughout the volume. It should be noted, however, that the early Rudd approach was characterised by his willingness to openly identify and debate his agenda and discuss his political values in a very public way. This provided a stark contrast with his predecessor, John Howard, who avoided engaging public debate on some of his more radical proposals, especially those such as privatisation, which had helped to reshape the Australian state by giving strong preference to individual over collective interests. This author has described this avoidance as constituting a 'legitimacy deficit' (Aulich 2010).

The second part of this volume focuses on changes to the institutions of government. It contains five chapters—all written by researchers who have made significant contributions to the series at previous times. John Halligan discusses the changes to the public sector in general and the Australian Public Service (APS) in particular. He identifies in the period tendencies towards steering strategically and moves towards centralising the APS, referring to this as a move towards 'one APS'. Halligan concludes that there was a massive reform agenda for modernising the Public Service and for building its capacity, especially in strengthening its role in policy making. He also identifies, however, much unfinished business in this reform agenda, which he generously labels as 'underdeveloped'. Significantly, neither of the two main parties indicated during the election campaign any willingness to progress the 'blueprint' for a new public service that had been initiated by Terry Moran, Secretary of the Department of the Prime Minister and Cabinet, so it remains to be seen whether or not this initiative will be a key agenda for the new Gillard government.

To bookend Halligan's discussion about the inner public sector, Roger Wettenhall again chronicles the state of the outer public sector, comprising the non-departmental public bodies (NDPBs). As in previous volumes in this series, here Wettenhall appends details of those NDPBs that have been established, changed or abolished in the period under review. In continuing this important research over a long period, Wettenhall's conclusion that 'the Commonwealth's NDPB sector is currently not working badly, though there are black spots' can be taken as a highly credible evaluation of the current state of this sector. Similarly, his conclusion that those centralising forces—also identified by Halligan—need to be carefully examined before significant decisions affecting the NDPB sector are implemented warrants serious attention by governments.

Former Clerk of the Senate, Harry Evans, discusses the issues faced by the Rudd government in managing a senate in which Labor was in a minority. Evans provides a succinct and plausible argument that lack of control of the Senate could be good for governments and that the Rudd government suffered little from senate obstructionism in comparison with its predecessor Howard governments. He makes the point that securing a majority senate could have contributed to the undoing of the last Howard government, as highly partisan measures, such as Howard's workplace relations legislation, can ultimately be harmful to their authors when there is little need to negotiate with others. If Evans's views can be translated to the incoming minority Gillard government then we could look forward to a period of 'good', if less stable, government.

Geoff Anderson and Andrew Parkin continue the analysis of intergovernmental relations that they began in the previous volume. They document the extraordinary level of activity initiated through the Council of Australian Governments (COAG) and the many initiatives that flowed from what was apparently a genuine attempt by the Rudd government to develop intergovernmental relations as one of its defining initiatives. They argue that much of the work is, however, unfinished or has run aground. Harsher critics have labelled the incursion of the Commonwealth into areas of state responsibility as one where 'the constraints of multi-tiered government placed Kevin Rudd's lofty goals out of reach' because they 'depended on the cooperation of other governments and organisations beyond his control' (Mulgan 2010:4–5). Indeed, Mulgan goes on to claim that Rudd's 'impossible ambitions...killed his prime ministership' because they exposed his ineffective leadership.

In previous volumes in the series, little attention has been paid to the opposition; typically, they appear as 'extras' to the main act. In this volume, we break with that tradition, and Gwynneth Singleton traces the fortunes of the opposition throughout the Rudd period using the polls as her signposts. She discusses the turbulence in the opposition parties that led to the election of three leaders in as many years, culminating with Tony Abbott. Singleton argues that the contrast between Abbott and his predecessors brings into focus the contested view of the primary role of Her Majesty's Opposition. Both Turnbull and Brendan Nelson were less adversarial and indicated that, at times, bipartisan approaches might be needed to develop policy in the national interest; Abbott, in contrast, vowed to lead an opposition that would exist primarily to oppose rather than to support the government (Daley 2010). Singleton also discusses the roles played by the opposition in contributing to policy development—perhaps a most prescient discussion in the light of the election of a minority Gillard government that will need to work more in coalition with minority parties in order to implement its agendas.

The third part of the book deals with the key policy issues faced by the Rudd government. Given the wide front on which the Rudd government worked, selecting key policy areas to be canvassed in this book has been challenging. We have favoured those that were controversial or represented significant change from the past or, as in the case of foreign policy, were intrinsically so significant that we felt they should be documented, even if there was a large degree of bipartisanship involved. We have selected education, the economy, Indigenous affairs, the environment and foreign policy as the focus of this policy section—perhaps an arguable choice but one we think best captures the mood for change that characterised the Rudd period.

The section is prefaced with a chapter on policy making itself: policy experts David Marsh, Chris Lewis and Paul Fawcett combine to analyse the ways in which Rudd made and implemented citizen-centred policy making—an initiative that had been included in Labor's 2007 policy platform. The authors draw from two politically salient cases—the 2020 Summit and the Community Cabinet initiative—to argue that the Rudd government used the discourse of increased participation in the policymaking process largely as a means of legitimising or promoting decisions that had already been taken. When considered with views discussed elsewhere in the volume that policy decisions under Rudd became focused on the cabal or 'kitchen cabinet' of four senior ministers, the conclusions reached by these authors represent a strongly negative evaluation of Labor's efforts to enhance network governance and community participation in policy making.

Rudd's government sought to implement a 'revolution in the quantity of our investment in human capital and in the quality of outcomes that the education system delivers' (Rudd and Smith 2007). On stepping down from the prime ministership, Rudd spoke of the achievements of his government and listed education as one of his successes. In the chapter on the 'education revolution', Carole Kayrooz and Stephen Parker map the many programs that were part of the 'revolution' in schools and the vocational education and training (VET) and higher education sectors. They conclude that the impressive list of activities undertaken by the Rudd government certainly represented a significant investment. They warn, however, that 'a massive spend on infrastructure does not make a revolution', and argue that Rudd's education program, while well intentioned, did not effectively address longstanding educational issues.

Anne Garnett and Phil Lewis continue the story of the economy and industrial relations under Rudd, and they give the Rudd government few plaudits for its economic achievements. In particular, they criticise policies that generated waste, fostered incompetent policy oversight and failed to invest in productive infrastructure, favouring, instead, policies of short-term spending stimulus. They do acknowledge that the Rudd government was quick to respond to the GFC and that this was one factor in Australia's success in comparison with other countries; they argue that the stimulus package did have some short-run effect in preventing unemployment rising more than it would otherwise have, but argue that much of the spending was needlessly wasteful and has damaged long-term growth.

Garnett and Lewis also acknowledge that others might provide more generous interpretations of Labor's economic policies; indeed, Nobel laureate Joseph Stiglitz was reported as saying that 'Labor did a fantastic job of saving Australia from the global economic crisis' (Sydney Morning Herald 2010)—a view echoed by former Liberal Prime Minister Malcolm Fraser (ABC 2010a). What this does is to underline the alternative views of the management of the economy that were presented to the Australian people before the 2010 election.

Andrew Macintosh, Deb Wilkinson and Richard Denniss combine to tell the story of climate change, the issue that contributed significantly to the fall of the Prime Minister and two leaders of the opposition. They acknowledge the high priority given to climate change by Prime Minister Rudd in referring to it as the 'greatest moral, economic and environmental challenge of our generation' (Rudd 2007), and note that the issue was to be one of the defining policies of the new era, whereby Rudd would demonstrate that the Labor Party was the champion of progressive reform. The chapter then describes how that policy was steadily diluted following substantial pressure from the opposition and from the Greens, until finally, the initiative was abandoned as Labor was unable to secure its legislation through both houses of Parliament.

Will Sanders and Janet Hunt write about one of the most significant early achievements of the Rudd government in finally responding to claims from Indigenous Australians to say 'sorry' for past policies that had so badly impacted on them. They argue, however, that the promise of a new focus on Indigenous matters slowly petered out, as the paradigm in which the policy was embedded remained unchanged, despite the rhetoric of partnership espoused by the Rudd government. In their chapter, Sanders and Hunt claim that a generational revolution is needed before appropriate policies can be developed to meet the present situation; they argue strongly for a new way of thinking about Indigenous affairs with policies that best manage the tensions between equality, choice and guardianship.

It is rare in a federal election campaign that foreign policy is so little mentioned. After assuming government, Rudd certainly developed a more nuanced and multilateral approach to foreign policy than that preferred by his predecessor. Andrew Carr and Chris Roberts assert that on major policies, however, such as the war in Afghanistan and on asylum-seekers, there was little to distinguish the main parties. Certainly, Rudd strode the international stage in relation to managing the GFC and to the Copenhagen climate change summit but, Carr and Roberts argue, in terms of concrete foreign policy change, aside from withdrawing combat troops from Iraq, Rudd over promised and under delivered.

The fourth and final part of the book focuses on Kevin Rudd and his leadership. Mark Evans argues that the Rudd 'debacle' clearly demonstrates that sustainable prime ministerial power rests on the incumbent's recognition that their powerbase is determined by a broad set of resource dependencies encompassing the core executive territory, media relations, the citizenry and the Prime Minister's party itself. He suggests that as soon as Rudd lost sight of the importance of his resource dependencies he started to lose his grip on power. Evans contrasts Rudd's failure to hold on to his leadership with the earlier successes of Bob Hawke and John Howard, and in so doing provides a template for serious consideration of successful leadership by future political leaders.

A series of failures

This volume features contributions from a number of academics—some regarding the Rudd government more warmly; most, however, less enthusiastic about its achievements. In reviewing all of the chapters included in this volume, it is clear that Rudd promised much but, due to a number of circumstances, his government disappointed overall. As Gillard so succinctly put it on assuming the prime ministership, 'it was a good government that in some areas had lost its way' (Kenny 2010). This raises the question about where Labor had lost it way, and it seems that it raises a series of themes, all of which point to failure of some sort or other.

A first failure was to promise so much and deliver so little in terms of hard outcomes. The Rudd government was afflicted by 'initiativitis' (Stoker 2000:6), or, as John Wanna describes in the next chapter, it became 'a government of announcements'. Governments gain kudos from announcing initiatives, but gain few from the implementation and evaluation of those same initiatives. Ministers queue to make announcements about new programs but are too rarely sighted when details about implementation are required. As noted by John Wanna in Chapter 2 and Mark Evans in Chapter 14, the Rudd agenda was breathtaking in its scope, and also in its hyperbole: 'the big education reforms', an ETS that would respond to the 'greatest moral challenge of our time', advancing causes such as provisions for the homeless and closing the gap between Indigenous and other Australians, assuming control of hospitals unless the states were able to demonstrably improve their management of those facilities, making schools more open and accountable. The list of projects labelled as high priority surely eroded the significance of each; opposition senate leader, Nick Minchin, noted the number of times Rudd had talked about different policy areas as his 'No. 1 priority' (van Onselen 2010). A second list—of implementation failures—could also be factored into any judgment of government achievements: the 'pink batts' fiasco, the buildings and computers for schools programs, Indigenous housing, and fuel and grocery watch schemes, among others, displayed failures in implementation with the Rudd government required to defend its performance in these key policy areas. This volume records a number of other programs that, while not the public disasters mentioned above, either petered out or lost momentum. Programs such as advancing reconciliation beyond 'sorry', healthcare reforms and a number of the COAG initiatives remain incomplete though at times they were touted as primary targets for reform. As Richard Mulgan (2010) notes, Rudd had a 'penchant for ambitious commitments that proved impossible to meet'—a theme that resonates through most chapters in this volume.

THE BOXING DAY TEST

Source: David Pope, *The Canberra Times*, 26 December 2008

A second failure was in communicating those successes that had been made. In particular, the quick response to the GFC—despite the waste that concerned Garnett and Lewis (see Chapter 10)—gave Australia a stronger chance to survive the GFC in sound economic condition. While there might have been some wasted opportunities in not investing sufficiently in long-term productive infrastructure development, it was not until the third week of the election campaign that Labor was prepared to cite its record of economic management as evidence that the electorate could trust it to manage the economy better than the opposition parties. Labor also did not trumpet other achievements such as those initially secured in health, reconciliation and in some COAG activities. Its 2010 election manifesto was more a statement about the future, as if somehow the past three years had yielded little for which Labor could claim credit.

A third failure lay in the role of ideas. It was clear that during the 2010 election campaign Gillard did not have or was not allowed to canvass new and radical ideas for her next government. Most commentators have lamented that the campaign was one that contained few serious policy debates, with both of the main parties relying on safety-first campaigns that revealed few policies that signalled significant change (or challenge!).[3] While Abbott's campaign was to repeat a mantra of opposition (to wasteful spending, debt, new taxes, and to asylum-seekers), Labor was unable to capture the spirit of change promised with a new prime minister aiming to get Labor 'back on track'. This was never better represented than in the 'debate' about border protection. We witnessed an unedifying discussion on immigration between the Prime Minister and the Leader of the Opposition—ironically, both immigrants—trying to outdo each other with their plans to curb the current levels of immigration! And all in the name of winning the votes of a few xenophobic Australians who happen to live in marginal electorates.

The final failure was in leadership. As Peter Hartcher (2010) argues, candidates for leader 'should have the ability to inspire and elevate society with a bold, engaging vision' rather than simply reflecting the current views of the community. For a party of change such as Labor, its loyal adherents can reasonably expect that it will promote to the broader community a vision for the future, likely based on traditionally held social democratic values. Clearly, the Rudd government did begin with a vision of an Australia that was moving away from the Howard–Thatcher notions of individualism towards a view of society in which collective activity was again to be recognised, encouraged and applauded. Rudd's earlier musings about the death of neo-liberalism fostered hope by many that Labor would lead Australia towards a new age of

---

3   Mungo MacCallum (2010) described the campaign thus: 'Never had the prime ministership of Australia been contested by such a pair of abject, craven, weak-kneed, whey-faced, chicken-hearted, lily-livered, jelly-bellied milksops.'

compassionate and collective government activity. It became clear, however, that as Labor jettisoned much of its vision—certainly with respect to issues such as the ETS and the management of immigration—disillusion began to set in among the electorate. As Jack Waterford (2010) asked presciently in May 2010 as Rudd's popularity began to crumble, 'has Labor any abiding belief?' This theme began to resonate with the electorate and it was hardly surprising that so many of Labor's 'true believers' deserted the party for alternatives such as the Greens, cast informal votes or failed to attend the polling booths at all.[4] This represented a failure of Rudd's leadership to bring his constituency with him. As Mark Evans suggests in Chapter 14, Rudd forgot that he was dependent on the resources and support of his party, his cabinet colleagues, the Public Service and the Australian electorate.

In the future, when we evaluate the Rudd government from the safer distance of time, a verdict that focuses on failure might appear to be too tough. Perhaps when Australia inevitably moves towards adopting some mechanisms to contain carbon emissions, or shifts to new-generational policies for Indigenous affairs, or finally recasts intergovernmental relations as a genuinely collaborative activity, some commentators will note that the seeds of these policies were sown during the Rudd period. Perhaps these commentators will wonder why these and other initiatives were not brought to fruition at the time; this will probably generate further discussion about broad issues such as the importance of well-planned policy implementation or the role of leadership in engaging the citizenry. More cautious governments might reflect on the dangers of overreaching by promising more than is reasonable or possible to deliver; or that openness in government in turn generates further demands for even more openness. It was clear that, with respect to transparency and accountability, Rudd was committed to the importance of performance management, introducing mechanisms such as mid-term reports, annual reports on 'closing the gap' and measuring the performance of schools and hospitals. When his constituency turned its attention to the Rudd government's performance, however, it found that Labor was still a 'work in progress' with few tangible indicators of successful implementation.

Many have noted the speed of Rudd's departure; this probably related most to his style of leadership. As Mark Evans has noted in Chapter 14, he preferred to work with a tightly held group of confidants and, in so doing, he alienated many of his cabinet and caucus colleagues. Perhaps when the challenge came to his leadership, many might have felt that he deserved support, given the difficulties that his government had surmounted, especially in relation to the GFC. When he sought this support, however, there were few willing to take

---

4   'The 2010 election appears to have had the highest number of informal votes in at least the last six federal elections' (ABC 2010b); and 'more voters refused to vote than at any election since 1925, the first election at which voting was made compulsory' (The Age 2010).

up his case for him. None will forget his long and emotional final speech or the forlorn figure he cut when showing up to Question Time the day after he had lost his prime ministership. For Rudd, this must have been his 'worst of times'.

Chris Aulich *is a Professor at the ANZSOG Institute for Governance, University of Canberra.*

References

Aulich, C. 2010. 'Privatisation in service delivery: lessons from Australia', in T. Moon Joong (ed.), *The Service Sector Advancement: Issues and implications for the Korean economy*, Korean Development Institute, Seoul.

Aulich, C. and Wettenhall, R. (eds) 2008. *Howard's Fourth Government: Australian Commonwealth Administration 2004–2007*, UNSW Press, Sydney.

Australian Broadcasting Corporation (ABC) 2010a. *Q & A*, ABC TV, 30 August, <www.abc.net.au/tv/qanda>

Australian Broadcasting Corporation (ABC) 2010b. 'Figures show 5pc of votes were informal', *ABC News*, 22 August, <www.abc.net.au/news/stories/2010/08/22/2989878.htm>

Daley, P. 2010. 'Abbott takes aim at a PM all at sea', *The Age*, 3 January, <www.theage.com.au/opinion/politics/abbott-takes-aim-at-a-pm-all-at-sea-20100102-lmgg.html>

Dickens, C. 2005 [1859]. *A Tale of Two Cities*, The Folio Society, London.

Hartcher, P. 2010. 'Should we expect more from our leaders?', *Sydney Morning Herald*, 28 July, p. 2.

Kenny, M. 2010. 'Julia Gillard replaces Kevin Rudd as Prime Minister of Australia', *AdelaideNow*, 24 June, <www.adelaidenow.com.au/news/national/rudd-faces-party-challenge-number-crunch/story-e6frea8c-1225883388264>

MacCallum, M. 2010. 'The wimp and the wuss', *Crikey*, 26 July, <http:www.crikey.com.au>

Mulgan, R. 2010. 'Impossible ambitions that killed a prime ministership', *The Public Sector Informant*, July, pp. 4–5.

Rudd, K. 2007. Address to the UN Bali Conference on Climate Change, Bali, 12 December, <www.australianpolitics.com/2007/12/12/rudd-address-to-bali-climate-change-conference.html>

Rudd, K. and Smith, S. 2007. *The Australian Economy Needs an Education Revolution*, Australian Labor Party, Barton, ACT.

Stoker, G. 2000. New Labour and local government modernisation, Paper presented to Local Government at the Millennium Conference, 21 February.

Stuart, N. 2010. *Rudd's Way: November 2007–June 2010*, Scribe, Melbourne.

Sydney Morning Herald 2010. 'Labor saved Australia: Nobel laureate Stiglitz', *Sydney Morning Herald*, 6 August, <www.smh.com.au/business/labor-saved-australia-nobel-laureate-stiglitz-20100806-11lkq.html>

The Age 2010. 'The great turnoff', *The Age*, 21 September.

van Onselen, P. 2010. 'Seeing right through Rudd's changing top priorities, *The Australian*, 24 February.

Waterford, J. 2010. 'Has Labor any abiding belief?', *The Canberra Times*, 5 May.

Appendix 1.1 Australian Commonwealth Administration series

Australian Commonwealth Administration 1983: Essays in review, Alexander Kouzmin, J. R. Nethercote and Roger Wettenhall (eds) 1984, School of Administrative Studies, Canberra College of Advanced Education in association with ACT Division, Royal Australian Institute of Public Administration, Canberra.

Australian Commonwealth Administration 1984: Essays in review, J. R. Nethercote, Alexander Kouzmin and Roger Wettenhall (eds) 1986, School of Administrative Studies, Canberra College of Advanced Education in association with ACT Division, Royal Australian Institute of Public Administration, Canberra.

Hawke's Second Government: Australian Commonwealth Administration 1984–1987, Roger Wettenhall and J. R. Nethercote (eds) 1988, School of Management, Canberra College of Advanced Education, and ACT Division, Royal Australian Institute of Public Administration, Canberra.

Hawke's Third Government: Australian Commonwealth Administration 1987– 1990, John Halligan and Roger Wettenhall (eds) 1992, School of Management, Canberra College of Advanced Education, and ACT Division, Royal Australian Institute of Public Administration, Canberra.

From Hawke to Keating: Australian Commonwealth Administration 1990–1993, Jenny Stewart (ed.) 1995, Centre for Research in Public Sector Management, University of Canberra, and Royal Institute of Public Administration Australia, Canberra.

The Second Keating Government: Australian Commonwealth Administration 1993–1996, Gwynneth Singleton (ed.) 1997, Centre for Research in Public Sector Management, University of Canberra, and Royal Institute of Public Administration Australia, Canberra.

The Howard Government: Australian Commonwealth Administration 1996–1998, Gwynneth Singleton (ed.) 2000, UNSW Press, Sydney.

Howard's Second and Third Governments: Australian Commonwealth Administration 1998–2004, Chris Aulich and Roger Wettenhall (eds) 2005, UNSW Press, Sydney.

Howard's Fourth Government: Australian Commonwealth Administration 2004– 2007, Chris Aulich and Roger Wettenhall (eds) 2008, UNSW Press, Sydney.

2. Issues and agendas for the term

JOHN WANNA

Kevin Rudd made at least two attempts to wrest the leadership of the federal Australian Labor Party (ALP) before he assumed the post of Leader of the Opposition on 4 December 2006. The first attempt was after the 2004 election and the much expected but 'inglorious exit' of the Leader of the Opposition, Mark Latham, in January 2005. Although Kim Beazley announced his intention to re-stand for the leadership, Rudd suddenly emerged as an 'undeclared' candidate in January 2005. But he was unable to attract any numbers (and by some accounts had secured as few as two votes) and quietly withdrew from the race, leaving Beazley unopposed for the post as 'the safe option' who struggled to regain momentum (Bynander and 't Hart 2007:65). Although some leadership destabilisation of Beazley occurred periodically between 2005 and 2006, Rudd apparently signed a written pledge of loyalty to him. Opinion polls, however, again turned against Beazley in 2006 and it was widely believed in Labor Party circles that the electorate had stopped listening to him. After an embarrassing series of gaffes by Beazley, Labor's extra-parliamentary factional heavies moved swiftly to depose him and install an alternative team. In November, polls showed Rudd was more popular than Beazley as preferred leader, and, on 1 December 2006, Rudd and Julia Gillard announced they would stand on a combined ticket for the leadership, claiming to the media that their tilt for the leadership was not a 'challenge' but a tactical mistake by Beazley's supporters that itself went wrong. It was an indicative sign of spin from the start and a sign that Rudd's leadership was always held hostage to the fickleness of polls. In the subsequent party-room vote held on 4 December, Kevin Rudd was elected leader of the parliamentary party by 49 votes to 39, with Gillard elected unopposed as his deputy. The two neophyte leaders immediately commenced a whistlestop road trip around Australia, which commenced a year-long gruelling campaign to win government.

Rudd's main aims as the new Leader of the Opposition were twofold. First, he had to convey the image that the 11-year-old Howard government faced a crisis of legitimacy, that it was 'out of touch' with ordinary families and was incapable of renewing itself (and the spectre of Peter Costello stalking Howard continually underscored this impression). Second, he had to rebuild

Labor's electoral credibility and prospects for victory. He set about achieving these aims with a ruthless efficiency and dispassionate single-mindedness. He wasted no opportunity to criticise, rebuff and even ridicule his opponents, at one stage joking he was enjoying playing with John Howard's head. And on the policy front during the campaign he chose to match the conservative government commitment for commitment, while allowing the Labor opposition to concentrate on a select number of wedge issues to lure swinging voters and recapture the 'Howard battlers'. As a 'small-target' tactic (similar to the one Beazley had run in the 2001 election to little effect), the strategy was a high-risk endeavour.

The Rudd government's agenda in its one and only two-and-a-half-year term was determined in strategic response to five catalytic periods: his 12 months as opposition leader building the party to take office; the detailed platform Labor took to the 2007 federal election or announced in the campaign; the chaotic maelstrom of the 'virtual honeymoon' of the first six months in office; the rapid response to the global financial crisis (GFC), which preoccupied the government from within six months into its term; and finally, dealing with the backlog of issues in the second half of the term that ended in misfortune. These five catalytic periods form the organising framework for this chapter—tracing how the many agendas evolved or morphed, were abandoned in about-faces or were replaced by new priorities in the government's term.

Orchestrating the 'great battle of ideas'

Over his period as Leader of the Opposition, Rudd began carefully positioning himself with important but diverse constituencies, including business sectors, unions, religious groups, working families, pensioners and the young. On the cusp of becoming leader, he had written a series of essays appearing in *The Monthly* magazine outlining his social and religious philosophy. In October in an essay entitled 'Faith in politics', he criticised the conservative exploitation of the 'culture wars' and the relentless attacks on the legitimacy of the left, manufactured, he believed, by John Howard together with the extreme 'right wing Christian' lobby (Rudd 2006a). He argued that the Christian right was trying to reshape Australia to suit its own agendas despite the fact that the conservatives had no monopoly on faith-based politics and that social democrats were equally entitled to expect the religious vote. He also suggested that Australians should look to admire religious martyrs who had demonstrated social compassion and courage in the face of danger, rather than look to the extremist religious groups who preached ideological divisiveness. Rudd himself volunteered that he revered the German theologian Dietrich Bonhoeffer for his integrity and commitment to his principles of equity and fairness. While the essay produced the predicted negative reaction from right-wing commentators, it signalled that Rudd was interested in the contest for ideas and in reaching out to various potential constituencies. Some interpreted this essay as a reverberation of Christian socialism, but he carefully underlined his socially conservative stance by ruling out the legalisation of same-sex marriage and promising to be a fiscal conservative.

He followed his 'Faith in politics' essay a month later with a more generic engagement with the 'battle for ideas in Australian politics', under the title 'Howard's brutopia'—derived from the eponymous condemnation of unchecked market forces under capitalism by Michael Oakeshott. In this essay, Rudd (2006b) outlined a historical and philosophical critique of free-market fundamentalism and economic neo-liberalism, particularly over the lack of appropriate balance in the fundamentalists' mind-set. The essay was also a trenchant attack on John Howard's neo-right policy agenda, which Rudd claimed was creating a divided Australia of 'two nations': the rich and the poor. According to Rudd, when Howard won a majority in the Senate in 2004, it

> enabled him to legislate away a century of hard-won protections for Australian families…Howard is also in the process of unleashing new forces of market fundamentalism against youth workers; families trying to spend sufficient time together; and communities trying to negotiate with single, major employers experimenting with their newfound powers. Breadwinners are now at risk of working less predictable shifts, spread over a seven-day week, not sensitive to weekends and possibly for less take-home pay. The pressures on relationships, parenting and the cost and quality of childcare are without precedent. (Rudd 2006b:8)

His critique was not merely a conventional restatement of the 'Your Rights at Work' campaign run by the Australian Council of Trade Unions (ACTU), but a more nuanced argument about the demoralising social impact of unleashed market forces. His alternative vision—outlined in a preliminary way in his maiden speech to the House of Representatives in November 1998—was based on the traditional social values of family, community, country, social responsibility, social inclusion, mutuality and even altruism. Individual initiative and reward should be balanced with social responsibility. Suddenly, Rudd was a 'philosopher and thinker' of some note. 'Brutopia' also intimated that the role of government needed to be *reframed*—a theme he would return to more forcefully in his subsequent economic essay on the causes of and solutions to the GFC (Rudd 2009).

In other speeches and in media commentary, Rudd also suggested that under Howard there were many 'no-go' issues that appeared to be anathema to the government's ideological stance. These were often topics that Howard or his senior ministers had politically ruled out as unacceptable to mention or even countenance. Such topics included climate change and carbon reduction, an apology to the 'Stolen Generations' and Aboriginal reconciliation more generally, asylum-seeker protection, workers' rights, cooperation with the states, the deployment of troops in Iraq and Afghanistan, enhancements to freedom of information, parliamentary reform, and reforms to government accountability and government advertising in particular. He had earlier gained some attention for his Don Dunstan Memorial Lecture in July 2005, which was devoted to cooperative federalism, and reflected his state government background. This speech had emphasised that Australia was engaged in a 'great battle of ideas', it denied convergence was occurring between the major parties, committed Labor to a fairness agenda based on a fair go, criticised Howard as a 'undiluted centralist', argued for the acknowledgment of a proper role for the states and suggested that future governments ought to 'end the blame game' and emphasise cooperative intergovernmental relations (Rudd 2005). This speech was followed up in his period as opposition leader with pledges to revitalise the Council of the Australian Governments (COAG) in order to drive reform agendas, while rationalising federal financial relations and reducing the number of types of Specific Purpose Payments.

Mostly these speeches and essays were positional statements aimed at creating a softer and alternative image to John Howard; they were a mixture of genuine beliefs and pragmatic calculation (and not dissimilar to the positional 'headland' speeches Howard gave in 1995; see Brett 2007; Johnson 2007).

The politics of campaigning: making Labor electorally appealing

As the election approached, Rudd promised a new style of leadership in place of the tired fourth-term Howard government. He was 'the man with the plan', as Labor campaign posters proudly proclaimed, before condensing the message to a much catchier moniker: 'Kevin 07'. His plan for the future was centred on improving the plight of 'working families' (an identified focus-group demographic) or at least acknowledging their problems and concerns, such as WorkChoices, the loss of rights at work, shiftwork, petrol prices, grocery prices, childcare affordability, even time for parents to read to their children. Much of the talk was reassurance. Rudd repeated his earlier commitment to improve commonwealth–state relations, announcing his government would work cooperatively with the state and territory governments across a range of policy areas (the 'end the blame game' mantra was in effect the translation of a complex issue into populist code to appeal to people on hospital waiting lists, those frustrated by delays or unable to get services, or who had been shunted between disconnected agencies). Working with the Labor premiers, he hatched a plan to establish a series of intergovernmental working groups to investigate priority policy areas, chaired by commonwealth ministers and eventually reporting to COAG on proposals and progress. On other accountability agendas, Rudd promised substantial reform to Parliament, to allow it to meet more frequently by increasing the number of sitting days, and to widen access to freedom of government information. He significantly committed Labor to reducing the number of ministerial advisers, and placing government advertising at arm's length by asking the Auditor-General to approve intended advertising campaigns before they commenced.

In the context of the 'small-target' campaign overall, Labor announced it would introduce an 'educational revolution', which was a grand slogan but largely bereft of details, except that senior high school students would each have a computer on their own desk. Waiting lists for elective surgery were to be reduced significantly with a $2 billion injection of new money, but if the states did not meet some mooted performance benchmarks then federal Labor was prepared to initiate a takeover of public hospitals, seeking authorisation through a referendum in 2009. A new high-speed national broadband initiative was to be implemented in the first term. A Labor government would establish two web-based market information schemes (Fuel Watch and Grocery Watch) to inform consumers of the best place to purchase these items. Labor also indicated it would adopt a 20 per cent renewable energy target by 2020 and commit to a carbon reduction scheme by 2011, but on the precise targets it would await the recommendations of the commissioned report by Ross Garnaut due in mid-2008. Labor further committed to a generous solar power rebate for those homeowners investing in self-sufficient solar power. And to end Australia's involvement in Iraq, Rudd promised to withdraw Australian troops by mid-2008—although forces would remain (and even be increased) in Afghanistan. On general policy matters, he promised to seek 'the best quality advice' from various sources and committed the government to 'one core thing—evidence-based policy' (ABC 2007b). Such 'evidence' would come from a growing list of reviews and inquiries that was being announced with regularity. Already, there was some speculation that Rudd was attempting to put off the hard policy decisions until well after the election so as not to destabilise his short-term 'me-too' campaign.

Rudd pronounced agreement with the Coalition government on so many policy fronts that he earned himself the label 'Howard-lite' (ABC 2007a; Tiernan 2008). He declared himself a fiscal conservative, who would maintain government surpluses and spend efficiently. He famously declared that he would 'take a meat axe' to the Public Service and would increase the efficiency dividend (a clawback provision) by 2 per cent to 3.25 per cent. He clarified that he was not aiming to impose a 'reduction in federal government services, I am talking about the administrative budgets of departments' (ABC 2007c). Labor indicated, however, that it wished to avoid developing an alternative tax policy in the lead-up to the election, but instead would accept the government's taxation framework while it reserved the right to review aspects of the revenue system once in office. This effectively neutralised tax as an election issue and prevented any scare campaign being mounted by the government against Labor on its taxation intentions. It also meant that when Costello pulled off a spectacular campaign coup by offering $34 billion in tax cuts over three years, Labor had effectively to match the bold move, which it largely did by the end of the first week of the campaign, tweaking the package very slightly through shaving a small cut from the most affluent earners. Indeed, Rudd made so many copy-cat announcements matching government commitments that Peter Costello asked in some exasperation what Labor would do if the government were not around to set the agenda (for an account of some of the political distractions of the campaign as it evolved, see Williams 2008).

Labor's specific platform for 2007 concentrated on the 'education revolution', signing of the Kyoto Protocol, repealing the WorkChoices legislation and substituting it with a 'simpler, fairer and more flexible' system, abolishing Australian Workplace Agreements, improving water management, and increasing spending on 'working families' and on health outcomes. Labor argued in the campaign that the Coalition was becoming irresponsible in economic management—a point underscored when the Reserve Bank lifted interest rates by 0.25 per cent in the middle of the campaign to depress overheated demand. In contrast with the Coalition, Labor continually promised to be responsible economic managers—balancing budgets, lowering taxes and facilitating market solutions. Rudd underscored his 'economically responsible' message during the campaign by not promising as much as the Coalition in tax cuts and new spending (ABC 2007b). He looked 'responsible' and could attack the government for being profligate.

The descent into a 'virtual honeymoon': a government of announcements in the immediate post-election phase

There was much euphoria in the Labor camp and amongst sections of the wider community with the change of government in November. Immediately on being sworn in by the Governor-General in early December, Rudd announced that seven COAG working groups would begin work immediately and work over Christmas–New Year (see Chapter 6 for detail). Rudd confirmed that on the first meeting day of the new Parliament he would make an apology to the Stolen Generations (without compensation) on behalf of the Australian Parliament and people, and would enable the legislature to meet more frequently with an extra sitting day (Friday) added to the two-week normal sitting timetable. He also selected his own ministry without a caucus vote and promoted some newer talent into the outer ministry and to parliamentary secretary positions. Notably, about half those in the full ministry were given new portfolio responsibilities from those they had shadowed, some with entirely new portfolio areas and others with significant changes to their allocated responsibilities.

The first six months provided a rush of intense activity, all conducted under impossible deadlines—driven by Rudd in an atmosphere of perpetual crisis. He declared the homeless were an initial priority and insisted all his ministers and backbenchers show concern and visit hostels. He and three ministers went to Bali to take part in international climate change negotiations and to sign the Kyoto agreement in mid-December 2007. Rudd gave a polished and impassioned speech at the parliamentary apology to the Stolen Generations in February 2008, showing statesman-like qualities with his empathy and sincerity. In conjunction with the Indigenous COAG working group, Rudd announced a three-pronged strategy to 'close the gap' on Indigenous disadvantage between Aboriginal living standards and those of the wider community (focusing on life expectancy, housing and schooling).

He announced a '2020 Summit' at which the 'brightest and best' would inject further priorities across 10 policy sectors, but carefully stage-managed and controlled. He unleashed the anticipated rash of reviews over this initial period—each designed not only to investigate policy options on given topics but also to buy time while the government worked out what it exactly wanted to do. And the announcements kept coming. Australian naval boats were sent into Antarctic waters chasing Japanese whalers, asylum-seeker restrictions were eased with a promise to end offshore detention, innovation was fundamental, industry would be assisted, unemployment was to be defeated, a war on drugs was trumpeted, a clamp-down on doping in sport was promised, water management became the government's most crucial agenda, and climate change was declared the 'great moral challenge' of the era. Impossible deadlines were set for the hundreds of issues within the cooperative federalism envelope, and many of the working groups were soon flagging under the load. One working group alone identified 27 separate areas for regulatory reform within four months of its existence (and paradoxically was relatively successful over the next few years). Australia's role internationally was talked up, and our relations with China and the United States were first-order issues. Root and branch taxation reform was suddenly urgent and Ken Henry was commissioned to undertake a comprehensive review of the taxation system. Suddenly, everything was 'priority one' (Jackman 2010:4). But often once announcements had been spruiked by Rudd or his senior ministers their attention span either quickly tired or was overtaken by the subsequent avalanche of further announcements.

In the meantime, progressing the myriad agendas was proving difficult. Parliamentary reform was quickly jettisoned, the extra sitting day was cancelled, and Parliament sat for no more days than usual. Negotiations with Telstra to roll out national broadband struck insurmountable difficulties; negotiations with state governments over the computer program for all senior secondary students hit frustrations; the innovation agenda for business and the public sector seemed to degenerate into nothingness; while 31 extra GP super clinics were announced, only a few were established in the next two years; funding for Aboriginal housing was committed but almost no houses were built; the national educational curricula faced opposition from state education bureaucracies and the My School web-based ranking or information site for individual schools was roundly criticised, most noticeably by principals and teacher unions. The emissions trading scheme (ETS) was progressively wound back and made more complicated with exemptions and extensive compensation arrangements; it was difficult to make sense of it. Then, after much strident rhetoric in the Parliament, the government eventually repealed the WorkChoices legislation and replaced it with the *Fair Work Act 2009*. Business groups remained angry because the government gave unions significant gains above those promised in the election, while unions were angry the government did not restore the old status quo (and the Deputy Prime Minister, Julia Gillard, was forced to make some embarrassing last-minute exemptions to preserve small businesses). Many inside government came to believe it had become pandemonium writ large. And Rudd began to attract the moniker 'Captain Chaos' and a reputation for micro-managing and indecision.

After six months in office, Rudd was accused of having failed to make the transition from campaigning mode to governing mode—meaning he was preoccupied with the politics of spin and the 24/7 media cycle and was prepared to keep making announcements as if he were still campaigning for office without much thought to implementing or prioritising them (Tiernan 2008). Others considered that he had offered no strategic narrative or 'guiding thread' to indicate a vision for his government (Burchell 2008). He was subsequently accused of beginning to resemble a 'home handyman in a house full of half-finished jobs, while still eager to begin more' (Phillip Coorey, cited in Marr 2010:73). His government earned a reputation for announcing policy decisions and then neglecting them or performing expedient about-faces. By the end of 2008, newspapers were tabulating the list of reviews and inquiries the Rudd government had commissioned—and the list was of the order of 150 separate inquiries, some of which were investigating substantial areas of policy to report back on recommendations for future policy directions. Hence, even before the GFC loomed large, the government had hit gridlock (Stuart 2010), although the 'virtual honeymoon' enjoyed by Rudd and his ministers stymied much overt criticism. Meanwhile, the electorate was prepared to suspend judgment and give the new government the benefit of the doubt.

Source: David Pope, *The Canberra Times*, 30 October 2009

The expeditious response to the GFC and the emergency stimulus agendas

Labor's first budget (2008–09) basked in the healthy surpluses inherited from the Howard era. The first tranche of the $31 billion tax cuts was delivered, significant boosts occurred to education, surpluses were parked in various foundation funds for the future, pensioners cynically were given no reprieve, and a continuing series of spending reviews would continue to deliver savings. No sooner was the budget out than the full impact of the sub-prime global credit crisis hit Australia. Against the backdrop of a collapse of confidence in world markets, fear of bank closures, lending and credit crises, expected lay-offs and depressed consumer spending, the government decided to act expeditiously. Bunkered down in crisis mode—using the strategic budget review committee of cabinet (the so-called 'gang of four') and key officials—the government held its collective nerve and quickly pulled together a concerted series of immediate responses that it believed would save Australia.

The agenda now was to provide a series of fiscal stimuli while offering assurances to financial markets and credit sectors. The responses included

- a huge $10.4 billion relief package in late 2008 allocated to pensioners ($4.8 billion), family assistance ($3.9 billion) and first-home buyers ($1.5 billion)
- $6.2 billion allocated to support the car industry over the next 10 years
- a further $42 billion emergency stimulus package in February 2009 (which included $28.8 billion for new infrastructure, $14.7 billion reserved for new school buildings, $6.6 billion on community housing, and $2.7 billion for the home insulation program)
- the second relief measure contained a further $12.7 billion in cash handouts to lower income earners, provided in cheques of $900; and a further $900 single-income family bonus was included; farmers received $950 hardship payments; and another bonus of $950 was provided for families with children at school.

The government also moved to assist various industries facing crisis. Bank guarantees were issued for all savings accounts; banking credit was secured; state government borrowings of up to $150 billion were guaranteed; lines of credit were organised for vulnerable sectors such as car dealers; there were proposals to establish a government-backed property fund for commercial properties; and the first-home-buyers' scheme was extended to the end of September 2009 after which its generosity gradually declined. Despite much urging from the opposition, the government ruled out including any additional tax cuts in the package, as the schedule of cuts promised in the 2007 election was still continuing.

Rudd and his Treasurer, Wayne Swan, both sought to take command in the crisis. They pleaded with employers not to retrench staff and retain as many in employment as possible—even on reduced hours. They urged unions to reduce wage claims for the duration of the crisis and encouraged retail spending while imploring banks not to foreclose on clients in risk of default. They also asked the Productivity Commission to investigate excessive executive salaries. In addition to the range of domestic responses, Rudd sought to affect a more coordinated international response to the crisis. He travelled to Washington, DC, to meet the new US President, Barack Obama, to discuss stimulus measures and then on to London to participate in the G20 Summit (which, largely at his and Gordon Brown's insistence, agreed to a coordinated, multinational stimulus strategy). He sought to have the G20 play a more significant role in global economic coordination and enhance Australia's voice in its deliberations.

In the end, the rapid response paid off, although the government received little credit. Australia recorded only one quarter of negative growth (a mere 0.5 per cent in the December quarter 2008)—not enough to qualify as a recession.

Housing approvals were down to about half the levels of 2003, but retail sales remained buoyant and shops reported record trading over the Christmas and post-Christmas sales periods. Car sales had dropped by 15 per cent over 2008 and then plunged by 24 per cent in the first few months of 2009, but then recovered. Some mining companies laid-off hundreds of employees, but the damage was contained. Overall, unemployment rose from 4.2 per cent to 5.8 per cent before falling back slightly—a much lower result than the estimate of 8.5 per cent forecast by Treasury.

Despite the Grech affair (when a senior Treasury official was outed after leaking bogus emails to the opposition; see AJPA 2009), Kevin Rudd emerged from the GFC with his popularity enhanced. He spent most of his time during the worst of the crisis in front of the media informing people of the dimensions of the crisis, attempting to manage expectations while reassuring them and trying to restore confidence. He claimed he was being 'fair dinkum with the Australian people'. His message was simple: the government was proactive and doing constructive things, but he kept warning Australia was 'not out of the woods yet'. He also released a further economic essay, entitled 'The global financial crisis' (Rudd 2009), which argued the real cause of the present 'seismic' crisis was due to the neo-liberal legacy of the previous three decades, which held that governments had but limited roles and that markets were supposedly able to effectively self-regulate. According to Rudd, these policies had failed and worsened the crisis because governments had withdrawn from protecting the public interest.

The government's second budget amid the crisis was very difficult. Treasury predicted a deficit for the current year (2008–09) of $32 billion (2.7 per cent of GDP) and two further deficits, of $53 and $57 billion in 2009–10 and 2010–11 respectively (about 5 per cent of GDP), followed by smaller deficits to 2012–13. Revenues were expected to drop by about $23 billion below forecasts for the year ahead and by a total of $210 billion over four years. Receipts from the GST would drop by $24 billion over four years—hitting state budget bottom lines as well. In contrast, expenses were estimated to rise by some $50 billion in the year ahead—causing the deficit. The size of the projected public debt, according to the government, was $188 billion by 2013. The most contentious news was that economic growth would recover relatively quickly—rising to 2.25 per cent in 2010–11 but then jumping to more than 4 per cent for the next four years— perhaps an optimistic projection.

Faced with such economic conditions, the policy agendas changed again. While aged pensions were increased by $32 a fortnight (fulfilling a commitment to review and restore pension purchasing capacity), and carers were given increased annual payments, the government did not increase other benefits to the disabled or unemployed (indeed, tougher eligibility criteria for disability pensions were announced). There were claims the government was privileging aged pensioners at the expense of other welfare recipients. Countering this view, the government announced it intended to increase the age at which older workers would qualify for the aged pension from 65 to 67 years, with the higher age being phased in from 2017 to 2023. This would keep more workers in the economy longer, along with some adjustments to superannuation entitlements. Four big spending commitments were then made: a further $23 billion to infrastructure over four years (but only $1.7 billion and $1.5 billion in the immediate two years); clean energy projects received $4.5 billion; higher education received an extra $5.3 billion; and an amount of $4.7 billion was set aside for the delayed new broadband initiative. Significantly, the Commonwealth announced it would limit the growth in government spending to just 2 per cent per annum over the next six years—putting a fiscal straitjacket around future government budgetary settings. It also made substantial cuts in departmental spending as part of its strategy to tighten government spending.

David Marr (2010:86), a (hostile) critic, regarded the GFC packages as the sole example of program courage displayed by the Rudd government. In the GFC policy response, the objectives were clear and imperative, and the particular agendas and policy responses were more open-ended and contingent. Rudd and his 'gang of four' triumphed because they took considered advice backed by experts, actually made decisions, and gave the impression of a government in control, even though the international environment was in turmoil and other nations were facing a catastrophic downward spiral. As Uren and Taylor (2010:80, 140–54) recount, the magnitude of the necessary stimulus injection was a moving feast, fluctuating by billions over a matter of a few hours and with the Prime Minister upping Treasury's initial recommendations by three to fourfold. Some of the responses look like garbage-can policy making, grabbing anything that sounds plausible or ready to go in the context of urgency. Beyond the cash handouts, Rudd and Swan were especially interested in double-impact spending initiatives (program injections that would create jobs and put cash into the economy while doing other good things, such as insulating homes to give better energy efficiency, or building new facilities at schools). These double-headed proposals led to a series of hastily thought through programs where insufficient attention was given to the implementation issues (such as occurred with the home insulation scheme, the Green Loans scheme and the Building the Education Revolution projects; see Chapter 10 in this volume for further details of the economic package).

Despite the problems posed by the GFC, Rudd refused to curtail his ambitious policy agenda, announcing that all commitments were still active, but gradually he would have to back off commitment after commitment until he was ousted in June 2010.

The demise: cascading misfortunes, victim of unintended outcomes

Emerging from the worst of the GFC, the Rudd government lost its way. After the stimulus packages, the government settled down to its pre-crisis agendas and added others for good measure, such as the Moran Review of the Public Service (see Lindquist 2010) and the endorsement of 'Big Australia' (growing to 40 million people by 2050). Yet this period was marked by sequential disappointments and lost opportunities. For the first time, the government was not in control of its agendas, and instead the inchoate agendas it had already spawned and that were already under way began to turn sour and be jettisoned. Things went into the 'too-hard basket' with some regularity. The fuel and grocery watch schemes were abandoned. Government advertising did not have to be vetted by the Auditor-General. The ETS legislation languished in the Senate and was defeated on two separate occasions. Rudd refused to countenance a double dissolution and eventually, in April 2010, announced that the ETS was indefinitely delayed—much to the dismay of his environmental supporters. Meanwhile, the Copenhagen climate change negotiations did not manage to agree on fixed global targets and generally the final communiqué was disappointing (see Chapter 11 for further detail of climate change policies).

Presented with the Henry review of the tax system, the government initially decided not to release it (which they eventually did in April 2010). When a list of just 10 items from the more than 130 recommendations was released, only a few were actual recommendations from the Henry team. Rudd infamously backed down on his promise to take over public hospitals, despite the lack of progress from the states on supposedly agreed performance benchmarks. There was no referendum, there was no commonwealth takeover, and while more funds were put on the table, the states managed to keep at bay the Commonwealth's attempt to place hospitals on an activity-based funding regime. The health agenda stoush suggested that Rudd was not interested in cooperative federalism at all and was cut from the same cloth as other centralist prime ministers (see Chapter 6 for a broader discussion of intergovernmental relations during the period).

And, inevitably, bad news attracted more bad news. Suddenly, a rising number of asylum-seekers again began arriving in boats, posing political problems for the government and accommodation issues for the resumed offshore processing of claimants. Telstra refused to cooperate with the National Broadband Network (NBN) and the government had to establish its own company at a total cost of more than $40 billion, which attracted minimal private sector interest. The media also unearthed a series of scandals concerning the home insulation and the Green Loans schemes (as part of the efficient energy initiatives). The initial concern was that money was being wasted on profligate implementation, but when inexperienced operators were attracted to the program, deaths in the industry occurred and the scandal could not be contained. Further problems with the cost overruns in the Building the Education Revolution (BER) program were a daily news item over the summer of 2009–10, with some estimates suggesting that costs had increased by some 900 per cent over a value-for-money costing. Schools in New South Wales especially complained they were given infrastructure they did not want or need or that required identical structures be demolished.

The 2010–11 budget added few new agendas except that the government expected to be in surplus a little sooner than expected. But no sooner was the budget released than the government unilaterally announced that a new national resource rental tax would be introduced, without consultation, with rubbery figures and with arbitrary criteria about who would be included and which firms excluded. The mining states with substantial state royalties were soon concerned at what they feared was a commonwealth takeover of mining revenues. The controversy generated by the resources tax eventually led to a more widespread questioning of Rudd's political judgment and encouraged the Gillard coup leaders to take swift action. And in response to the advertising campaign from the mining companies, the government showed it was little different to previous ones with indulgent public advertising.

Conclusion

Kevin Rudd will be regarded as having one of the most ambitious and divergent lists of agendas of any first-term prime minister. He will also undoubtedly go down as a prime minister who promised much, but who actually achieved relatively little. He is already remembered for the string of promises he failed to keep, or proposals he abandoned. Rudd's extensive agendas, in the words of one Labor party staffer, 'generated a lot of expectations when we were elected in 2007' (The Weekend Australian 2010:10). It was always going to be hard to live up to these heightened expectations. There was criticism that while the agendas were prolific, there was no overall vision or narrative to make sense of the frenetic activity to the electorate.

It is also the case that for the first two catalytic periods (in opposition and in the campaign itself), Rudd largely drove the political and policy agendas. After that, the agendas overwhelmingly drove his government, and, although the initial responses to the GFC were widely applauded, the increasing difficulties in agenda management in the last year of his term proved terminal. Perhaps with hindsight, as Prime Minister, he could identify his priority reform agendas but often dithered and 'was incapable of pushing through tough reforms' (Jackman 2010:3).

Ultimately, Rudd's demise was due to many factors, not merely his Herculean agendas. He was undone by his hubris and a lack of a consultative style, by the siege mode he created inside government, by constantly believing he knew best, and by the slipping away of electoral confidence in his leadership. The inability to deliver on many of the announced agendas merely fed into the culture of disappointment he inadvertently generated. His sudden demise highlighted the negative aspects of his leadership, but at the same time obliterated the many positive things he achieved along the way, especially his calm economic management when Australia faced the global crisis. But once that appeared to be over, the electorate quickly moved on to other issues and took his role for granted.

After Labor suffered a major reversal at the August 2010 election, some senior Labor figures argued that, in retrospect, the government had been incredibly busy on so many fronts (often driven by polls and focus-group research), but had lost interest in focused reform that would help Australia's competitiveness and sustainability. In one important sense, this lack of a coherent legacy was one of the main reasons Labor found it difficult to mount a convincing campaign in the August 2010 election. The Rudd legacy became a millstone around the neck of Julia Gillard as she attempted to carve out her own agendas.

John Wanna *holds the Sir John Bunting Chair of Public Administration, School of Politics and International Relations, The Australian National University, and is Professor in Public Policy at Griffith University.*

References

Australian Broadcasting Corporation (ABC) 2007a. 'Tricky times ahead for Rudd and Labor', *7.30 Report*, ABC TV, 2 August, <www.abc.net.au/7.30/content/2007/s1995501.htm>

Australian Broadcasting Corporation (ABC) 2007b. Transcript of interview with Kevin Rudd, *7.30 Report*, ABC TV, 21 November, <www.abc.net.au/7.30/content/2007/s209654.htm>

Australian Broadcasting Corporation (ABC) 2007c. 'Cutting bureaucracy won't hurt services', *Australia Votes 2007*, ABC TV, 21 November, <www.abc.net.au/stories/2007/11/21/2097424.htm>

Australian Journal of Politics and History (AJPH) 2009. 'Political chronicle—Commonwealth of Australia', [John Wanna], *Australian Journal of Politics and History*, vol. 55, no. 4, pp. 584–638.

Brett, J. 2007. 'Exit right: the unravelling of John Howard', *Quarterly Essay*, no. 28.

Burchell, D. 2008. 'A thousand days', *The Weekend Australian*, 22–23 March.

Bynander, F. and 't Hart, P. 2007. 'The politics of party leader survival and succession: Australia in comparative perspective', *Australian Journal of Political Science*, vol. 42, no. 1, pp. 47–72.

Jackman, C. 2010. 'Why we still need to talk about Kevin', *Australian Literary Review*, 4 August, pp. 3–4.

Johnson, C. 2007. 'John Howard's values and Australian identity', *Australian Journal of Political Science*, vol. 42, no. 2, pp. 195–209.

Lindquist, E. A. 2010. 'From rhetoric to blueprint: the Moran Review as a concerted, comprehensive and emergent strategy for public service reform', *Australian Journal of Public Administration*, vol. 69, no. 2, pp. 115–151.

Marr, D. 2010. 'Power trip: the political journey of Kevin Rudd', *Quarterly Essay*, no. 38.

Rudd, K. 2005. The case for cooperative federalism, The Don Dunstan Memorial Lecture, Don Dunstan Foundation, Adelaide, July.

Rudd, K. 2006a. 'Faith in politics', *The Monthly*, October.

Rudd, K. 2006b. 'Howard's brutopia', *The Monthly*, November.

Rudd, K. 2009. 'The global financial crisis', *The Monthly*, February.

Stuart, N. 2010. *Rudd's Way: Labor in power 2007–2010*, Scribe, Melbourne.

The Weekend Australian 2010. 'Mending the Labor Party's broken heart', *The Weekend Australian*, 28–29 August.

Tiernan, A. 2008. The Rudd transition: continuity and change in the structures of advice and support to Australian prime ministers, Senate Occasional Lecture Series, May.

Uren, D. and Taylor, L. 2010. *Shitstorm*, Melbourne University Press, Carlton, Vic.

Williams, P. 2008. 'The 2007 Australian federal election: the story of Labor's return from the electoral wilderness', *Australian Journal of Politics and History*, vol. 54, no. 1, pp. 104–25.

Part II. The Institutions of Government

3. The Australian Public Service: new agendas and reform

JOHN HALLIGAN

A change of federal government can be expected to produce new directions for the Australian Public Service (APS), and this is more likely after lengthy periods of opposition provide the incubation for new policy and the impetus for initiating change. The 1972, 1983, 1996 and 2007 turnovers stand out as significant turning points for the APS.[1]

Kevin Rudd's first term was notable for the change of focus expected of a new government, and the distancing and differentiating of public governance and administration from that of the Howard government (cf. Halligan 2008a). But the aspirations were much higher—to anticipate the long-term challenges and to shape the future (Stuart 2010:2)—which sharply distinguished it from the Howard government. Three factors were significant. First, the government came to office with a governance reform agenda that encompassed aspects of the Public Service. Second, there was momentum for change coming out of the Prime Minister's drive for performance and strategic focus across a wide range of policy issues. Third, there was the unleashing of a formal reform process and the resulting 'blueprint' that were associated with the head of the Public Service, Terry Moran.

This chapter first considers the advent of a new government and the contribution that it initially sought to make to machinery and principles of governance, and then examines the launching of a major reform process that produced the blueprint for reform (AGRAGA 2010). Judgments about how this ambitious agenda were worked through in practice can only be provisional, and for this exceptional term indicate the need to differentiate evaluation at the level of ideas and initiatives from those of implementation and practice. The working assumption was that Rudd was guaranteed more than one term and that implementation would continue across several terms. As well there

---

1 For details, see earlier volumes in this series (Appendix 1.1).

was the unravelling of the government's policy and program intentions, which cannot be detailed within this chapter, yet they came to overshadow what was accomplished.

The reform trajectory and transitions for the APS

Where the APS has come from and how it appeared to be travelling during the first term prior to the blueprint are the subjects of this and the following sections. In the first decade of the contemporary reform initiatives (the 1980s), the dominant theme was management improvement. The commitment to neo-liberal reforms in the 1990s led the Public Service to become decentralised, marketised, contractualised and privatised—most clearly under the Howard government. A deregulated personnel system and a new financial management framework extended agency devolution. A diminished role for central agencies was one result.

The transition from this approach proceeded in three phases. The first phase (early 2000s) blunted the impact of 'New Public Management' (NPM) and was characterised by less emphasis on competition and outsourcing, responding to new pressures (for example, international threats to security) and a greater focus on effectiveness. A heavy-handed approach to controlling the Public Service was supplanted by more reflection and balance in public management.

The dominant themes of the second phase (mid-2000s) can be summarised as integrating governance. First, central agencies were resurrected through expanding their roles—the Department of the Prime Minister and Cabinet (PM&C) in policy coordination, and more prominent roles for other central agencies in espousing principles, and monitoring and guiding budgeting, performance and values. Second, systematic monitoring of implementation was introduced as politicians focused on public perceptions of service delivery, and the Cabinet Implementation Unit was used to ensure delivery of government policies and services. A third element was the rationalisation of public bodies and more direct control for ministerial departments over agencies following a review of the corporate governance of statutory authorities. The fourth element was a whole-of-government approach to working across portfolio boundaries, which was influenced by new priorities and pursued through traditional coordination and instruments such as task forces (Halligan 2006, 2008a; O'Flynn 2009).

The third phase encompassed more extensive integration and capacity building for the Public Service, but as part of the new Rudd government's agenda—

discussed in the next section. Three factors need to be acknowledged in examining the Australian context. First was the long-term effect of the Coalition government's pursuit of a neo-liberal agenda of NPM involving devolution, outsourcing, privatisation and favouring the private sector (although there were several continuities and a continuation of trends apparent under the previous government).

A second factor was the overall impact of the financial and economic crisis on government budgets and on attitudes towards state intervention. The projected budget surplus in 2008 of $22 billion was converted to a deficit as two economic stimulus packages were implemented in 2008–09.

The third factor was the Labor government's agenda. The Rudd government introduced its own interpretation of the issues with new agendas to transform public dialogue, an emphasis on national approaches to improving delivery and performance, and objectives in a range of fields including the APS and governance. Its wide policy agenda covered a 'stronger' and 'fairer' Australia and preparing for future challenges (including in education, health, climate change and water) as outlined in the mid-term progress report (Australian Government 2009). Other agendas such as a national urban policy were also added (Moran 2010a).

The Rudd government's new agenda of institution and capacity building

The government arrived with an agenda for addressing a number of areas of public governance. In style it was quite different from Howard in the handling of the transition with the Public Service, perhaps reflecting Rudd's earlier experience as chief of staff for a Queensland premier. There was no immediate displacement of departmental secretaries, and the language was one of positive engagement with machinery-of-government changes, signalling new policy emphases—for example: climate change and energy efficiency, and broadband, communication and the digital economy.[2]

In Rudd's response to the national and global environment, he argued for the transition between two epochs and orthodoxies, the latter representing different traditions on the roles of government and the market. Neo-liberalism, which sought to subject the state to private markets, was countered by the conception of a 'social-democratic state' as the best option for developing capacity in which the government funds, regulates and provides services (Rudd 2009a).

---

2 Detailed lists of creations, changes and abolitions of departments and agencies are included as Appendices to Chapter 4.

Several elements envisaged for the future Public Service and government were reinvigorating the Westminster tradition (including an independent and professional public service, merit-based selection, and continuity of employment); policymaking processes based on evidence and a culture of contestability; enhancing strategic policy capability; strengthening integrity and accountability; broadening participation through inclusive policy processes; and service delivery focused on outcomes.

Integrity, accountability and Westminster

The strength of an administrative tradition grounded in Westminster has been apparent in Australia when governments have overstepped the limits of acceptability (for example, the backlash to the purge of secretaries by the Coalition in 1996, and the response to the role of political advisers in the mid-2000s). System correction was again apparent with Labor's initial approach. The Rudd government promised to preserve tradition, which meant that it was able to make changes at the top without incurring public debate about the process. Five new departmental secretaries were appointed within the first 20 months after the 2007 election in a process that involved the movement of 11 senior executives as the government sought to place appropriate officials in significant positions.

The office of John Faulkner, the Special Minister of State, was used to pull together a range of integrity and governance responsibilities under one minister: the Public Service, codes of conduct, privacy and various procedures for handling transparency and accountability (for example, freedom of information and regulations). A new Code of Conduct for Ministerial Staff and Standards for Ministerial Ethics were introduced.[3]

As part of its accountability and integrity agenda, the Rudd government recognised the effect of the increasing numbers and roles of ministerial staff on the relationship between ministers and public servants, and the lack of consideration to formalising their responsibilities. The number of advisers was reduced and their conduct subjected to regulation following Rudd's election (Maley 2010). The new Code of Conduct for Ministerial Staff, introduced in mid-2008, stipulated that 'ministerial staff do not have the power to direct APS employees in their own right and that APS employees are not subject to their direction'. Political advisers were now expected to be accountable where they had a policy role (APSC 2008). Yet ministerial staff numbers grew during the

---

3 Other measures included establishing a register of lobbyists and new guidelines to cover campaign advertising.

term as offices sought to handle the demands (and they were formally increased after the 2010 election to cope with the more fluid political environment) (Kerr 2010).

Public service coherence and consolidation: one APS

The lament across the service—the reasons differing between location and level—was of the limitations of a devolved agency structure. Chief executives and departmental secretaries had control over conditions of employment, which produced substantial variations in salary packages. The head of the Public Service, Terry Moran (2009), asserted that there was 'one-APS, and… we need to bring more meaning to that statement. The APS is not a collection of separate institutions. It is a mutually reinforcing and cohesive whole.' The level of agency and departmental autonomy (see Aulich et al. 2010) had generated some concerns, including those relating to constraints on the mobility of APS officers because of variations between agencies in pay and conditions. The Prime Minister echoed these themes: 'there is a clear need for a stronger collective identity within the APS…There are still too many impediments and disincentives for employees moving between agencies'. He added the need 'to foster a greater sense of cohesion and esprit de corps across the APS' (Rudd 2009b:11, 13).

The demise of designated outsourcing

One of the strongest symbols of NPM was outsourcing. The Rudd government sought to reduce this dependence, initially by commissioning a UK expert, Peter Gershon, to undertake a review of the use of information and communication technology (ICT). It recommended a 'major program of both administrative reform of, and cultural change from, a status quo' to reduce costs across the APS by $16 billion of the annual computer and communications expenditure (Gershon 2008:iii). Legal services were also being brought more in-house following a review.

The government moved to reverse the external reliance by a major reduction in outsourcing of ICT in the Public Service. The goal of the Finance Minister, Lindsay Tanner, was for the number of ICT contractors to be cut by 50 per cent by the end of 2011. Full-time public service staff would replace them. This 'is designed to correct imbalances caused by the previous Government's radical decentralisation of the sector', which derived from the 1997 decision to outsource IT infrastructure services through competitive tendering processes (Tanner 2009). This devolved environment of the public sector was now seen as a key challenge to achieving government outcomes. The decentralised financial managementsystem was perceived to run the risk that the 'government may not be fully leveraging its substantial purchasing power to achieve value for money in its procurement...the excessive decentralisation that was embraced by our predecessors inevitably resulted in significant waste, duplication and inefficiencies in the procurement of goods and services' (Tanner 2009).

National integration

A new phase in intergovernmental relations was initiated with the intention of strengthening vertical relationships within the federation. The reform agenda of the Council of Australian Governments (COAG) was at the forefront of the government's modernisation and policy agenda. The focus on developing intergovernmental relationships and improving national policy and delivery of the federal system was given impetus because, for a time, the same party controlled all nine governments (for detailed coverage of COAG matters, see Chapter 6 of this volume).

At the interface between levels, the Australian Intergovernmental Agreement on Federal Financial Relations was designed to improve the wellbeing of Australians through collaborative working arrangements and enhanced public accountability covering outcomes achieved and outputs delivered. The arrangement provides for accountability at the federal level with state-level flexibility regarding delivery and indicators (APSC 2010).

A secondary dimension has been the argument for extending professional connections across the several public services. The APS is viewed as 'part of a broader professional family of public services'. Modern challenges require working together to give 'real voice to the concept of "one-APS" and building a broader professional ethos must involve knocking down barriers which prevent mobility' (Moran 2009).

Performance management and transparency

Australia has been more committed to performance management than most Organisation for Economic Cooperation and Development (OECD) countries pursuing this agenda since the mid-1980s with increasing refinements. The official model is a fully developed performance-management system based on a framework of outcomes and outputs covering individual and organisational dimensions and management interrelationships (Bouckaert and Halligan 2008; Hawke and Wanna 2010).

As to how performance information was used, the picture was one of both evolution and continuing shortcomings, including variations among agencies in how they engage performance. A review of the Application of the Outcomes and Outputs Framework (ANAO 2007) reported variability in descriptions of outcomes and outputs, outcomes and outputs structures, operational integration and use of this information in decision making. In practice, the implementation was not fully realised and officials often worked around the framework rather than through it.

The change of government produced an agenda to improve budget transparency (termed 'Operation Sunlight') that drew on a report by the then Senator Andrew Murray (Tanner 2008). The diagnosis of the existing framework was blunt:

> Some outcomes are so broad and general as to be virtually meaningless for Budget accounting purposes leading taxpayers to only guess what billions of their dollars are being spent on...

> There is also imprecise reporting of targets and little reporting back against key result areas. Loose outcome descriptions can also foster incentives for money to be shifted between outcomes for political purposes or for spending such as government advertising to be undertaken for overt political purposes without parliamentary approval...

> The outcomes and outputs framework was intended to shift the focus of financial reporting from inputs...to outputs and outcomes i.e. actual results. While this is worthy in theory, it has not worked. Basic information on inputs was lost in the changeover, and reporting of outcomes is seriously inadequate. (Tanner 2008:4)

The main objectives included improvements to the outcomes and outputs framework, the readability and usefulness of budget papers and the transparency of estimates (see Operation Sunlight: DoFD 2010).

The Australian response to the limitations of its performance management framework has been to seek improvements to it. Rather than outcomes as a focus being discarded, they remain with augmented features to the framework. Programs were revived for portfolio budget statements and, along with outcomes, form the basis for reporting. Political leaders reinforced a performance focus, and there was greater interest in targets and league tables, and service delivery focused on outcomes. The pursuit of more effective performance management maintains the directional path of 30 years, but it continues to be a work in progress.

Open government

A declaration of open government was made in mid-2010 with three components: citizen engagement, accessibility of government information and new technology. A new multidimensional culture of 'public sector openness, transparency and engagement' was proclaimed, which for citizens was intended to offer pro-disclosure, and collaborative (in designing policy and service delivery), engaged (online, the 'collaborative web') and consultative and participative government (AGIMO 2010; Tanner 2010).

The task force's report recommendations on Government 2.0 were accepted (Government 2.0 Taskforce 2009). A concrete result was the creation of the Office of the Information Commissioner, which, with freedom-of-information (FOI) reforms, was thought to be sufficient to restore 'trust and integrity in government' (Tanner 2010).

The Prime Minister and central steering

This role was reinforced under Rudd following a major organisational audit of the Department of the Prime Minister and Cabinet, which indicated that it was 'heavily focused on the day-to-day activities of government, and that [its] capacity to provide strategic policy advice could be improved' (PM&C 2008:3). A Strategy and Delivery Division was established to advance administrative priorities that were more strategic, long term and proactive. The overall objective was a strong department for supporting the Prime Minister's reform agenda for the nation with monitoring of progress assuming significance (Halligan forthcoming).

Rudd's leadership approach was close to a 'priorities and planning style' in which first ministers are 'in a strong political position and choose to pursue an ambitious, creative, and comprehensive legislative program' (Campbell 1988:59). This style favours central agencies and their role in 'assembling coherent policies and programs'. Ultimately, a strategic governance form of central steering is dependent on executive leadership, and how the priorities and the planning style are sustained over time.

The indications of the 'court government' reported for Canada, where power has been concentrated in the Prime Minister and 'carefully selected courtiers' (Savoie 2008:16), has relevance to Australia. One issue under Rudd was the extent to which informal processes had displaced formal cabinet decision making. On the one hand, cabinet meetings were reported as having increased 47 per cent in 2008–09, while cabinet committee meetings were up 211 per cent (PM&C 2009), yet there were consistent reports that a 'kitchen cabinet' of key ministers made key decisions. Moreover, the Prime Minister's office was depicted as having

> acquired more comprehensive authority and power. Never, even in John Howard's day has so much power been concentrated in the Prime Minister's private office. Not in his department, although it too is accumulating unprecedented power, but among the tight core of

minders, advisers and managers focused exclusively on the political survival of the government and the Prime Minister. Above anything else (Waterford 2008:8).

Rudd's reliance on inexperienced political advisers was regarded as a factor in his displacement, and surfaced as an early but transient election issue in 2010.

Blueprint for reform

With the government's extended agenda of change, it was concluded that there were significant capability weaknesses and a lack of coherent direction for the Public Service to justify the appointment of an advisory group. According to the Prime Minister, 'the next stage of renewal of the APS requires more than just piecemeal change. We need a more sweeping reform driven by a long-range blueprint for a world class, 21st century public service' (Rudd 2009b:12).

The review of the reform of Australian government administration was announced in September 2009 as a six-month process (Rudd 2009a), a discussion paper was released the next month (AGRAGA 2009), and the report *Ahead of the Game: Blueprint for the reform of Australian government administration* was released in late March 2010 (AGRAGA 2010). The head of the Department of the Prime Minister and Cabinet chaired the advisory group.[4]

Why does Australia have an explicit and fully fledged reform process? Leaving aside Australian state governments and territories that have been running reform agendas in recent years (for example, Western Australia and the Northern Territory), there appears to be nothing comparable internationally. Yet Australia is far less constrained (or crippled) than others by the fallout and large deficits from the global financial crisis, and is not driven by the need to cut the Public Service (by up to 25 per cent for departments in the United Kingdom).

One interpretation is that a party out of power for 11 years might wish to launch a reform agenda in order to differentiate itself from the previous regime, yet the government was already undertaking the reforms discussed earlier. Of direct relevance were the expectations of an activist government, and in particular a prime minister with a highly ambitious policy and reform agenda. The expansive program was already making demands on the Public Service that exceeded capacity and exposed weaknesses. A further explanation that assisted in understanding the rationale for the review was its chair. Terry Moran came from a commonwealth central agency and later ran the Victorian Premier's Department before becoming Secretary of the Department of the Prime Minister

---

4   For details of the process, see the comprehensive review by Lindquist (2010).

and Cabinet. Unusually, the new head had both a strong mandate and an understanding of how to manage a large and complex public sector and the systemic requirements and interplay between the elements.

Initially, there was a highly aspirational flavour to the review. The subtitle of the discussion paper was 'Building the world's best public service' (AGRAGA 2009). The paper correctly observed that 'in most international comparisons, our public service fares very well', but it wanted further improvement: 'Australia's public service can legitimately aspire to be no less than the best public service in the world.' This raised questions about which countries to compare Australia with given its high standing, and how to comprehend what is best practice overall for a civil service. It is difficult to point to specific models of high-performing and quality civil services that offer rounded and relevant options, and there are problems with ignoring the country traditions in which models are embedded (for example, the Nordic emphasis on trust) or government structures (unitary compared with federal systems). Eventually, the review settled for being 'ahead of the game' (AGRAGA 2010).

The actual diagnosis suggests lack of capacity and accountability, a series of deficits (for example, a shortfall in capability), a lack of high performance, and creeping bureaucratisation and compliance issues (termed 'red tape') (AGRAGA 2009, 2010; Rudd 2009b). These tendencies could be seen as reflecting the 'sedimentation' that permeates much recent academic interpretation as the layers of different models of public management are superimposed over time (Halligan 2010).

The review picked up a number of matters already the subject of discussion, debate and reports. The catalogue of items compiled in the blueprint report included efficiency dividends (JCPA 2008), revising APS values (IPAA 2009), reducing red tape (MAC 2007), the roles of secretaries, including stewardship as a response to short-term thinking (on secretaries, see Egan 2009; Halligan 2008a; Podger 2009; Sedgwick 2010), weaknesses in policy making (Banks 2009), and the consequences of different conditions of employment for joint activity (Blackman et al. 2010; Moran 2009).

The blueprint covers 28 recommendations in nine reform areas that are organised under four themes: citizen needs; leadership and strategic direction; capability; efficiency and high standards (Appendix 3.1). By its nature, this is not an exercise that has yet generated innovations that would rank internationally. Centrelink, for example, was originally hailed overseas as a one-stop, multipurpose delivery agency for providing services to several purchasing departments, and for seeking customer-focused delivery that provided integrated services (Halligan 2008b). This is not to say that innovation will not emerge in the implementation process, and the commitment to being innovative is high (MAC 2010).

There are, of course, ideas that are new to the APS, but are based on practice elsewhere. The question of relating to citizen engagement has been around for some time (Briggs 2009), but conducting satisfaction surveys has been borrowed from Canada and New Zealand. The capability reviews from the United Kingdom have been adopted, but the concept is being substantially adapted to Australian needs.

Four types or orders of reform can be distinguished. The first—system maintenance—is the most basic and focuses on finetuning and reconditioning. As previously discussed, there was an accumulation of items waiting for the right opportunity to be formalised (cf. Kingdon 1984). Reform enhancement— the second type—is about introducing new instruments and techniques. This includes giving impetus to reform agendas that need a driver—for example, citizen engagement. A third type—system design and maintenance—addresses systemic coherence and balance in which there is systematic refurbishing of the components. This type is in the tradition of a comprehensive review and provides a reform context in which finetuning and new techniques can be introduced.

A fourth, paradigm reform represents a fundamental form of change that subsumes the others, and can be observed in the historic shift to new public management. To put this in a contemporary perspective, the Australian agenda falls well short of the United Kingdom—ever a risk-taker in reform—which could yet produce a case of paradigm change in its radical action in 2010 to reconfigure the public sector. But note that economic conditions are the mother of innovation. The distinctive pathways of the two countries reflect different levels of public spending, the impacts of the economic crisis and the size of their budget deficits.

Australia fits the third type as a large-scale crafting of the system. The influence of Moran as a systemic thinker and operator is important here. He argues that the blueprint for the Public Service is 'more than the sum of the parts' (Moran 2010b).

What is original about the review is the exercise itself, both in the conception of comprehensive design and maintenance and in the execution. The blueprint is a prolegomenon to an extended reform process managed by the Public Service. There is a rolling agenda for change with a large range of elements that encompasses many players (in particular, two leadership groups: a new Secretaries Board and APS 200—a senior leadership forum for supporting the secretaries).

By the advent of the caretaker period prior to the August 2010 election, numerous processes were under way to implement the blueprint recommendations.

The most significant was the augmentation of the Australian Public Service Commission's powers by government endorsement of the blueprint. It was made the lead agency for about half the recommendations, with $39 million allocated under the 2010 budget (although subsequently cut by Prime Minister, Julia Gillard, when projecting fiscal rectitude in the election campaign).

Results of the term

Several emergent features remain underdeveloped: central steering, public service capacity, flexible delivery and external relationships.

Steering strategically

Central steering was reformulated under Rudd, who emphasised strategy, policy capability, targeted performance and the design of governance nationally and federally. Rudd's leadership style followed a 'priorities and planning style' (Campbell and Halligan 1992) in which first ministers operate from a position of strength to pursue an ambitious and comprehensive program, which favours the role of central agencies in providing coherence and direction. Following an organisational audit of the Department of the Prime Minister and Cabinet, which indicated the need for improving its capacity to provide strategic policy advice, a Strategy and Delivery Division was established to advance priorities that were more strategic, long term and proactive. The overall objective of a strong department for supporting and monitoring the Prime Minister's reform agenda intensified as the term proceeded.

Internal public service: strengthened but wanting

The institution of the Public Service has been strengthened by attention to boundaries, political and private sector relationships and traditions. There were, however, high expectations for performance and for improved innovative policy capacity (the subject of a Management Advisory Committee 2010 project that inquired into public sector innovation and an appropriate culture; also ANAO 2009; DIISR 2010). The perceived deficit in capacity was a factor in the Moran review of the Public Service.

Managing flexibly and across boundaries

The importance of the business case for government initiatives remained and could entail 'market design'. Markets were to be managed to achieve government objectives (the notion of markets as policy instruments that can be managed is not new). The Treasurer, Wayne Swan (2008), embraced the use of markets that were 'properly designed and well regulated'. While there were precedents for this approach (for example, the Job Network), the designed and regulated market was used in a range of areas (with Swan regarding commonwealth–state relations as being redesigned using 'a more market-driven framework' that combined incentives and accountability).

External relations with citizens: a work in progress

A government agenda has been to broaden participation through inclusive policy processes, and the Prime Minister has diagnosed citizen relationships as a field for further attention. This area is challenging for the central-government tier in a federal system, although delivery agencies (for example, Centrelink) have extensive experience. The Government Task Force on Government 2.0 addressed the use of Web 2.0 techniques for supporting community consultation and collaboration (Government 2.0 Taskforce 2009), and this was a feature of the Moran review.

Implications and contradictions of Rudd's governance

The full implications of these reform strands cannot be examined within one chapter, beyond noting that the government was operating on the assumption of more than one term in office in order to address perceived deficiencies. For the Public Service, the two main leaders—the Prime Minister and his chief official adviser—exercised pivotal influence (not unlike John Howard and Peter Shergold). Rudd displayed the features of a priorities and planning style (before defaulting to electioneering), while Moran deployed the powers of his headship of the Department of the Prime Minister and Cabinet to strengthen its roles and launch a pervasive review of the system. The complementary roles of the political executive and the Public Service leadership are apparent: the political and policy agendas directed by the Prime Minister and the machinery reforms being led by the departmental secretary, although endorsed by the government.

Several issues remained unresolved. First was the question of potential conflicts between objectives that invariably arise with a comprehensive reform agenda. The effect of the Rudd agenda was a doubled-edged sword. On the one hand, it reinforced traditional values: a professional public service and accountability and transparency; while on the other, it was seeking to reduce the size of the service while making heavy demands on public servants and renewing the emphasis on performance. One trade-off was that the consolidation and reaffirmation of Westminster principles meant higher expectations for a modernised public service.

A second issue was how best to balance the several relationships involved in governing. For example, in addressing the relative roles of line and central agencies, the question was what forms of rebalancing are appropriate. Whereas before the degree of decentralisation was perceived to be problematic, now the matter was more one of curbing potential centralising tendencies.

The contradictions in the Rudd style were a defining feature of the term: the commitment to enhancing the Public Service, against the eventual reliance on court politics of a few advisers (cf. Savoie 2008 on Canada and the United Kingdom); the richness of the array of initiatives, against the lack of consummation under a government thought to be guaranteed a second term. The most disturbing aspect for public governance was the loss of impetus as the Rudd government compromised its agenda in the run-up to the election and experienced acute implementation failure with programs (for example, the roll-out of the home insulation program and the Building the Education Revolution program). The Prime Minister forsook policy and planning for short-term opportunism and pragmatism reminiscent of Howard in his last election year (Halligan 2008a), and similarly experienced an *annus horribilis*. The catastrophic failures of governance climaxed with the replacement of Rudd as Prime Minister and the unexpected retirement of two ministers: John Faulkner, Minister for Defence, and Lindsay Tanner, Minister for Finance—both of whom had played significant roles in reform.

Source: David Pope, *The Canberra Times*, 18 May 2010

Conclusion

Judgments about the Rudd term need to recognise the dimensions presented in this chapter. A number of new measures were articulated and implemented and have contributed to the quality of governance. Others were in process with an indeterminate result and/or were sidelined by the policy and political crises leading up to the election. The blueprint is a medium-term venture that stretches well beyond the present parliamentary term, but this will be subject to the level of funding, which was drastically cut by Prime Minister Gillard during the 2010 election campaign, and to the level of political endorsement and support in her second term.

Stability of office-holding in the transition to power and the common ground between alternative governments have been significant factors in sustaining the trajectory and implementation of Australian agendas in the reform era. Despite a succession of models and variations in the leadership styles of prime ministers' different ideological approaches, the cumulative results have been relatively consistent.

The interpretation in this chapter has taken into account the promise of a reform agenda—much of it unfulfilled—and that its realisation is attendant on how the new Prime Minister envisages the way forward. Much of the blueprint agenda can be pursued by the Public Service if committed leadership exists. Prime Minister Gillard has indicated that the emphasis on the Department of the Prime Minister and Cabinet would be modified under her leadership and with the low funding priority accorded to APS reform, the fate of the reform program (like much of the Rudd term) remains indeterminate.

John Halligan *is Professor of Public Administration at the University of Canberra.*

References

Advisory Group on the Reform of Australian Government Administration (AGRAGA) 2009. *Reform of Australian government administration: building the world's best public service*, Discussion Paper, Commonwealth of Australia, Canberra.

Advisory Group on the Reform of Australian Government Administration (AGRAGA) 2010. *Ahead of the Game: Blueprint for the reform of Australian government administration*, Commonwealth of Australia, Canberra.

Aulich, C., Batainah, H. and Wettenhall, R. 2010. 'Autonomy and control in Australian agencies: data and preliminary findings from a cross-national empirical study', *Australian Journal of Public Administration*, vol. 69, no. 2, pp. 214–28.

Australian Government 2009. *Mid Term Progress Report*, June, Commonwealth of Australia, Canberra.

Australian Government Information Management Office (AGIMO) 2010. *Declaration of Open Government*, Department of Finance and Deregulation, Commonwealth of Australia, Canberra, <http://www.finance.gov.au/e-government/strategy-and-governance/gov2/declaration-of-open-government.html>

Australian National Audit Office (ANAO) 2007. *Application of the outcomes and outputs framework*, Audit Report No. 23, Australian National Audit Office, Barton, ACT, <http://www.anao.gov.au/uploads/documents/2006-07_Audit_Report_23.pdf>

Australian National Audit Office (ANAO) 2009. *Innovation in the Public Sector: Enabling better performance, driving new directions*, Australian National Audit Office, Barton, ACT.

Australian Public Service Commission (APSC) 2008. *Code of Conduct for Ministerial Staff*, Circular 2008/7, Australian Public Service Commission, Canberra.

Australian Public Service Commission (APSC) 2010. *Case Study: Australia's new cooperative federal financial agreement: focusing on better outcomes for citizens*, Australian Public Service Commission, Canberra.

Banks, G. 2009. *Challenges of Evidence-Based Policy-Making*, Commonwealth of Australia, Canberra.

Blackman, D., Buick, F., Halligan, J., O'Flynn, J. and Marsh, I. 2010. Australian experiences with whole of government, Paper presented to Panel Track 32, Working Across Boundaries: Barriers, enablers, tensions and puzzles, IRSPM Conference, University of Bern, April.

Bouckaert, G. and Halligan, J. 2008. *Managing Performance: International comparisons*, Routledge, London.

Briggs, L. 2009. *All Those Who Stand and Wait—Putting citizens at the centre*, 21 May, John Curtin Institute of Public Policy,

Curtin University of Technology, Bentley, WA.

Campbell, C. 1988. 'The search for coordination and control: when and how are central agencies the answer', in C. Campbell and B. G. Peters (eds), *Organizing Governance: Governing organizations*, University of Pittsburgh, Pa, pp. 55–79.

Campbell, C. and Halligan, J. 1992. *Political Leadership in an Age of Constraint: Bureaucratic politics under Hawke and Keating*, Allen & Unwin, Sydney.

Department of Finance and Deregulation (DoFD) 2010. *Operation Sunlight*, Department of Finance and Deregulation, Commonwealth of Australia, Canberra, <http://www.finance.gov.au/financial-framework/financial-management-policy-guidance/operation-sunlight/index.html>

Department of Innovation, Industry, Science and Research (DIISR) 2010. *Australian Innovation System Report*, Department of Innovation, Industry, Science and Research, Commonwealth of Australia, Canberra.

Department of the Prime Minister and Cabinet (PM&C) 2008. *Annual Report 2007–2008*, Department of the Prime Minister and Cabinet, Commonwealth of Australia, Canberra.

Department of the Prime Minister and Cabinet (PM&C) 2009. *Annual Report 2008–2009*, Department of the Prime Minister and Cabinet, Commonwealth of Australia, Canberra.

Egan, J. 2009. *Review of Work Value for the Office of Secretary: Australian government departments of state*, Prepared for the Commonwealth Remuneration Tribunal, Sydney.

Gershon, P. 2008. *Review of the Australian Government's use of Information and Communication Technology*, Commonwealth of Australia, Canberra.

Government 2.0 Taskforce 2009. *Engage—Getting on with Government 2.0*, Australian Government Information Management Office, Canberra.

Halligan, J. 2006. 'The reassertion of the centre in a first generation NPM system', in T. Christensen and P. Lægreid (eds), *Autonomy and Regulation*, Edward Elgar, Cheltenham, UK.

Halligan, J. 2008a. 'Australian Public Service: combining the search for balance and effectiveness with deviations on fundamentals', in C. Aulich and R. Wettenhall (eds), *Howard's Fourth Government*, UNSW Press, Sydney, pp. 13–30.

Halligan, J. 2008b. *The Centrelink Experiment: An innovation in service delivery*, ANU E Press, Canberra.

Halligan, J. 2010. 'Reforming management and management systems: impacts and issues', in P. Ingraham and J. Pierre (eds), *Public Change and Reform: Moving forward, looking back: a festschrift to honor B. Guy Peters*, McGill-Queens University Press, Montreal.

Halligan, J. (forthcoming). 'Central steering in Australia', in C. Dahlström, B. G. Peters and J. Pierre (eds), *Steering from the Centre: Central government offices and their roles in governing*, University of Toronto Press, Ontario.

Hawke, L. and Wanna, J. 2010. 'Australia after budgetary reform: a lapsed pioneer or decorative architect?', in J. Wanna, L. Jensen and J. de Vries (eds), *The Reality of Budgetary Reform in OECD Nations: Trajectories and consequences*, Edward Elgar, Cheltenham, UK, pp. 65–91.

Institute of Public Administration Australia, National Council (IPAA) 2009. Submission to the Advisory Group Reform of Australian Government Administration, November.

Joint Committee of Public Accounts and Audit (JCPA) 2008. *The efficiency dividend and small agencies: size does matter*, Report 413, Commonwealth of Australia, Canberra.

Kerr, C. 2010. 'More work to cope with political paradigm shift', *The Australian*, 27 September, p. 5.

Kingdon, J. W. 1984. *Agendas, Alternatives, and Public Policies*, Little Brown & Co., Boston.

Lindquist, E. 2010. 'From rhetoric to blueprint: the Moran Review as a concerted, comprehensive and emergent strategy for public service reform', *Australian Journal of Public Administration*, vol. 69, no. 2, pp. 115–51.

Maley, M. 2010. 'Australia', in C. Eichbaum and R. Shaw (eds), *Partisan Appointees and Public Servants: An international analysis of the role of the political adviser*, Edward Elgar, Cheltenham, UK, pp. 94–113.

Management Advisory Committee (MAC) 2007. *Reducing Red Tape in the Australian Public Service*, Commonwealth of Australia, Canberra.

Management Advisory Committee (MAC) 2010. *Empowering Change: Fostering innovation in the Australian Public Service*, Commonwealth of Australia, Canberra.

Moran, T. 2009. Challenges of public sector reform, Speech to Institute of Public Administration Australia, Canberra, 15 July.

Moran, T. 2010a. City strategic planning, Speech to Council of Capital City Lord Mayors Towards a National Urban Policy Summit, 27 May.

Moran, T. 2010b. Presentation to APS staff by Terry Moran, Secretary of Department of the Prime Minister and Cabinet, Canberra, 21 May.

O'Flynn, J. 2009. 'The cult of collaboration in public policy', *Australian Journal of Public Administration*, vol. 68, no. 1, pp. 112–16.

Podger, A. 2009. *The Role of Departmental Secretaries: Personal reflections on the breadth of responsibilities today*, ANU E Press, Canberra.

Rudd, K. 2009a. 'The global financial crisis', *The Monthly*, February, pp. 20–9.

Rudd, K. 2009b. John Paterson Oration, Australia and New Zealand School of Government Annual Conference, Canberra, 3 September.

Savoie, D. 2008. *Court Government and the Collapse of Accountability in Canada and the United Kingdom*, University of Toronto Press, Ontario.

Sedgwick, S. 2010. Australian public sector reform, Presentation to 2010 Government Business Conference, 6 May.

Stuart, N. 2010. *Rudd's Way: November 2007–June 2010*, Scribe, Melbourne.

Swan, W. 2008. Address to the Per Capita Conference, Brisbane, 30 October.

Tanner, L. 2008. *Operation Sunlight: Enhancing budget transparency*, December, Commonwealth of Australia, Canberra.

Tanner, L. 2009. Address by the Hon. MP Minister for Finance and Deregulation, Public Sector Procurement Conference, Sydney, 28 July.

Tanner, L. 2010. Declaration of open government, Media release, 16 July, Parliament House, Canberra, <http://www.financeminister.gov.au/archive/media/2010/mr_412010.html>

Waterford, J. 2008. 'On a west wing and a prayer', *The Canberra Times*, 16 May, p. 8.

Appendix 3.1

Nine reform areas and 28 recommendations in the 'Blueprint'

A high-performing public service			
Meets the needs of citizens	Provides strong leadership and strategic direction	Contains a highly capable workforce	Operates efficiently and at a consistently high standard
1. Delivering better services for clients 1.1 Simplify Australian government services for citizens 1.2 Develop better ways to deliver services through the community and private sectors 1.3 Deliver services in closer partnership with state, territory and local governments 1.4 Reduce unnecessary business regulatory burdens 2. Creating more open government 2.1 Enable citizens to collaborate with government in policy and service design 2.2 Conduct a citizen survey	3. Enhancing policy capability 3.1 Strengthen strategic policy 3.2 Build partnerships with academia, research institutions and the community and private sectors 3.3 Improve policy implementation 4. Reinvigorating strategic leadership 4.1 Revise and embed the APS values 4.2 Articulate the roles and responsibilities of secretaries 4.3 Revise employment arrangements for secretaries 4.4 Strengthen leadership across the APS 4.5 Improve talent management across the APS 5. Introducing a new APSC to drive change and provide strategic planning 5.1 New APSC with responsibilities to lead the APS	6. Clarifying and aligning employment conditions 6.1 Ensure employment bargaining arrangements support one APS 6.2 Assess the size and role of the Senior Executive Service (SES) 7. Strengthening the workforce 7.1 Coordinate workforce planning 7.2 Streamline recruitment and improve induction 7.3 Expand and strengthen learning and development 7.4 Strengthen the performance framework 7.5 Encourage employees to expand their career experience	8. Ensuring agency agility, capability and effectiveness 8.1 Conduct agency capability reviews 8.2 Introduce shared outcomes across portfolios 8.3 Reduce internal red tape to promote agility 9. Improving agency efficiency 9.1 Review the measures of agency efficiency 9.2 Strengthen the governance framework 9.3 Small agencies to improve the efficiency of their corporate functions

Source: AGRAGA (2010).

4. Continuity and change in the outer public sector

ROGER WETTENHALL

Introduction

This chapter continues the record of changes in the outer public sector carried through all previous volumes in the *Australian Commonwealth Administration* series. As in all previous volumes, here the 'outer public sector' is conceived of as that part of the public sector that is made up of non-departmental public bodies (NDPBs)—a broad category comprising mainly statutory authorities and corporations, government-owned companies and executive agencies, all of which fall outside the central establishment of ministerial departments and a few parliamentary departments. The word 'quango' is sometimes used as an alternative general class name.

A difficulty with all relevant classification exercises is, however, that the NDPB category does not lend itself to the drawing of clear boundaries. If we envisage the public sector as a wheel-like structure containing an inner area made up of the departments with their policy, system-maintaining and some operational functions, and an outer area made up of all the non-departmental bodies performing operating, regulatory and other system-serving functions— sometimes thought of as constituting a large governmental 'fringe'—then there is opaqueness both between the inner and outer areas and at the far edge of the outer area.[1]

Such opaqueness occurs closer to the centre of government when some public functions are placed in divisions of departments that are sufficiently separately branded to have some of the characteristics of NDPBs. Closer to the outer fringes of government, it occurs in several ways. We find varieties of public–private mixing, with bodies in which the central government or an NDPB

---

1 The inner and outer areas as described here are sometimes referred to as 'core' and 'non-core'; however, I believe that terminology diminishes the importance of the outer area, so I avoid it in this chapter (except in quotations).

shares ownership and operations with one or more non-governmental (private) bodies; these 'mixed enterprises' have traditionally been seen as parts of the outer public sector if the public stake comes to more than 50 per cent. And the mixing could rather be with 'non-government' in its other sense—that of the 'third sector' inhabited by a mass of not-for-profit bodies. Indeed, it is sometimes difficult to determine whether an organisation is an NDPB or a third-sector body. Yet another set of boundary issues arises from the field of inter-jurisdictional sharing: some NDPBs are creations of two or more governments, so that reality is offended if we try to locate them in a single public sector. Examples of all these types of opaqueness are provided in the discussion below, which also notes other problems of terminology and classification in the NDPB arena.

Notwithstanding these difficulties of comprehension, virtually all governments have NDPBs. It has been widely observed that, though they might not be much liked, the processes of government could scarcely operate without them. Exploring this part of a public sector is an exercise in understanding how the machinery of government works and, as with earlier editions of the *Australian Commonwealth Administration* series, it is appropriate to begin this present exploration with an indication of changes that occurred in the establishment of the central departments in the transition from the Howard governments to the Rudd government. How NDPBs connect with this departmental establishment— as a class and individually—is always a central issue to be confronted in an exploration such as this.

Following a brief description of the departmental arrangements, this chapter goes on to consider issues of terminology, classification and general agency policy that have arisen in the NDPB experience of the Rudd government. The Uhrig *Review of the Corporate Governance of Statutory Authorities and Office Holders* and reactions to it (Uhrig 2003; Wettenhall 2005a, 2005b) came close to dominating the NDPB experience of the fourth Howard government. Necessarily, therefore, this chapter asks whether that fascination with Uhrig continued into the dispositions of the new government, or whether other forces took over as shapers of structures and relationships. The chapter also identifies the new creations, reorganisations and abolitions of the period and seeks generally to illustrate the pervasiveness of the population of NDPBs throughout the whole intertwined system of government, economy and society.

A general theme is that, while there have been many changes, the whole commonwealth experience with NDPBs during the Rudd government period suggests that the evolution of NDPB policy and practice mostly follows a line of continuous development over a much longer period.

The departmental establishment

Whereas the last Howard government had 16 portfolios and corresponding portfolio departments with two other departments (Human Services and Veterans' Affairs) arranged as 'outliers' within one or other of the portfolio departments, the Rudd government began with 17 portfolios and portfolio departments and two outlier departments (Climate Change and Veterans' Affairs). Several of the Howard portfolios and portfolio departments continued as before, though with some redistribution among the departments of statutes administered—in particular, the Attorney-General's Department gained many new responsibilities as it inherited a range of additional statutes to administer relating to territories and to emergency services. Within the portfolio departments, most ministers were assisted by other ministers of non-cabinet rank[2] and by parliamentary secretaries—for example: the Minister for Justice and Customs assisted the Attorney-General in the administration of that department and had a dedicated relationship with some of the NDPBs associated with it, which were described on the departmental web site as 'portfolio agencies'.

Appendix 4.1 lists the departments of the Rudd government and shows their relationship to those of the previous government. While a few of the listed titles have had very long lives (Attorney-General's and Treasury go back to the time of Federation), the Rudd list probably went further than that of any other commonwealth government in applying titles that reflect contemporary policy issues and associations (such as Broadband, Deregulation, Innovation and Climate Change—the last expanded late in the period to Climate Change and Energy Efficiency). It could be speculated that these titles reflected the initial enthusiasm to be different and tackle particular pressing problems, but that they would not endure long, leading to a sense of instability within the affected departments and their associated bodies.

For completeness, Appendix 4.1 also lists the parliamentary departments, though their involvement in the NDPB story is fairly limited; it does not go much beyond the existence of a Parliamentary Service Commissioner and the fact that the Public Accounts Committee, which the parliamentary departments service, has particular prescribed functions relating to the office of the Auditor-General.

---

2   Foreign Affairs and Trade is an exception, with two ministers of cabinet rank.

Away from the centre: terminology, classification and related issues

On underestimating the size and importance of the outer public sector

The size of a total public sector and its importance for the economy and society of the state it serves are frequently underestimated by people at or near the centre of a governmental system—people such as politicians, administrators and commentators, who focus on the inner part as though it is all that really matters. And this underestimation often leads to the sometimes quite damaging assumption, when the outer part is finally remembered, that language, forms and principles applying appropriately to the inner apply equally appropriately to the outer. There are important distinctions and the machinery of government will not function as well as it might if they are not adequately recognised.

The first report of the Advisory Group on Reform of Australian Government Administration appointed by Prime Minister Rudd in mid-2009 illustrated this problem (Moran 2009). Consistently with 'whole-of-government' thinking, the group used the terms 'public sector' and 'public service' virtually interchangeably. Of course, the Public Service is part of the public sector, but it is only a part. In this sort of treatment, which has been very common recently, the needs and importance of the outer areas of the public sector inevitably suffer serious neglect.[3]

In preparing its second and final report, the Advisory Group apparently heeded criticism that it had been careless about such machinery-of-government matters (Gourley 2009; Wettenhall 2010). Now it focused appropriately on its central mission—the Public Service proper—with fairly sparse commentary about the rest:

> Within Australian Government administration, the Australian Public Service (APS) is a core institution...Of the approximately 300,000 Australian Government employees, around 160,000 are employed in the APS...Remaining Australian Government employees operate under other Commonwealth agency specific legislation (such as *The Australian Federal Police Act 1979*), and those employed under other arrangements (for example Commonwealth companies such as Medibank Private Limited) who work closely with APS employees. (Moran 2010:viii, 3)

---

3 The Uhrig report, which played such an important role in the relevant history of the fourth Howard government, could not make this mistake because its terms of reference directed it specifically to NDPBs: statutory authorities and statutory office holders.

There was a general exhortation that 'efficiency in the public sector is critical to ensure the best possible outcomes are achieved for the level of input'. Of course, the word 'agency' was used, but in adding that the search was for 'efficiency across the APS and within agencies' (Moran 2010:67), the implication was that the concern was with departments and those agencies staffed *within* the Australian Public Service.[4] As will be noted elsewhere in this book, one major reform strategy was for a strengthening of the Public Service Commission to play a leadership role; however, as a former commissioner has noted under the intriguing title 'Inside or outside the tent' (Podger 2009:159–82), there are ambiguities about its governmental centrality and the notional autonomy that comes with its statutory authority status. Beyond that, in calling for '[e]fficiency in the creation of inter-jurisdictional entities; [a] governance framework that is efficient and promotes fit-for-purpose organisations…and [m]ore efficient small agencies' (Moran 2010:67), a final recommended reform strategy did come some way towards acknowledging the kinds of issues to which this chapter directs attention.

An item of international recognition secured late in the Rudd government period attested to the prestige that can come to members of the NDPB establishment. In the 2010 UN Public Service Awards competition, two accolades came to Australia: to the Australian Electoral Commission and the National Blood Authority (Ludwig 2010). Both are statutory authority members of this establishment, with the particular status of 'statutory agencies' (on which see below).

Towards framework statutes

The circumstance that some NDPBs are staffed as part of the Public Service and some are not contributes to the fairly general misunderstandings. Using a variant style of terminology, there are 'off-public service' NDPBs as well as 'on-public service' ones, just as there are 'off-budget' agencies as well as 'on-budget' ones. This has been accommodated in part by the development within the Commonwealth system since 1997 of the division between agencies subject to the *Financial Management and Accountability (FMA) Act* (they are part of the Commonwealth fiscus so 'on-budget') and those subject to the *Commonwealth Authorities and Companies (CAC) Act* (not part of the Commonwealth fiscus, with independent financing arrangements so 'off-budget').[5] With some exceptions, the on-public service/off-public service division corresponds with the on-budget/off-budget division. The 1997 statutes represent a culmination of efforts to establish some order in the management of the public sector as a whole that had been under way at least since the time of the Coombs Royal Commission,

---

4   Conflicting uses of the term 'agency' present another problem (see Wettenhall 2005b).
5   Though there may be budget interactions, as when governments buy some services from them, make grants or loans to them for particular purposes, or receive dividends and loan repayments from them.

and it is a distinct improvement that the way of thinking it encourages is now widely established within the Commonwealth system. Unfortunately, the hardline advocates of whole-of-government 'solutions' to perceived problems of government often do not seem to understand the distinctions and the need for separate recognition of the outer parts.

The major organisational categories recognised in the two framework acts are as follows.[6]

FMA Act

- portfolio (ministerial) departments (in Department of Finance and Administration/Deregulation terminology: 'departments of state')
- parliamentary departments
- non-commercial statutory authorities, usually without boards, also called 'statutory agencies' when staffed under the *Public Service Act*
- executive agencies
- prescribed agencies (a category that includes the executive agencies and FMA-connected statutory authorities, but goes further to embrace some large departmental branches with considerable managerial autonomy; see further below).

CAC Act

- statutory authorities with separate fiscuses, usually incorporated with boards (so also statutory corporations)
- government-owned companies limited by guarantee
- government-owned companies limited by shares.

The Department of Finance and Administration/Deregulation (DoFA/DoFD) has provided a very useful service since 2003 in producing two-sided coloured 'flip charts' recording movement in these categories. It has also been producing a comprehensive *List of Australian Government Bodies and Governance Relationships* (DoFD 2009a) that goes much further in providing a detailed breakdown of each ministerial department, with information about branches, agencies and functions performed—extending to ministerial councils, intergovernmental bodies, joint ventures and partnerships, and much else. Though they thus cover much more, the lists provide useful data about the NDPB establishment.

DoFA entrenched its position as machinery-of-government nerve centre for the Commonwealth administration when it provided the secretariat for the Uhrig inquiry during the fourth Howard government. It subsequently provided

---

6   As discussed below, for one reason or another, a few Commonwealth entities have escaped inclusion under either system.

enduring policy underpinning for the conceptual skeleton provided by Uhrig—it was well aware of the high level of criticism the Uhrig report had attracted (Uhrig 2003; Wettenhall 2005a:46)—by developing a set of guidelines for ministers and senior departmental officials considering the creation of new administrative bodies (DoFA 2005). This statement of governance arrangements was to prove highly influential when the system moved into new leadership under Rudd and Labor.

A major objective was to promote greater consistency and greater collaboration between departments in thinking about such developments. There was a presumption in favour of maintaining new functions within departments wherever possible and a further presumption that, where there was a strong case for a separate body, the FMA framework with employment under the *Public Service Act* was the preferred option. It was consistent with Uhrig and with whole-of-government thinking that agencies with high autonomy were to be used sparingly. The CAC framework came into its own where commercial-type activities and mixed-ownership activities were involved and corporate boards were deemed necessary—though there is a suggestion that, in the event, DoFD needed much persuading that CAC conditions were necessary even where mixed ownership applied.[7]

The government arrangements statement contained one significant reversal. Fuelled by 'New Public Management' (NPM) influences, there had been a marked movement from the late 1980s away from the statutory-body form towards the company form, even where public ownership remained constant. Now, however—in a return to the policy enunciated in the Walsh policy guidelines of the Hawke period (Walsh 1986)—the presumption is that 'it is preferable to establish a body as a Commonwealth authority rather than as a Commonwealth company', and a company should be established only 'in exceptional circumstances' (DoFA 2005:xiv).[8]

This reversal was already apparent before the 2007 change of government, but some terminological confusion remained. Unfortunately for clear understanding of machinery-of-government issues, the popular language did not change much and press reporting often continued to describe statutory bodies erroneously as 'companies' (for examples of this treatment of Australia Post and CSIRO in just three days in the Canberra press, see Ja 2010; Mannheim 2010). It is likely that some confusion arose from a passage in the 2009 DoFD list in which three statutory bodies—Australia Post, CSIRO and Indigenous Business Australia—were referred to in a paragraph beginning with the words 'companies limited

---

7   In the case of the Australian Curriculum Assessment and Reporting Authority.

8   For a fairly similar earlier episode in which the criterion for exemption was stated as a 'necessity only, as opposed to convenience', see Wettenhall (1987a:37–8). The problem is, of course, that terms such as 'necessity' and 'exceptional circumstances' are incapable of precise definition.

by shares'. The point being illustrated was not that they were companies themselves, but that each of them had a number of subsidiary bodies organised as companies (DoFD 2009a:vii).

The notion of 'prescribed agency' is another development of classificatory significance. Prescription is by regulation under the *FMA Act* and, as noted, the category includes executive agencies, statutory bodies other than those under the *CAC Act* and parts of departments considered to 'be legally or administratively independent to a level that justifies financial autonomy' (DoFA 2005:51).[9] To complicate the picture, DoFD recognises two other kinds of quasi-separate parts of departments—'business operations' and 'functions with separate branding'—that nonetheless lack prescribed agency status. Examples of the three types of quasi-separate parts of departments drawn from the DoFD list are given in Appendix 4.2.

The organisational history of some of these entities reflects the opaqueness of the border between departments proper and non-departmental portfolio agencies. Thus the Australian Agency for International Development (AusAID) had a statutory authority forebear, the Australian Development Assistance Agency, for a short period in the 1970s (Viviani and Wilenski 1978), and statutory authority status has again been suggested for it from time to time; in the controversies affecting the Therapeutic Goods Administration in 2006, it was often assumed by the media—incorrectly —that it was 'an independent body' (Wettenhall 2007:72); and the Australian Government Information Management Office was an executive agency for a short period after 1999. To the unofficial observer, it is a surprise that some other sections of departments are not (or so far have not been) accorded a degree of separate recognition in this way; a case in point is Emergency Management Australia, now part of a National Security and Criminal Justice Group within the Attorney-General's Department.

Some uncertainties of identification and classification can be attributed simply to the transitional nature of parts of the NDPB arena. Thus the Australian Climate Change Regulatory Authority was set up in anticipation of the passing of the climate change legislation, but in the event the government's plans stalled in the Senate and there was embarrassment in dealing with the staff already appointed. Again, the creation of an Australian National Preventative Health Agency, to be a commonwealth statutory agency but with close links to the intergovernmental Health Ministers' Conference, was proposed in legislation introduced in 2008 (Boxhall and Scully 2009), but that too was blocked in the Senate. The proposed Australian Business Investment Partnership Limited—the so-called Ruddbank—suffered the same fate: the government was to have had

---

9   Another very useful DoFD document brings together the *FMA Act* and the body of regulations under that Act. Among other things, these regulations are used to establish the 'prescribed agencies'. See DoFD (2009a).

a 50 per cent stake and the 'big four' banks 12.5 per cent each in a mixed-ownership company intended to be manager of a fund to help commercial property companies struggling to refinance their loans in the global financial crisis (GFC) environment. And the High Court ruled in 2009 that the Australian Military Court set up in the late stages of the fourth Howard government was unconstitutional, forcing the Rudd government to plan a new military justice tribunal system that accorded with the Constitution. As a final example of the transitory character of some NDPB arrangements, the Defence Honours and Awards Tribunal was set up by ministerial direction and began operations in 2008; the intention was that it would be formally established by legislation 'at a later date' (DHAT 2008), but that did not happen in the period being reported on here.

Long-used practices in the use of the terms 'board' and 'commission' have undergone changes as the official codifying exercises have progressed. 'Board' was entrenched as the organisational centrepiece of one of Uhrig's two templates, whereas 'commission' is not now likely to have that status in the Commonwealth jurisdiction. DoFA/DoFD officers who advise on machinery-of-government changes and have responsibility for producing these lists and flip charts now speak of authorities internal to departments as well as those external to departments, with some bearing the formal title 'commission' falling into the internal group.[10]

The term 'commission' does, however, continue to have another application. In longstanding practice in Australia and analogous countries, it has been used as a class name for bodies appointed to conduct inquiries into administrative and policy issues and problems, as in 'royal commission' (Prasser 2006). Their authority usually comes from letters patent issued by a head of state, not from a statute or company registration, and they are not usually considered to be part of the NDPB establishment. Notably in the period of the Rudd government, the National Health and Hospitals Reform Commission—its terms of reference set by the Council of Australian Governments (COAG)—operated with this sort of status (NHHRC 2008). An older regular NDPB, however, the Australian Law Reform Commission (ALRC 2010), has been giving consideration to ways of improving the use of such inquiry agents in the Commonwealth jurisdiction.

The opaqueness of the outer border of the public sector can be illustrated by two telling examples. The DoFD list includes Beyond Blue Limited, an intergovernmental (commonwealth, states, territories) company limited by guarantee and established in 2000 to 'provide a national focus…to increase the capacity of the broader Australian community to prevent depression and

---

10   My thanks to Marc Mowbray-d'Arbela and John Kalokerinos of the Legislative Review Branch of DoFA/ DoFD for many fruitful discussions exploring this and related machinery-of-government issues.

respond effectively to it' (DoFD 2009a:424). The list does not include the Alcohol Education and Rehabilitation Foundation (AER), which describes itself as a 'not-for-profit company established by Federal Government legislation in 2001 with a mandate to "change the way we drink"' and as 'the leading national voice for promoting research into and awareness of safe and responsible consumption of alcohol and prevention of licit substance abuse' (AER 2010).[11] Although this AER is not in the DoFD list, another one is! This is the also-intergovernmental (and statutory) Australian Energy Regulator (DoFD 2009a:593)—demonstrating once more the ubiquity of the non-departmental 'fringe' and the classificatory difficulties it creates.[12]

The Parliament's Joint Committee on Public Accounts and Audit has used an entirely different sort of classification in its consideration of the impact of the efficiency dividend first imposed in 1987–88 and increased in incidence by the Rudd government in 2008–09. In this matter, governments have drawn no distinction between departments and NDPBs, though because the system applies only to funding that comes from parliamentary appropriations many NDPBs, especially the more commercial ones now operating under the *CAC Act*, have not been much affected. In its own deliberations, the committee has been particularly concerned about the impact of the dividend on 'small agencies' and it has used the term 'non-executive agencies' to apply to all agencies specifically established to be independent of the executive government—a meaning that has little or no relationship to 'executive agencies' as used in the *Public Service* and *FMA Acts* and in the DoFD lists. For the committee, the groups mainly affected—and mostly suffering badly because of the effects of the efficiency dividend system—are oversight agencies (for example, the Audit Office and the Ombudsman), cultural agencies (the National Museum, National Gallery, National Library—all statutory-authority administered), the courts and scientific agencies (JCPAA 2008).

In the very early days of the Rudd government, legislation to amend the *CAC Act* that had been prepared in the late Howard period was introduced by incoming Finance Minister, Lindsay Tanner. The *CAC Act* was now amplified by bringing its requirements relating to reporting by and accountability and transparency of commonwealth companies into line with changed requirements for all companies under the general *Corporations Act*; by introducing a new class of 'general policy

---

11   These bodies are examples of what I identified as 'sideline' public sector companies, in contrast with the 'frontline' companies operating government business enterprises or GBEs (in Wettenhall 2003:32–6). One described itself as 'a private non-profit company established by the government'. The chief executive of another asked seriously: 'Are we public or are we private?'

12   For another example of this sort of classification uncertainty, see Chapter 12 of this volume for the account by Will Sanders and Janet Hunt of the creation of a 'new national Indigenous representative body' (a successor to the Aboriginal and Torres Strait Islander Commission) as a company limited by guarantee rather than a statutory authority, and said to be 'supported, but not quite so directly created, by the Commonwealth Parliament and government'.

orders' covering instructions applying to public sector bodies generally; and by amending the definition of 'commonwealth company' to exclude subsidiaries of either existing companies or existing statutory authorities (*Authorities and Companies Amendment Act* [Cth] 20/2008; Tanner 2008:199–200). Similarly, there was an early adjustment to the *FMA Act* relating to agency transaction procedures, requiring agencies to establish audit committees and introducing provisions to cover circumstances in which agencies cease to exist (*Financial Framework Legislation Amendment Act* [Cth] 90/2008).

Emphasising this chapter's theme of continuity and change operating together, a Financial Framework Legislation Amendment Bill that had been long in preparation was introduced into the Parliament near the very end of the Rudd government. It would change some of the processes involved in the CAC and FMA systems and also vary the status of more NDPBs within those systems (notably the Australian Institute of Criminology, the Criminology Research Council, the Australian Law Reform Commission and the National Transport Commission). As these were not issues that divided the political parties, it could be assumed that this bill would eventually become law irrespective of the outcome of the August 2010 election.

There would be more to come. A 'tidying-up operation' headed by the machinery-of-government team in DoFD had been under way for much of the Rudd period and was unlikely to be much affected by the outcome of the election. Planning was already under way for further changes, such as the merging of Centrelink and Medicare and the closure of more small government-owned companies.

Waning of the Uhrig influence?

The fourth Howard government had followed the Uhrig recommendations broadly (Wettenhall 2008:34–8), resulting in the closure of some NDPBs, the abolition of the boards of others so that their managements stood much closer to ministers and their departmental chiefs, and a general enhancement of ministerial authority over the whole NDPB arena. After the change of government, we heard little about the Uhrig agenda; one explanation was that mostly all that could be done had already been done; and of course it had conservative political associations. DoFA's (now DoFD's) governance arrangements document had Uhrig connections, however, and that was readily embraced by the Rudd ministers, so no radical process changes were to be expected.

The DoFD list (2009a:vii–viii) indicated a fairly significant movement away from the CAC arrangements (bodies with separate financial governance systems) to FMA arrangements, but that covered much of the fourth Howard period as well as the earlier part of the Rudd period so that it did not tell us much about differences in the styles of the two governments. That would need to be ascertained from a closer study of the creations and categorisations of the Rudd period.

Notwithstanding its deficiencies (Gourley 2009:19; Wettenhall 2005a:46), the Uhrig report was swimming with the tide. Uhrig surveyed and reported at a time when the great excitement with NPM doctrines such as devolution was being overtaken by the new search for whole-of-government solutions to administrative problems, motivated in part by the heightened national security situation and in part by growing awareness that those NPM doctrines had been taken to excess (on which see Chapter 3 of this volume). Paraphrasing *The Canberra Times'* editor-at-large, Jack Waterford (2009), devolution was out and central control was back in. In this climate, it was always likely that forces lined up against granting significant autonomy to administrative agencies would win over those in favour of greater autonomy.

There was no driving force in the NDPB arena in the period of the Rudd government to match the Howard-backed Uhrig in the previous period. The Finance Minister, Lindsay Tanner, whose department was producing these lists and flip charts, was, however, clearly influential. Tanner was active in many areas of public sector change and reform (see Chapter 3 of this volume). On NDPBs, he expounded on his developing views in some major speeches in late 2009, one of which involved the formal launch of the 2009 list at a conference of the Australian Institute of Company Directors in Canberra. The list was, he asserted, an important aid to improving the transparency of the Commonwealth government and its preparation had forced departments to examine their portfolio structures carefully and critically. The lesson was that they should try to accommodate new tasks within themselves before rushing to create new authorities; also that continuing review was necessary 'to bring some consistency' to the structure of agencies and their governance arrangements (Franklin 2009; Tanner 2009a; see also Hawthorn 2009). The whole exercise, he said, had been important in establishing 'a solid understanding of the current landscape of government' (Tanner 2009a:2).

Consistency is an important principle, but it might not count for much where there are strong arguments for special arrangements in particular cases. Thus, going somewhat against the general trend, Tanner advocated movement of the Future Fund from the *FMA Act* to the *CAC Act* so that it would have a degree of autonomy from government and ministers similar to that enjoyed by the Reserve Bank. Tanner was on record also as favouring a review of the system of making appointments to the boards of public sector bodies, and was associated with the bold decision to appoint Peter Costello, long-term Treasurer in the vanquished Howard government, to the board of the Future Fund (Wright 2009). Developments relating to the Australian Broadcasting Corporation (ABC) and the Special Broadcasting Service (SBS) furthered this process; the government acted in 2008 to set up a merit-based system for appointments to the boards of these two authorities for which political impartiality was considered especially important. An independent nomination panel was to consider all applications for board positions against a core set of selection criteria and provide the minister with short lists of recommended candidates. If the minister wanted to go outside those short lists, he needed the Prime Minister's specific agreement, with a statement of reasons to be tabled in Parliament and, in the case of a chair position, the Leader of the Opposition had to be consulted (DBCDE 2010). This can be seen as a major step in reinforcing notions of autonomy and non-partisanship that are so often associated with bodies in the non-departmental public sector. Whether it will become a model for application beyond the ABC and the SBS remains to be seen.

Source: David Pope, *The Public Sector Informant*, June 2009

Privatisation, sovereign wealth funds, Chinese influences and the effects of the GFC

Mention of the Future Fund furnishes a reminder that the idea of privatisation—now mostly off the Australian political radar—still has some traction, even if it is in part delusional. We have been encouraged to believe that Telstra is now fully privatised, but the fact is that residual government shareholdings after the third-tranche sale (worth about $9 billion in late-2009 prices) were lodged in the very clearly publicly owned Future Fund, not sold to private buyers. The Future Fund is now firmly recognised as Australia's 'sovereign wealth fund', so it joins a variety of international publicly owned investment funds operating around the world and now grouped for study under this new class name.[13] Privatisation proposals still emerge as fundraising schemes in the Australian states, but the only significant commonwealth manifestation occurred late in the period of the Rudd government as the Liberal–National Party opposition renewed calls for the sale of the government-owned health insurer confusingly known as Medibank Private.

Perhaps surprisingly, Chinese influences have been important. At a time when the output of Australia's mineral industry is so keenly sought by industrialising China, that country offers a reminder of the continuing great significance of state-owned enterprises in the world. Again and again, we have seen that Chinese state-owned enterprises such as the Aluminium Corporation of China (or Chinalco) are seeking to buy into private Australian mining firms. Clearance for such deals is required from the Australian Foreign Investment Review Board (FIRB; not a statutory body), and some such bids have been successful. Concern is not infrequently expressed, however, that the Chinese state-owned enterprises involved are really agents of the Chinese state, so their introduction into Australia gives the Chinese government great advantage in its dealings with the Australian government and Australian private firms. Assurances have been sought that these firms are free to operate in the market in their own best interests, but those assurances have not been forthcoming with any clarity (for example, AAP 2009; Garnaut 2009; Kroeber 2009). Further, it seems that, on the Chinese side, proceedings seen in the West as part of normal commercial negotiations can be regarded as encroaching on state national security secrets and leading to draconian punitive action (O'Malley and La Canna 2009). For those following these matters, the issue of relationships between governments and the NDPBs inhabiting the relevant public sectors is thus dramatically revived in Australia, having been imported from a foreign source.

The GFC of 2007–09 had major effects on the administrative systems of many countries as governments faced the need to redesign their systems for regulating financial institutions, acquired major shareholdings in failing banks and car manufacturers and actually brought some of those institutions totally into their public sectors; so, around the world as the GFC worked itself out, there were major impacts on the establishment of NDPBs. In Australia, however, the regulatory system based on NDPBs such as the Reserve Bank and the Australian Prudential Regulation Authority appeared to have been working well, with the Commonwealth government's $42 billion stimulus package operating

---

13   The term 'sovereign wealth fund' was first used in an article in a 2005 issue of the *Central Banking Journal* (see Rozanov 2005; Truman 2009).

mainly through direct payments to individuals, firms and state and territory governments and, where necessary, a mass of contracting-out arrangements. The whole GFC experience certainly aroused interest in NDPB-related issues such as the matter of applying lessons from past experience with mixed enterprises to aid policy makers in dealing with the new world crop of such enterprises,[14] but in the event Australia escaped fairly lightly and the GFC did not of itself produce a need for major reconstruction in the NDPB arena.

New creations, reorganisations and abolitions

At the close of the fourth Howard government, there were 90 CAC bodies (including 64 statutory bodies and 26 companies) and 77 bodies (other than departments) listed under the *FMA Act*, making a total of 167 in these two major groups of commonwealth NDPBs (Wettenhall 2008:54, based on DoFA lists and flip charts). As hinted at above, there would also be several others not prescribed for either CAC or FMA treatment, some of them gathered around that rather indistinct border between the departmental part and the non-departmental part of the Commonwealth public sector, and yet more inhabiting that even more indistinct 'no-man's-land' at the outer edge of the public sector.

The Governor-General's speech opening the new Parliament in February 2008 gave some hints of relevant measures to come when it indicated that the Rudd government was giving high priority to strengthening the nation's long-term economic prospects by inter alia introducing 'a plan of action on skills and infrastructure'; that it would be introducing an entirely new 'workplace relations system'; and that 'a Freedom of Information Commissioner [would] be appointed to take overall responsibility for access to government information and [to] improve review processes' (Jeffery 2008:2, 5, 10). Other NDPB developments had been anticipated in several policy documents issued in the lead-up to the late-2007 election—for example, the 'New Directions for the Arts' document referred to by the Minister for the Environment, Water, Heritage and the Arts in introducing legislation to reorganise government support for the film industry (Garratt 2008:832). That was one of many statutes affecting the NDPB arena that came quickly after the opening.

Changes in the Rudd period involved the creation of some new NDPBs with allocations to one or other of the CAC and FMA categories, sometimes resulting from conversions of others; the abolition of some NDPBs; and several shifts between the two categories. In many cases, the change process has been uncontroversial, unlikely to attract much public attention and not much

---

14 See discussion in Wettenhall (2010).

affecting the performance of functions even where accounting arrangements have changed significantly. In other cases, however—for example, in the restructuring of industry regulatory and support arrangements—there has been substantial change to working systems, sometimes accompanied by protracted political debate reflecting deep divisions between government and opposition parties in the legislature.

The tables assembled in Appendix 4.3 seek to identify the new creations and conversions, status shifts and abolitions in summary form. The next section notes some of the major features of this change process, so supplements the data in these tables. The record is drawn primarily from data assembled in the statute book and parliamentary debates over the period of the Rudd government, with space considerations preventing comprehensive referencing of all sources used. As far as possible, I have attempted to concert my record with that in the DoFD list; however, a perfect correlation is not possible because that list covers a different (though overlapping) reporting period. Also, building on a point made earlier, the outer border of the public sector is so opaque that a major research project would be necessary before there could be certainty that *all* relevant changes in that area had been identified.

Features of the change process

The first few weeks of the new Parliament saw speedy passage of legislation creating several of these new authorities, and several main features of the change process were already apparent. There was continuity with the earlier Howard period to the extent that quite a few of the changes were being planned within the bureaucracy—in part as a legacy of the Uhrig review—before the change of government.

Several features impacting on organisational or titular arrangements need immediately to be noticed. First, some of the changes affected clusters of NDPBs, not just single ones. In industrial relations, water management and film industry support particularly, new agencies were created, old ones displaced and some functions shifted between agencies, so that several were affected in a single adjustment. Second, drafting habits affected patterns of nomenclature, in that the tendency to eliminate class words such as 'board', 'commission' and 'authority' from formal titles gathered pace—witness Fair Work Australia, Safe Work Australia, Skills Australia, Infrastructure Australia, Screen Australia, National Film and Sound Archive Australia, Wheat Exports Australia and Health Workforce Australia.

The trend towards the reduction or elimination of boards and the concentration of authority in the hands of chief executives continued, although there was much variation within that general pattern. In the official thinking, boards now seemed to be clearly differentiated from commissions, about which there was some ambiguity. In some cases (for example, Skills Australia, Infrastructure Australia, Wheat Exports Australia), the agency comprised a chair and members (along with supporting staff) with no statutory reference to either board or commission. In the rearranged Fisheries Management Authority, the board was replaced by a commission and CEO, the minister having discretion to appoint the same person as both chair and CEO. In the rearranged Australian Sports Anti-Doping Authority, the CEO is now declared unambiguously to be the agency head. This trend is associated with the increasing currency of 'statutory agency'—a convenient title for agencies staffed under the *Public Service Act* introduced in the revision of that Act in 1999. Linking two of these features, the Minister for Infrastructure, Transport, Regional Development and Local Government, Anthony Albanese, described the rearranged Australian Transport Safety Bureau as 'a separate statutory agency…[with] a commission structure' (Albanese 2009:1110). All this is consistent with Uhrig's 'executive management template' in which CEOs are accountable directly to ministers, and of course consistent also with both the movement from CAC to FMA status and the general thrust towards whole-of-government arrangements.

The changes to the Civil Aviation Safety Authority (CASA) buck the general trend, reinstating a board previously disposed of after continuing clashes between board members and the minister (see Wettenhall 2000:83–4, 2005d:82). After an inquiry, a senate committee reported that CASA lacked significant policy direction, that layers of management had increased since removal of the old board and that the CEO was now forced to wear two hats—both policy and executive direction; it concurred with the majority stakeholder view that restoration of the board would enhance CASA's governance and accountability (SSCRRAT 2008:32–6, 48). Perhaps Uhrig should have undertaken a few actual case studies of this sort!

Boards generally continue in the agencies remaining under the *CAC Act* and especially in those of an intergovernmental character. There has been a long history of intergovernmental NDPBs serving the Australian federation—a notable early example being the River Murray Commission established by an agreement between the Commonwealth and three state governments in 1914, ratified by legislation passed in each of the four legislatures and with each government then appointing a commissioner. Over the past few decades, other such bodies have appeared, usually at the instigation of one or other of the 'ministerial councils' that now link commonwealth, state and territory ministers in related portfolios, with the related bodies directed by and reporting to those councils. It has increasingly been left to the Commonwealth to enact creating legislation as necessary, building in the rights of all involved governments to participate in board appointments, to issue directions and receive reports.

Though the formula has differed from case to case, in the period under review, that has happened with the Murray–Darling Basin Authority, the Australian Curriculum Assessment and Reporting Authority, Safe Work Australia, Health Workforce Australia and Infrastructure Australia.

COAG has been involved in several of these creations and itself spawned another NDPB—the non-statutory COAG Reform Council—in the late Howard period. With the task of monitoring, assessing and reporting on the performance of all Australian governments, the council reports to the Prime Minister as chair of COAG and has a secretariat in the Department of the Prime Minister and Cabinet (Griffith 2009). Together with the tendency to use the Commonwealth Parliament as the creating instrument for these intergovernmental agencies, this arrangement must be seen as part of the increasing dominance of the Commonwealth within the federation.

Impulses for change have come from virtually all points of the political compass. As indicated elsewhere in this book, industrial relations featured as one of the battlegrounds between the political parties in the lead-up to the 2007 election, and it was inevitable that the array of agencies operating in that area would undergo major change after the governmental transition. It was a recommendation of a consultant who reported in 2007 on the relationship between CASA and the Australian Transport Safety Bureau that led to clarification of the latter's status as an 'independent' statutory authority (Albanese 2009:1110). A report from another NDPB, the Productivity Commission, was a significant influence on the decision to establish Health Workforce Australia (Productivity Commission 2005; Roxon 2009:3616). Of course, not all such proposals are accepted; the Independent (but government-appointed) Sports Panel reporting in 2009 wanted the Australian Institute of Sport separated from the Australian Sports Commission, but that recommendation was rejected (Crawford 2009; Ellis 2010).

Other impulses were generated by community influences mostly away from the main interests of the political parties—some attracting sufficient support to be translated into legislative and administration action. Thus an alliance comprising mostly food industry leaders, health professionals and the immediate past governor-general spearheaded the process that led to creation of the National Organ and Tissue Donation and Transplantation Authority (ABC 2010).[15] Not so successful was the advocacy of a Stolen Generations Reparations Tribunal by a group consisting of the Public Interest Advocacy Centre and the Australian Human Rights Centre, which pushed through a senate inquiry and a private member's bill in the Senate but with no governmental or strong parliamentary inclination to be supportive (Stewert 2008:5520).

---

15   This creation would also have had the strong support of a prime minister who had himself been the recipient of an organ transplant (The Canberra Times 2010).

Other proposals circulating but not consummated included those for a public sector regulator to review breaches of the financial regulations by government departments and agencies, a parliamentary standards commissioner to scrutinise use of electoral allowances by MPs, a children's commissioner to be associated with the Human Rights Commission, an Australian space agency and (from the Leader of the Opposition, Tony Abbott) a commission to advise on sustainable population growth levels (Cronin 2010).

A safe prediction is that there will always be a large outer public sector. It serves many community interests—governmental and other. So the big question is not so much how many constituent units that assemble within it, but how they relate to central government and the ministers that direct it. The issue of the relationship between agency and supervising minister has received much attention in the NDPB literature over the years, and of course a leading effect of Uhrig was that commonwealth ministers were generally strengthened in this relationship. There has been a gradual attrition of agency autonomy over the years since the first Australian statutory corporations were protected in so many ways from ministerial intervention in operational matters.

Through most of the twentieth century, it could be said that Labor governments generally favoured more intrusive controls than non-Labor ones. It would, however, be difficult to draw that distinction today. Whatever policy, partisan and personality issues separate the main political parties, Labor and non-Labor have shared not only in the attractions of managerialism that came with the NPM movement but also in the subsequent push for whole-of-government solutions generated in large part by the security situation. In this they are like peas in a pod: in this part of the NDPB experience, there has been substantial continuity over the transition from Howard to Rudd. It would be interesting to study the NDPB situation in the states to see whether they also reflect this trend.

Agencies in action: a massive contribution to good governance

A mid-2010 DoFD flip chart recognises 91 bodies under the *CAC Act* and 81 (other than departments) under the *FMA Act* (DoFD 2010); also, as noted above, there will be some other NDPBs not (or not yet) gathered in these groups. All the constituents of this establishment of 170-plus agencies go about their allotted tasks mostly quietly and unostentatiously, making a huge collective contribution to society, the economy and the processes of good governance generally.

At any particular time, of course, it is likely that a small number will be attracting much public and media attention. This could be because the political parties are involved in contests about their missions or because they have been creating waves themselves through their own occasionally dysfunctional actions. But it could also reflect the fact that, for some, the attraction of public notice is virtually unavoidable in the light of the missions allotted to them. As Peres (1967:362) pointed out many years ago, NDPBs range along a spectrum running from tight definitions of mission that allow very limited policy discretions to much looser definitions that allow competing conceptions of activity or confer judgmental responsibilities—and those in the latter group can be said to have a 'high controversy quotient'. Where NDPBs have been particularly newsworthy at some time during the period of the Rudd government, it could have been for any of these reasons.

A final indication of the importance to the society and the economy of the population of commonwealth NDPBs, and of the diversity of activities of members of that population, comes from a random selection of a few that have attracted much public and media attention—a lot of it positive but also some negative—in the period under review. It is likely that the Reserve Bank takes pride of place in this group, mostly because of its ongoing role in determining basic interest rates. Others to attract much attention have included Centrelink, CSIRO, the Australian Federal Police, the National Capital Authority, the Murray–Darling Basin Authority, and Fair Work Australia and its forebears and associates in implementing industrial relations policies.

Concluding comment: need for a 'college' of NDPBs?

Machinery-of-government systems are cyclical in nature, moving backwards and forwards between centralising and decentralising phases (Aulich and Wettenhall 2009:103–9), and we can expect the outer NDPB sector to expand and enjoy greater autonomy in the decentralising periods. The Australian Commonwealth system is no exception and the current focus on the whole of government can be seen as a centralising force. On the evidence, it has not led to any significant decrease in the number of NDPBs, but there has been a strong tendency to reduce the autonomy of the individual units. There are, of course, usually aberrant cases (such as, in this period, the Reserve Bank, the Future Fund and, reversing an older aberrant decision, CASA).

There is always a question of balance. Governments need to have sufficient authority to ensure overall harmony in public sector operations. But that should not deprive the units of room to discharge their functions with a reasonable degree of autonomy and effectiveness. Again, on the evidence, the Commonwealth's NDPB sector is currently not working badly, though there are black spots. It is, however, under threat from those who want to push the whole-of-government argument strongly. There seems to be little awareness that there is a counter-case to be made. Uhrig is still the exemplar here, always concerned to enhance ministerial authority and prepared to draw conclusions about the whole sector notwithstanding lack of effort to communicate with most of it. Others who give scant attention to the outer public sectors entrench this approach to its general detriment.

As agents as various as the Coombs Royal Commission, Uhrig and Tanner have pointed out, we need to be sure there is a strong case for establishing an NDPB before removing a function from direct (and often quite flexible) ministerial/departmental administration. When we do, however, we need to be aware that we have opted for a different pattern of administration. The evidence suggests that, away from the more obviously distinctive group of government business enterprises, that awareness is lacking.

In the long history of NDPB arrangements, there have been occasions when—either out of consciousness of threat to the group or from a sense of good order—all or most of the non-departmental units in a particular jurisdiction have come together in what might be seen as a 'college' to explore problems they have in common, develop some common stances and gain attention for their collective effort to serve society, the economy and the system of governance that would not otherwise come to them. In several countries, the public (state, government-business) enterprises have done this (Wettenhall and O Nuallain 1987); in the Australian Commonwealth, it happened during the Coombs Royal Commission's investigation (Wettenhall 1981:16–18) and again when there was much dissention over the efforts of the Hawke government to enunciate a general agency policy (Painter 1986). Perhaps this should be happening now, to balance the effects of Uhrig, the Moran inquiry and all the other centralising forces that are at work.

Roger Wettenhall *is Emeritus Professor in Public Administration at the University of Canberra and a Visiting Professor at the university's ANZSOG Institute for Governance.*

References

Albanese, A. 2009. Second Reading Speech on Transport Safety Investigation Amendment Bill, House of Representatives, *Debates*, 12 February.

Alcohol Education and Rehabilitation Foundation (AER) 2010. 'Call for applications for position of Chief Executive Officer', *The Canberra Times*, 17 April.

Aulich, C. and Wettenhall, R. 2009. 'The public sector's use of agencies: a dynamic rather than static scene', *Public Organization Review*, vol. 9, no. 2, pp. 101–18.

Australian Associated Press (AAP) 2009. 'Review board grills Chinalco over juicy Rio Tinto stake', *The Canberra Times*, 3 March.

Australian Broadcasting Corporation (ABC) 2010. 'Organ donor transplant problems', Transcript, *Health Report*, ABC Radio National, 3 May.

Australian Law Reform Commission (ALRC) 2010. *Making inquiries: a new statutory framework*, ALRC Report 111, Australian Law Reform Commission, Sydney.

Boxall, A.-M. and Scully, S. 2009. Australian National Preventative Health Agency Bill 2009, *Bills Digest*, no. 34, Parliamentary Library, Canberra.

Coombs, H. C. 1976a. *Report*, AGPS, Canberra.

Coombs, H. C. 1976b. *Royal Commission on Australian Government Administration: Appendix volume one*, AGPS, Canberra, pp. 312–64.

Crawford, D. 2009. *The Future of Sport in Australia*, Department of Health and Ageing, Commonwealth of Australia, Canberra.

Cronin, D. 2010. 'Coalition reveals targets for cuts', *The Canberra Times*, 20 May.

Department of Broadband, Communications and the Digital Economy (DBCDE) 2010. *ABC and SBS Board Appointments*, Department of Broadband, Communications and the Digital Economy, Commonwealth of Australia, Canberra, <www.dbcde.gov.au/television/abc_and_sbs_board_appointments>

Defence Honours and Awards Tribunal (DHAT) 2008. Initiating Directive, Defence Honours and Awards Tribunal, Canberra, <www.defence-honours-tribunal.gov.au/initiating-directive>

Department of Finance and Administration (DoFA) 2005. *Governance Arrangements for Australian Government Bodies*, Department of Finance and Administration, Commonwealth of Australia, Canberra.

Department of Finance and Deregulation (DoFD) 2009a. *List of Australian Government Bodies and Governance Relationships*, (Third edition), Department of Finance and Deregulation, Commonwealth of Australia, Canberra.

Department of Finance and Deregulation (DoFD) 2009b. *Financial Management and Accountability Legislation, October 2009*, Department of Finance and Deregulation, Commonwealth of Australia, Canberra.

Department of Finance and Deregulation (DoFD) 2010. *CAC Act* and *FMA Act* charts, 15 March, Department of Finance and Deregulation, Commonwealth of Australia, Canberra.

Department of Prime Minister and Cabinet (PM&C) 2007. Administrative Arrangements Order, 3 December, Department of Prime Minister and Cabinet, Commonwealth of Australia, Canberra.

Ellis, K. 2009. House of Representatives, *Debates*, 16 September, p. 9713.

Ellis, K. 2010. *Australian Sport: The pathway to success*, Commonwealth of Australia, Canberra, <www.health.gov.au/internet/main/publishing.nsf/Content/pathway-to-success>

Franklin, M. 2009. 'Tanner cracks down on public sector agencies', *The Australian*, 15 October.

Garnaut, J. 2009. 'The dragon set to devour Rio [Tinto]', *Sydney Morning Herald*, 12 February.

Garratt, P. 2008. Second Reading Speech: National Film and Sound Archive Bill, House of Representatives, *Debates*, 20 February, pp. 831–4.

Gourley, P. 2009. 'The Moran review: the good, the bad and the ludicrous', *The Public Sector Informant*, November.

Griffith, G. 2009. *Managerial Federalism: COAG and the states*, Parliament of New South Wales, Sydney.

Hawthorne, M. 2009. 'Comrade Tanner', *The Age*, 15 October.

Ja, C. 2010, 'Economist "harassed" by CSIRO over paper', *The Canberra Times*, 11 February.

Joint Committee of Public Accounts and Audit (JCPAA) 2008. *The efficiency dividend and small agencies: size does matter*, Report 413, Parliament of the Commonwealth of Australia, Canberra.

Jeffery, M. 2008. Governor-General's speech, Senate, *Debates*, 12 February, pp. 3–10.

Kroeber, A. 2009. Extended interview with Arthur Kroeber, Managing Director of Dragonomics, Beijing, ABC Radio National, 10 November.

Ludwig, J. 2010. APS recognised in United Nations 2010 Public Service Awards, Media release, 7 June, Parliament House, Canberra.

Mannheim, M. 2010. 'Aust Post rules out compromise', *The Canberra Times*, 8 February.

Moran, T. 2009. *Reform of Australian Government Administration: Building the world's best public service*, Advisory Group on Reform of Australian Government Administration, Department of the Prime Minister and Cabinet, Commonwealth of Australia, Canberra.

Moran, T. 2010. *Ahead of the Game: Blueprint for the reform of Australian government administration*, Department of the Prime Minister and Cabinet, Commonwealth of Australia, Canberra.

National Health and Hospitals Reform Commission (NHHRC) 2008. *National Health and Hospitals Reform Commission*, Woden, ACT, <www.healtrh.gov.au/internet/main/publishing.nsf/Content/nhrc-1>

O'Malley, S. and La Canna, X. 2009. 'China's view of secrets under fire', *The Canberra Times*, 11 July.

Painter, M. (ed.) 1986. 'Public management forum: guidelines for government business enterprises', *Australian Journal of Public Administration*, vol. 45, no. 4, pp. 281–343.

Productivity Commission 2005. *Report on Australia's Health Workforce*, Productivity Commission, Melbourne.

Peres, L. 1967. 'The resurrection of autonomy: organization theory and the statutory corporation', *Public Administration* [Sydney], vol. 17, no. 4, pp. 360–70.

Podger, A. 2009. *The Role of Departmental Secretaries: Personal reflections on the breadth of responsibilities today*, ANU E Press, Canberra.

Prasser, S. 2006. *Royal Commissions and Public Inquiries in Australia*, LexisNexis Butterworth, Sydney.

Roxon, N. 2009. Second Reading Speech: *Health Work Force Australia Act*, House of Representatives, *Debates*, 13 May.

Rozanov, A. 2005. 'Who holds the wealth of nations?', *Central Banking Journal*, vol. 15, no. 4.

Rudd, K. 2010. Ministerial changes, Media release, 26 February, Parliament House, Canberra.

Senate Standing Committee on Rural and Regional Affairs and Transport (SSCRRAT) 2008. *Report on Administration of Civil Aviation Safety Authority and Related Matters*, Parliament of the Commonwealth of Australia, Canberra.

Stewert, R. 2008. Second Reading Speech: Stolen Generations Reparations Tribunal Bill 2008, Senate, *Debates*, 24 September.

Tanner, L. 2008. Second Reading Speech: Commonwealth Authorities and Companies Amendment Bill, House of Representatives, *Debates*, 13 February, pp. 199–200.

Tanner, L. 2009a. Speech to Australian Institute of Company Directors Public Sector Governance Conference, Canberra, 14 October.

Tanner, L. 2009b. The Future Fund: delivering for Australia, Address to National Press Club of Australia, Canberra, 25 November.

The Canberra Times 2008. 'Govt sets investing principles', *The Canberra Times*, 18 February.

The Canberra Times 2010. 'Rudd says his problems "hardly significant"', *The Canberra Times*, 16 August.

Truman, E. M. 2009. *Sovereign wealth funds: the need for greater transparency and accountability*, Policy Brief 07-8, Peterson Institute for International Economics, Washington, DC.

Uhrig, J. 2003. *Review of the Corporate Governance of Statutory Authorities and Office Holders*, Department of Finance and Administration, Commonwealth of Australia, Canberra.

Viviani, N. and Wilenski, P. 1978. *The Australian Development Assistance Agency: A post mortem report*, RIPA, Brisbane.

Walsh, P. 1986. *Statutory Authorities and Government Business Enterprises*, AGPS, Canberra.

Waterford, J. 2009. 'On a west wing and a prayer', *The Canberra Times*, 16 May.

Wettenhall, R. 1987a. 'Federal Labor and the statutory corporation under Matthew Charlton', in *Public Enterprise and National Development: Selected essays*, Royal Australian Institute of Public Administration (ACT Division), Canberra.

Wettenhall, R. 1987b. 'Statutory authorities and government business enterprises: some observations on recent policy papers', in *Public Enterprise and National Development: Selected essays*, Royal Australian Institute of Public Administration (ACT Division), Canberra.

Wettenhall, R. 2003. '"Kaleidoscope", or "now we see them, now we don't!"': Commonwealth public sector involvement in company formation', *Canberra Bulletin of Public Administration*, no. 110, pp. 29–44.

Wettenhall, R. 2005a. 'Parliamentary oversight of statutory authorities: a post-Uhrig perspective', *Australasian Parliamentary Review*, vol. 20, no. 2, pp. 39–63.

Wettenhall, R. 2005b. 'Statutory authorities, the Uhrig report, and the trouble with internal inquiries', *Public Administration Today*, no. 2, pp. 62–76.

Wettenhall, R. 2007. 'Non-departmental bodies under the Howard governments', *Australian Journal of Public Administration*, vol. 66, no. 1, pp. 62–82.

Wettenhall, R. 2008. 'Non-departmental public bodies as a focus for machinery-of-government change', in C. Aulich and R. Wettenhall (eds), *Howard's Fourth Government: Australian Commonwealth Administration 2004–2007*, UNSW Press, Sydney, pp. 31–56.

Wettenhall, R. 2010. Submission to Advisory Group on Reform of Australian Government; 'Whole-of-Government' and Non-Departmental Public Bodies, Submission 0079, Department of the Prime Minister and Cabinet, Commonwealth of Australia, Canberra, <www.dpmc.gov.au/consultation/aga_reform/submissions/cfm>

Wettenhall, R. (forthcoming). 'Mixed enterprise and the global financial crisis: relevance for the 21st century of a 20th century institution', *Asian Review of Public Administration*, vol. 21, no. 1.

Wettenhall, R. and O Nuallain, C. (eds) 1987. *Getting Together in Public Enterprise*, IIAS, Brussels.

Appendix 4.1

Departments under the Rudd government*

Table A4.1.1 Ministerial (portfolio) departments

Final Howard arrangements	Rudd arrangements (3 December 2007)
No change	Agriculture, Fisheries and Forestry
No change	Attorney-General
Was Communications, Information Technology and the Arts	Broadband, Communications and the Digital Economy
No change	Defence(with Veterans' Affairs as separate outlier department)
Was: 1) Education, Science and Training 2) Employment and Workplace Relations	Education, Employment and Workplace Relations
Was Environment and Water Resources	Environment, Water, Heritage and the Arts
Was Families, Community Services and Indigenous Affairs	Families, Housing, Community Services and Indigenous Affairs
Was Finance and Administration (with Human Services as separate outlier department)	Finance and Deregulation
No change	Foreign Affairs and Trade
No change	Health and Ageing
Was outlier of Finance and Administration	Human Services
No change	Immigration and Citizenship
Was: 1) Industry, Tourism and Resources 2) Transport and Regional Services	Infrastructure, Transport, Regional Development and Local Government
+	Innovation, Industry, Science and Research
Prime Minister and Cabinet	Prime Minister and Cabinet (with Climate Change^ as a separate outlier department)
+	Resources, Energy and Tourism
No change	Treasury

Table A4.1.2 Parliamentary departments#

Department of the House of Representatives
Department of the Senate
Department of Parliamentary Services

* Compiled from document showing the track-change variations made to the Administrative Arrangements Order of 21 September 2006 (Howard) to produce the Administrative Arrangements Order of 3 December 2007 (Rudd).

+ No corresponding department; instead, parts of other departments used to constitute the new one.

^ Expanded to *Climate Change and Energy Efficiency* on 26 February 2010 (Rudd 2010). Note that the ministerial reshuffle of 6 June 2009 did not involve changes in the departmental arrangements.

Unchanged.

Appendix 4.2

Examples of quasi-separate parts of departments recognised in the DoFD lists

Prescribed agency (not executive agency or statutory body)

- Australian Agency for International Development (AusAID) within Department of Foreign Affairs and Trade
- Defence Materiel Organisation (DMO) within Department of Defence
- Geoscience Australia within Department of Resources, Energy and Tourism
- IP Australia within Department of Innovation, Industry, Science and Research
- Royal Australian Mint within Department of the Treasury

Business operation

- Australian Quarantine and Inspection Service (AQIS) within Department of Agriculture, Fisheries and Forestry
- Therapeutic Goods Administration (TGA) within Department of Health and Ageing

Function with separate branding

- Artbank within Department of Environment, Water, Heritage and the Arts
- Australian Antarctic Division within Department of Environment, Water, Heritage and the Arts
- Australian Bureau of Agricultural and Resource Economics (ABARE) within Department of Agriculture, Fisheries and Forestry
- Australian Government Information Management Office (AGIMO) within Department of Finance and Deregulation
- Defence Science and Technology Organisation (DSTO) within Department of Defence
- National Portrait Gallery within Department of Environment, Water, Heritage and the Arts

Appendix 4.3*

Table 4.3.1 Creations and conversions: statutory authorities

Name Under the CAC Act	Creating act	Comment
Screen Australia	12/2008	Body corporate and statutory agency, replacing Australian Film Commission, Film Australia Ltd and Film Finance Corporation Ltd
National Film and Sound Archive	14/2008	Body corporate and statutory agency, created out of part of Australian Film Commission
Albury–Wodonga Development Corporation	90/2008	A long-existing statutory corporation, coming into CAC framework for first time
Australian Curriculum Assessment and Reporting Authority	136/2008	Body corporate, to develop national school curriculum; may charge fees and recruits own staff
Civil Aviation Safety Authority	19/2009	Body corporate with board restored (it had been removed in 1993)
Name Under the FMA Act		
Australian Fisheries Management Authority	36/2008	Moved from CAC Act to FMA Act; still a body corporate and now a statutory agency, with CEO replacing earlier authority board; now supported by a commission
Australian Accounting Standards Board (AASB, Office of)	61/2008	Moved from CAC Act to FMA Act; no separate corporate identity; now a statutory agency; acquired some functions from Financial Reporting Council
Auditing and Assurance Standards Board (AUASB, Office of)	61/2008	As for AASB
National Organ and Tissue Donation and Transplantation Authority	122/2008	Statutory agency constituted by a CEO and staff, assisted by a statutory Advisory Council
Murray–Darling Basin Authority	139/2008	Body corporate and statutory agency, representing a merger of earlier MDB Commission and MDB Authority; intergovernmental and reports to MDB Ministerial Council. There are satellite statutory bodies: Basin Officials Committee, Basin Community Committee and Commonwealth Environmental Water Holder
Safe Work Australia	175/2008 and 84/2009	A statutory agency replacing Australian Safety and Compensation Council; intergovernmental and reports to Workplace Relations Ministerial Council
Australian Transport Safety Bureau	20/2009	Formerly a marginal structure in transport ministry, now clearly separate as a statutory agency

Fair Work Australia	28/2009	With a quasi-judicial bench and replacing Australian Fair Pay Commission, Australian Industrial Relations Commission, Australian Industrial Registry and Workplace Authority; general manager and staff constitute a statutory agency
Fair Work Ombudsman (Office of)	28/2009	A statutory agency replacing Workplace Ombudsman
Australian Customs and Border Protection Service	33/2009	Formerly Australian Customs Service
Australian Sports Anti-Doping Authority	113/2009	Moved from CAC Act to FMA Act; a statutory agency with CEO now unambiguously as agency head; board replaced by subsidiary Advisory Group and Rule Violation Panel^
Australian Information Commissioner (Office of)	52/2010	To begin November 2010 and to include Commissioner for Information, Privacy Commissioner (no longer a separate office) and Freedom of Information Commissioner
Advisory structures on the margins of departments		
Infrastructure Australia	17/2008	With a statutory office of Infrastructure Coordinator
Skills Australia	10/2008	
Education Investment Fund Advisory Board	154/2008	As part of GFC stimulus package
Health and Hospitals Fund Advisory Board	154/2008	As part of GFC stimulus package
Coordinator-General for Remote Indigenous Services	68/2009	A statutory official with office to be staffed within Department of Families, Housing, Community Services and Indigenous Affairs

* Details of company changes taken from DoFD (2009a:x–xiii).

^ Previous form described as a CAC–FMA 'hybrid' by Ellis (2009:9713).

Table 4.3.2 Creations and conversion: executive agencies

Old Parliament House	Gazette proclamation 1 May 2008; subsequently renamed Museum of Australian Democracy at Old Parliament House

Table 4.3.3 Creations and conversions: government-owned companies (all under *CAC Act*)

AAF Company (Army Amenities Food Co.)	Created 1 July 2008
Australian Learning and Teaching Council Ltd	Created 1 July 2009; previously Carrick Institute for Learning and Teaching in Higher Education Ltd
Australian Solar Institute Ltd	Created 10 August 2009
Australian Sports Foundation	Created 18 February 1986; brought under CAC Act on 23 July 2009
National Breast and Ovarian Cancer Centre	Created 25 August 2000; brought under CAC Act on 1 July 2008
NBN Co. Ltd	Created 9 April 2009 to develop the national broadband network; intended to have mixed public–private ownership
Tuggeranong Office Park Ltd	Created 22 March 1989; brought under CAC Act on 3 December 2008
Outback Stores Pty Ltd	Previously a subsidiary of Indigenous Business Australia; created as a separate company under CAC Act on 1 March 2010

Table 4.3.4 Abolitions (not recorded in creations and conversions list above)

Statutory authorities	
Dairy Adjustment Authority	Act 123/2008
Prescribed authorities (FMA Act)	
Biosecurity Australia	De-prescribed on 1 July 2009
Companies	
Health Services Australia Ltd	Became subsidiary of Medibank Private Ltd on 1 April 2009
Maritime Industry Finance Co. Ltd	Delisted 24 April 2008
Net Alert Ltd	Delisted 18 December 2008
Telstra Sale Co. Ltd	Delisted 27 May 2009
Three Innovation Investment Fund (IIF) firms	

5. The Rudd administration and the Senate: business as usual[1]

HARRY EVANS

Introduction

Like most federal governments, the Rudd administration did not possess a party majority in the Senate. This is usually seen as a problem for governments—a source of trouble and frustration, giving rise to the possibility of a dissolution of both Houses under the deadlock-resolving provisions in Section 57 of the Constitution, if the Senate rejects, unacceptably amends or fails to pass government legislation within the terms of that section. Nowadays, a party majority in the Senate is taken to mean control of the chamber because of the strength of party discipline. In the past, however, non-Labor governments particularly could not always control their senators so that even with a party majority governments could find themselves in difficulties in the Senate.

A case can be made that lack of control of the Senate is good for governments: it compels them to justify their legislative proposals rather than ram them through (legislation is often improved even by amendments moved by opponents); it encourages the seeking of broader support for policies and the compromise that often improves programs; it imposes greater accountability and thereby helps avoid mistakes and lapses in propriety and legality; and it counters the temptation to legislate highly partisan measures ultimately harmful to their authors (the now leading example being the last Howard government's workplace relations legislation). Discussion of senate/government relations, however, invariably concentrates on the negatives.

Of all governments, the Rudd administration had the least justification for any claim that the Senate was the cause of its problems. Admittedly, the numbers

---

1 Information in this chapter is drawn from publications by the Department of the Senate, principally *Business of the Senate* and *Work of Committees*, which are cumulated annually and which can be found on that department's web site (<www.aph.gov.au/Senate>). Analysis and commentary are, of course, the responsibility of the author.

in the Senate were particularly difficult for this government. For the first eight months of its life, it had to make do with the Coalition parties' senate majority of one left over from the last Howard administration, until the Senate places turned over in accordance with that house's fixed term. That situation was not a serious disadvantage, as it gave the incoming ministry breathing space to formulate its ambitious agenda. After 1 July 2008, if the Coalition opposed a government measure, the proposal had to gain the support of all seven minor-party senators—five Greens, one Family First Party and one independent—to form a majority to be carried. The loss of only one of those votes, where the Coalition parties were opposed, was fatal to any government proposal under the constitutional provision whereby equally divided votes in the Senate negatives the motion before the chamber, while the loss of two meant that any non-government measure would have a majority.

There are four areas in which a non-government majority in the Senate may challenge the government: the amendment or rejection of government legislation; the conduct of inquiries into matters that might expose government weaknesses; Senate demands for information, particularly as a condition of passing legislation; and disallowance of delegated legislation. The Senate may express its disapproval of government activities in extreme cases by censure motions, but these have no effect other than to draw attention to alleged failings.

Legislation

The first major item on the new government's agenda was the replacement of the Howard workplace relations legislation. This went relatively smoothly, as the minor parties had opposed the key elements of that legislation in the first place. Subsequently, the course became more difficult, due mainly to the complexity of legislation, particularly for the emissions trading scheme.

The figures for government bills rejected by the Senate always convey an impression of moderation, as the overwhelming majority are passed. In 2008, 11 bills were rejected compared with 159 passed; in 2009, there were 15 rejected and 136 passed; and in 2010 only three—all hangovers from 2009—were rejected and 114 passed. In many cases, multiple bills contain one measure; the emissions trading scheme consisted of 11 bills, accounting for the high number of rejections in 2009.

These raw statistics give no clue of the importance of the measures, and some major government proposals were rejected. The most significant was the emissions trading scheme—twice rejected in 2009, thereby providing the government with a 'trigger' for a double dissolution by which it could seek a more friendly senate from the electorate. Any claim of obstruction there, however, was undermined by the announcement in 2010 that the legislation would be postponed, largely because of lack of international cooperation, which was one of the grounds on which the Coalition parties voted against it. Other measures providing triggers related to changes to private health insurance.

Some bills rejected were later passed with or without senate amendments, including those relating to the government's nation-building expenditures, the luxury car tax, government borrowings by the issue of bonds, household stimulus payments, cost recovery in the Pharmaceutical Benefits Scheme, the establishment of Safe Work Australia, income support for students and the Medicare levy surcharge. Some bills rejected were not presented again, or not in a form allowing the achievement of a trigger, which could lead observers to question the government's commitment to them. Those not presented again included a bill to establish the Australian Business Investment Partnership as part of the government's anti-recession program and another to set up a national monitor on fuel prices.

Some major bills were passed with senate amendments accepted by the government—notably those concerning income support for students in 2009 and paid parental leave in 2010. The latter came to be regarded as virtually the only big legislative achievement of the government. As its term went on, the Rudd ministry showed a greater readiness to accept amendments originating in the Senate, including those suggested in senate committee reports, which were often adopted before the bills in question reached the Senate. This procedure was used by previous administrations. There were no serious new senate/government disagreements over legislation in 2010. The government was learning how to manage the Senate; and the learning process usually takes most of a first term.

That the Rudd government was let off lightly with its legislation, apart from the problematical emissions trading scheme, can be demonstrated by a comparison with the first three Howard administrations, which did not have senate majorities. Those governments built up 'storehouses' of double-dissolution triggers, which were never used, all relating to major government policies, so that those policies could simply not be enacted. In the 1996–98 Parliament, there were four bills providing triggers, relating mainly to workplace relations—the most significant and contentious issue throughout the Howard era. In the 1998–2001 Parliament, that subject appeared again as the sole trigger. In 2001–04, there were seven— relating to workplace relations again, the full sale of Telstra, border protection, disability entitlements and protection of small businesses under the trade practices regime. Many other bills were passed with senate amendments the government would rather not have had, indicating a pragmatic approach of taking what it could get through the Senate in some areas while refusing to compromise on the 'big-ticket' items.

Complaints by Rudd ministers about 'senate obstruction' were muted compared with those of the Howard era, and this accurately reflected the real situation.

Source: David Pope, *The Public Sector Informant*, June 2009

Inquiries

Governments lacking senate majorities have always had to cope with senate inquiries that exposed their failings and delayed their measures. As already suggested, this traditional parliamentary activity is often beneficial to a government by keeping the ministry on its mettle, but governments habitually resist it. Inquiries are usually conducted through committees, and the public hearings have an immediate impact, reinforced by the subsequent committee reports, as they allow those with any kind of interest in a matter to critique the relevant government measures.

It is now accepted, even for the most part by governments, that all complex or contentious government legislation, and all major government policies and programs, will be referred to senate committees for public hearings. In this regard the experience of the Rudd government was not unusual, but its significant policies and proposals were very complex and contentious, and committee hearings were bound to expose difficulties. All of the forms of senate committee inquiry—hearings on bills, hearings on terms of reference referred by the Senate to both standing and select committees and estimates hearings— were used to scrutinise those policies and proposals.

Standing committee hearings on matters referred by the Senate included those on the government's response to the global financial crisis, the financial guarantees given by the government and its stimulus expenditure, Murray–Darling Basin management and water policy generally, and the tender process for employment services contracts. Select committees, which are appointed for specific inquiries into particular matters, scrutinised the proposed national broadband network, climate policy and state government financial management (that is, the handling of commonwealth money by state Labor governments). While these kinds of inquiries inform the public, they also compel the government to explain in detail what it is doing and why. In all of these areas, the Rudd government had considerable explaining to do.

This experience was not different from that of the Howard governments that lacked a senate majority. Every major proposal of those administrations—such as the GST and the workplace relations overhaul—was subjected to the most intense committee scrutiny. Inquiries causing particular difficulties for the government included: those into tax reform (spread over several committees); the operation of the Tax Office; unfair dismissal law; funding of government schools; cuts to childcare funding; global warming policy; the 'children overboard' affair; government advertising, which became a major electoral issue with the huge expenditure on advertising the WorkChoices legislation; and the regional partnerships program—the inquiry into which led to a devastating Auditor-General's report, released just before the 2007 election, with significant damage to the government. So the Howard ministries were vexed by senate inquiries no less than that of Rudd, and probably more so.

Governments now spend a great deal of time and energy (and money) attempting to control the information flow, to ensure as far as possible that the information reaching the public is favourable to them or at least has a favourable 'spin'. Senate inquiries, which the government cannot control, break down that information management and give the public a different and fuller picture. Shortly before the fall of Prime Minister Rudd, a senate hearing revealed that the Department of Climate Change and Energy Efficiency was not told in advance of the decision to postpone the emissions trading scheme, making that decision appear even more erratic.

Demands for information

The Senate makes demands for information by means of orders for the production of documents—an ancient procedure whereby ministers are ordered to lay before the Senate, and thereby make public, specified documents or those relating to a particular matter. The passage of one of these orders—almost always relating to a matter of some contention—usually indicates that the non-government parties think that the government is hiding something. Often the orders refer to information refused to a committee. Mostly governments comply with the orders, but sometimes they refuse, which raises suspicions that there really is something to hide. A senate resolution requires that a refusal be accompanied by a recognised public interest ground. There is a range of legitimate public interest grounds, such as prejudice to legal proceedings and damage to international relations, but it is up to the Senate to decide whether a ground is justifiably raised in the particular case. If the Senate is not satisfied, it may impose procedural penalties on the government. The most serious penalty would be a refusal to pass government legislation.

In that regard the Rudd government soon found itself in difficulties. The Senate required the production of information on the economic modelling of the emissions trading scheme and on the proposed national broadband network. The government refused, initially at least, mainly on the ground of commercial confidentiality—an excuse now regarded as slippery because of past misuse. This provided the Senate majority with a seemingly reasonable basis for not passing the relevant legislation. The emissions trading legislation was rejected in 2009 and a motion was passed declaring that legislation for the national broadband network would not be considered until the required information was produced.

Other orders in 2008 and 2009 related to subjects that caused great difficulties for the government, such as the green loans, the home insulation program and the school building scheme. In 2008, there were nine orders eliciting five government refusals; in 2009, there were 32 orders with seven government refusals. The 22 orders passed in 2010 provide a check list of the accumulated issues causing the government problems: government advertising, particularly when the government exempted itself from its own rules with respect to the proposed mining tax, after claiming to have cured the advertising abuses of the Howard era; the proposed national broadband network again; the home insulation program again; green loans again; asylum-seekers; taxation reform; and many others.

There were several claims by the government that documents should not be produced, with some of the usual suspects—the difficult issues—appearing again. Not all of those claims were based on coherent public interest immunity grounds—a concept that the government and its public servants still do not fully understand.

In 2008, when the Coalition parties suddenly rediscovered parliamentary accountability, orders were passed requiring the publication of lists of government appointments and grants. There could hardly be any argument against this and the government complied. These orders, like an earlier, pre-Rudd one on government contracts, are of continuing effect so will operate as an additional accountability measure on future governments.

Again, a comparison with the Howard administrations suggests that the Rudd government was treated lightly. In 1996–98, there were 48 orders for documents, five of which were not complied with by the government; in 1998–2001, there were 56 orders and 15 not complied with; and in 2002–04, there were 89 orders of which 46 were not complied with. The figures indicate a growing resistance by the Howard ministries to senate demands for information. In several cases, initial refusals to produce the documents in question were followed by capitulation after pressure was applied, particularly by way of committee hearings. The orders often related to matters causing severe difficulties for the government, such as the waterfront affair of 1998, proposed welfare changes in 1999, the magnetic resonance imaging machine affair of 1999–2000 and higher education funding in 1998 and 2002–03. Two customs and excise tariff bills were deferred until relevant information was produced. Frequent claims of commercial confidentiality in relation to government contracts led to a senate order for all contracts to be listed on the Internet, with any claims of confidentiality to be explicitly stated and subject to scrutiny by the Auditor-General; after initial resistance, this order has since been complied with. Nothing in the Rudd era equals this record of conflict between the Senate and the government over the disclosure of information.

Disallowance of delegated legislation

Government policies are frequently given effect by delegated legislation—instruments made by ministers under authorisations contained in statutes. Such instruments are subject to disallowance by either house of the Parliament, which means that the Senate has the opportunity to veto the policies contained in them, just as it has the power to veto proposed primary legislation contained in bills.

The Rudd government did not promulgate many contentious statutory instruments, probably because its major plans required primary legislation. In 2008, the Senate disallowed only three instruments, involving government policies relating to road user charges, dental services and higher education grants. In 2009, seven disallowance motions were carried, three of which related to significant policy issues: construction industry regulation, export control charges and increased fees for cataract surgery. The last-named issue, which carried over into 2010, led to a long battle between the Senate majority and the government, with the Senate disallowing successive instruments and the government seeking ways to bypass the disallowance procedure; the government eventually compromised on the matter. In 2010, two instruments were disallowed, relating to aviation security and therapeutic goods.

By way of comparison, during the three Howard administrations that lacked senate majorities, there were 27 instruments disallowed by the Senate, many involving major policy matters, so there was nothing unusual about the Rudd government's treatment in this area.

Censure motions

As already noted, censures of ministers or the government collectively by the Senate have no immediate effect, but they provide a measure of the degree of conflict and difficulty experienced by the government with the Senate.

During the life of the Rudd government only one censure motion was passed by the Senate, relating to the delivery of climate change policies, particularly the roof insulation program and the green loans scheme, which must rate as some of the greatest public administration failures ever—well deserving of parliamentary disquiet.

During the first three Howard administrations, ministers were censured on 11 occasions, for offences ranging from failures to produce information in response to senate orders and administrative breakdowns to participation in the Iraq war on false or undisclosed grounds.

If censure motions were to be regarded as the sole index of senate/government conflict, it would be taken that the Rudd government led a relatively peaceful life in the Senate.

A minor factor

Defeats and difficulties in the Senate are therefore only a relatively minor part of the story of the Rudd administration. The defeat that stands out is the rejection of the emissions trading scheme—declared by the Prime Minister to be his greatest moral issue. That episode, however, is overshadowed by the subsequent announcement that the project would be deferred. The form of that announcement was puzzling. The government could simply have stated that it was still committed to the scheme but would wait until the electors gave it a more favourable senate. The adverse reaction to the announcement was speedily followed by the overthrow of the Prime Minister by his party. That is the event that will occupy historians of the period. In the history of the Senate, the Rudd era will be seen as exhibiting a normal pattern of activity of that house: 'business as usual.'

Harry Evans *was Clerk of the Senate from 1988 to 2009.*

6. Federalism: a fork in the road?

GEOFF ANDERSON AND ANDREW PARKIN

Over its long history, the Australian Labor Party has had a complicated and sometimes inconsistent engagement with federalism (Galligan and Mardiste 1992; Parkin and Marshall 1994). The Rudd Labor government, over its truncated lifespan of less than three years, earned itself a special place in this history by embodying and projecting many elements of this complicated inconsistency.

At times, and especially in its first two years, the Rudd government, led by its prime minister, was seemingly intent on fabricating a collaborative approach that could be characterised as being in the national interest but respecting the role of the states and not especially aggrandising the role of the Commonwealth. At other times, and especially near the end, the Rudd government was more inclined to lambast the states as impediments to the national achievement of a more efficient, consistent and effective policy reform as Rudd sought a greater direct role for the Commonwealth. In some ways typical of his whole prime ministership, Kevin Rudd expressed a variety of positions at and between these polar extremities with, on each occasion, a degree of forcefulness and apparent sincerity. Thus, in the end, as in so many other respects, the Rudd approach to federalism was strangely enigmatic.

John Howard's final years as Prime Minister had seen him hone a philosophy of 'aspirational nationalism' as the rubric shaping his distinctive approach to Australia's federal system of government (Parkin and Anderson 2008). Kevin Rudd's unprecedented experience at the state level in observing and managing commonwealth–state relations as a senior adviser to the Queensland government had provided good reason for federalists to anticipate that as Prime Minister he would lead a government that might seek to reverse this centralist inheritance.

A year before becoming the leader of the Labor Party, Rudd had set out the case for cooperative federalism. While he did not subscribe to the 'mindless mantra of states' rights', he described himself as a committed federalist, believing that 'a properly functioning federation can advance the cause of progressive politics…not retard it' (Rudd 2005). Harking back to the cooperative federalism achievements under the Hawke and Keating Labor governments, Rudd suggested that a new commitment to cooperative federalism would provide the mechanism for the next wave of progressive policy reform. The Council of Australian Governments (COAG)—the heads-of-government forum comprising the Prime Minister, the state premiers and the territory chief ministers—was, he declared, the 'only viable model' for achieving the reform program (Rudd 2005). On winning the leadership of the Labor Party in 2006, Rudd identified enhancing federalism to be a priority. 'We can't just sit back and watch the Federation wither away', he declared (ABC 2006).

During the election campaign of 2007, commonwealth–state relations presented both an opportunity and a threat to Rudd and Labor. On the one hand, there was the opportunity to argue that only a federal Labor government could guarantee the cooperation necessary to eliminate the 'blame game' between the Commonwealth and the uniformly Labor-governed states and territories. On the other, there was the looming negative of what John Howard was to call the spectre of 'wall-to-wall Labor governments without a check or balance' (Shanahan 2007).

Less than a week after being sworn in as Prime Minister, Rudd called a meeting of state and territory leaders 'to set a new framework for co-operative commonwealth–state relations' and 'take practical steps to end the blame game' (Rudd 2007a). The stage was thus set for a possible new era in collaborative commonwealth–state relations.

Now fast forward to June 2010, five months short of the third anniversary of the triumphant 2007 election, when Kevin Rudd reluctantly stepped down as Prime Minister. The months leading up to this denouement had once again brought federalism to the fore in a pre-election atmosphere, but not this time within a context of cooperative commonwealth–state relations. Rather, the intergovernmental ambience had been soured by the fallout from Rudd's proposal—announced three months previously, on 3 March 2010—that the Commonwealth would establish a National Health and Hospital Network, and for that purpose appropriate one-third of the GST revenues that had previously flowed exclusively to the states. The proposal severely strained fraternal ties with the Labor-governed states and saw the Liberal government of Western Australia (which had come into office under Premier Colin Barnett, in September 2008) reject Rudd's plan outright. Two months later, the Rudd government's budget announcement on 2 May of a proposed (and ultimately ill-fated) Resource Super Profits Tax (RSPT) interjected a commonwealth tax into the states' mining royalty domain and brought the resource-rich states of Queensland and Western Australia, and the aspiring resource-rich state of South Australia, into open disagreement with the Commonwealth. Across the Nullarbor, there were once again the 'rumblings of secession' (Williams 2010).

This contrast of the impact on federalism between the beginning and the end of Rudd's term as Prime Minister is indicative of an unusual policy and political trajectory. But the picture needs to be completed by a consideration of the intervening period. The two years following the 2007 election saw the relationship between the Commonwealth and the states conducted in a less combative atmosphere than had been the case under the Howard government and, for the most part, a rhetoric of cooperation characterised public exchanges, which seemed genuine enough. Prime Minister Rudd elevated a reinvigorated COAG to a central role to drive the implementation of a challenging, ambitious policy agenda. Rudd's commitment to cooperation found tangible expression in a new financial agreement with the states that redrew the architecture of a key mechanism of commonwealth–state relations in favour of greater state autonomy, albeit overlaid with a new structure of 'national partnerships' with familiar commonwealth-controlled financial strings attached. In addition, Rudd made gestures towards a more respected and visible role for the local government sphere. The rest of this chapter details some of the key actions taken and assesses what was achieved.

A number of key issues highlight the complexities of the Rudd government's approach to federalism. Rudd's development of COAG as a central and positive institution of commonwealth–state relations contrasted with John Howard's more grudging acknowledgment of its usefulness (Anderson 2008; Parkin and Anderson 2007:32–3). A new financial arrangement granting more flexibility to the states in how they expended Specific Purpose Payments (SPPs)—long resisted during the Howard years[1]—was a genuine pro-federalist innovation. This was, however, counterbalanced by a new set of highly conditional National Partnership Payments (NPPs) and by the later proposed breach of the financial agreement in terms of a GST clawback to fund public hospitals. In other key areas where effective reform requires substantial commonwealth–state cooperation—health, education and the Murray–Darling Basin—there were both contrasts and continuity with the approach of the previous Howard government.

COAG and the governance of the federation

As a shadow minister, Rudd had described COAG as the only viable alternative to what appeared to be an increasingly dysfunctional federation (Rudd 2005). The COAG meeting that he called less than a week after being sworn in as Prime Minister confirmed COAG's intended enhanced status, with state and territory leaders joined for the first time by treasurers as full participants. In an echo of his election campaign rhetoric, Rudd announced:

---

1   Notwithstanding a serious Treasury-inspired proposal along these lines put forward in 1999 (Parkin and Anderson 2007:305).

> I want to use this COAG meeting to set a new framework for co-operative commonwealth–state relations and take practical steps to end the blame game. The time for buck-passing must come to an end. The time for real work to deal with real problems facing the nation must begin. (Rudd 2007a)

The Prime Minister moved quickly at that first meeting to change some key structures in the management of intergovernmental negotiations. As proposed by Rudd, COAG established a series of working parties charged with developing strategies and implementation plans. Each working party was chaired by a commonwealth minister with a senior state or territory official—not a corresponding state or territory minister—acting as their deputy. The COAG *Communiqué*, in a masterful piece of understatement, described this quite remarkable innovation as 'a break with previous practice' (COAG 2007). As the new Prime Minister told the media following the meeting:

> We intend to turn COAG into the workhorse of the nation…We see this as part of the working machinery of the Australian nation. If you're serious about delivering national outcomes it means making sure that the states and territories and the Commonwealth are in harness together, and that's what we propose. (Rudd 2007b)

After this initial gathering in December 2007, COAG proceeded through a series of quarterly meetings. By the end of Rudd's second year in office, COAG had met nine times and, by the time Rudd had been replaced as Prime Minister, he had chaired 10 meetings. This compares with a mere two meetings in Howard's first two years as Prime Minister and the total of only 14 meetings during the 11 years of the Howard government.

The Rudd government's view of COAG as a key institution of national government was quite explicit. Addressing the 2020 Summit, the Prime Minister took credit for having 'breathed life into the once fractious COAG process'. He told Summit participants that 'governments are now working together to drive reform and achieve real outcomes for Australia' (Rudd 2008a). The Treasurer, Wayne Swan, in delivering the first budget of the Rudd government, claimed 'a reinvigorated and cooperative COAG process' as the basis for a new framework for commonwealth–state financial relations and for substantial progress on the reform agenda to enhance productivity and improve services in a wide range of areas (Swan 2008a:11–13). The Deputy Prime Minister, Julia Gillard, told her New Zealand counterparts at an Australia New Zealand Leadership Forum in June 2008 that COAG 'is becoming a dynamic part of our nation's system of government' (Gillard 2008).

Changing the financial architecture

The Howard government—as had most previous governments at least since the 1970s—had been unapologetically adamant that commonwealth grant contributions were a legitimate vehicle for pursuing commonwealth policy and program priorities.[2] As Leader of the Opposition, Rudd had received a report during the 2007 election campaign from an Advisory Group on Commonwealth–State Relations[3] that had recommended significant reforms in the structure and administration of SPPs (Keating et al. 2007). While Rudd indicated that he would act on those recommendations, the speed with which he subsequently acted, and the breadth of the changes that he sponsored, came as something of a surprise.

Following the first COAG meeting, Rudd announced that the Commonwealth would embark on a significant program of reform that included a radical shift in the structure and management of SPPs. His explanatory statement also demonstrated how his prior experience of the protocols of commonwealth–state relations and the structures of COAG were defining his approach to government:

> Special Purpose Payments are part of the deep structure, folklore and mysticism of commonwealth–state relations. If you've worked in these areas before, as I have, they are the source of frustration at multiple levels, given the multiplicity of them and the way in which they've been designed. Now, we intend to take a different view. We want to see our SPPs rationalised in the future. (Rudd 2007b)

By the COAG meeting in Adelaide in March 2008, consensus had been reached on the key elements of this proposed new financial agreement (COAG 2008a). At the heart of the reform was a decision to radically consolidate the more than 90 SPPs into just a small number of omnibus SPPs, each permitting the states significant internal inter-program flexibility. The outcome was the creation of just five SPPs covering the key areas of health care, schools, skills and workforce development, disabilities services, and affordable housing (COAG 2008d).

For a time, it appeared that external shocks might derail the reform process. On 27 March 2008, the Prime Minister announced that Australia faced 'a global financial

---

2   Particularly controversial had been commonwealth-imposed grant conditions unrelated to the immediate policy or program at hand. For example, conditions for funding for infrastructure projects that insisted that state government agencies could not accept tenders and/or expressions of interest from contractors unless their agreements with unions and employees were in line with the Commonwealth's preferred position on industrial relations (Parkin and Anderson 2007:306).

3   Geoff Anderson was a member of this advisory group. The other members were Dr Michael Keating, former head of the Department of the Prime Minister and Cabinet (Chairman), Meredith Edwards, former Deputy Vice-Chancellor of the University of Canberra, and Professor George Williams, Anthony Mason Professor of Law at the University of New South Wales.

crisis that poses very significant challenges for the global economy as well as our own' (Rudd 2008b). The government's response, however—via further attention to economic reform, enhanced competitiveness and increased productivity—appeared to have positive implications for federalism. Essential to this reform agenda, as the Treasurer explained, was 'a reinvigorated COAG process' that could 'unlock the benefits of modern federalism' so that, as partners, the Commonwealth and the states could overcome the challenges that the world economy presented (Swan 2008b). These remarks by the Treasurer followed the COAG meeting in Adelaide on 26 March, which, in retrospect, was probably the collaborative high-water mark of commonwealth–state relations under the Rudd government.

The details of the arrangements agreed in Adelaide were to be finalised at the COAG meeting planned for November 2008. As that meeting approached, the global financial crisis (GFC) that the government had described first as a challenge and then as a complication (Wanna 2009) had become a clear source of tension. Following the October meeting of COAG, media reports of a confidential brief on funding options prepared for the states suggested that they were seeking an additional $23 billion as the price for signing up to the Prime Minister's COAG agenda (Taylor 2008). Rudd was moved to describe this as 'one of the larger try-ons of the century' (ABC 2008b).

Despite these tensions, the Intergovernmental Agreement on Federal Financial Arrangements was formally concluded at the COAG meeting in November 2008, its path smoothed by the commitment of the Commonwealth to an additional $7.1 billion in SPP grants over the following five years (COAG 2008d). The reforms spelt out in the agreement were quite fundamental. Alongside the formal confirmation of the dramatic reduction (via consolidation) in the number of SPPs was a system of reporting against mutually agreed outcomes and performance benchmarks by an independent COAG Reform Council (CRC) in which the performance of both levels of government would be assessed.

The post-2000 GST-based system of fiscal federalism created by the Howard government, under which the states were guaranteed all of the GST proceeds, was clearly a positive development for the states by strengthening their financial, and hence policy, autonomy (Parkin and Anderson 2007:295–7). The Rudd government's SPP reforms of 2008 went a significant step further, allowing the states greatly enhanced discretion and autonomy in the utilisation of commonwealth-awarded SPP funds. The agreement to a system of financial incentives and rewards for pursuing reform—long sought by the states—also embodied a major conceptual breakthrough by attempting to shift the scrutiny of SPP-funded programs to their policy and service impact and away from the previous focus on compliance with detailed acquittal conditions that the Commonwealth had attached to its financial inputs.

There was, however, an interesting and significant counterbalancing initiative from the Commonwealth that accompanied the consolidation and freeing up of the SPPs.

A new category of commonwealth conditional payments to the states—badged as National Partnership Programs (NPPs)—was established. The Commonwealth's intention here was to drive nationally significant reforms in areas that were unambiguously commonwealth priorities via the provision of financial rewards to the states (COAG 2008e). As a result, there are now three categories of NPPs: National Partnership Reform Payments, which aim to facilitate reforms or reward states that deliver on 'nationally significant reforms'; NPP payments, which support the delivery of specified outputs or projects; and a third category of projects that support election commitments or other specific payments that 'support national objectives and provide a financial contribution to the states to deliver specific projects' (Swan 2009:11). The constitutional authority for all of these payments remains Section 96—the same authority that has underpinned the SPPs. The number of NPPs grew quickly, and in many ways the NPPs are becoming reminiscent of what much of the previous SPP regime used to look like.

Health and hospitals

In the 2007 election campaign, Kevin Rudd had declared an intention to end the 'blame game' in health either by agreement with the states or by a constitutional referendum to give the Commonwealth the power to impose a solution. The management of Australia's public hospitals and health system and the commonwealth–state relationships and agreements that underpinned it were thus always going to be defining issues for the Rudd government. The Prime Minister's self-imposed deadline of June 2009 as the date by which the reforms would be achieved added urgency and created a political timetable that was always going to be difficult to meet.

The first COAG meeting following the election agreed on the terms of reference for a National Health and Hospitals Reform Commission (NHHRC). This included a requirement that the NHHRC address overlap and duplication including in regulation between the Commonwealth and states.

Subsequent COAG meetings saw increases in the funding provided to the states for health. This suggested that the Prime Minister preferred to improve the performance of the states via enhancing their capacity rather than via the option of the foreshadowed alternative of a constitutional referendum battle. Meanwhile, the NHHRC was developing its plans for the nation's health and hospital system. In April 2008, it provided advice to the Commonwealth Minister for Health on a framework for the new Australian Health Care Agreement by way of a report entitled *Beyond the Blame Game* (NHHRC 2008a). In December 2008, the NHHRC released an interim report (NHHRC 2008b) that offered three options for systemic reform. These were shared responsibility with clearer accountability, the Commonwealth taking sole responsibility with delivery through regional authorities or a complete takeover by the Commonwealth (NHHRC 2008b:274).

The final report of the NHHRC was due in June 2009, coinciding with the deadline the Prime Minister had set for his announced timetable for reform or a referendum. The difficulties that announcement would create soon became apparent. One significant problem was that there had never been any clear criteria established for what would constitute successful reform sufficient to signal an end to the 'blame game'. The health agreement at COAG in November 2008 specified a number of performance measures against which the Commonwealth and the states had agreed to report to the COAG Reform Council. This process would, however, begin in the 2009–10 financial year—too distant to satisfy the politics surrounding the June 2009 deadline. Instead, in the vacuum that was created, the media focused on the release of the annual report on hospitals by the Australian Institute of Health and Welfare (AIHW), particularly the evidence that in the politically sensitive area of elective surgery waiting times had increased (ABC 2009; AIWH 2009). The Prime Minister's response that he was 'dead-set determined to get on with the business of long-term reform', that the government would 'roll up our sleeves', and his claim while he had received the NHHRC's final report that 'we need to be methodical, careful, working our way through these recommendations' (ABC 2009) served only to highlight the contrast with the 2007 commitment.

It was against this background that the Prime Minister unveiled the Commonwealth's plans for a new National Health and Hospital Network on 3 March 2010, claiming that this would be the most significant reform of the health system since the introduction of Medicare in the 1980s. The plan proposed that the Commonwealth would take the dominant funding responsibility for all public hospitals and put significantly more funding into the system. It also, however, directly challenged the role of the states because their hospital systems would instead be run by local networks. Most significantly, the Commonwealth would hold back about one-third of the GST revenues to be placed in a new National Hospital Fund to be spent only on health and hospitals (Rudd 2010). The outline of the policy came with a renewed warning to the states: if they refused to agree to the reform then a referendum would be held at the same time as the forthcoming election to give the Commonwealth all the power it needed to act (Rudd 2010).

An agreement was eventually reached at the COAG meeting held on 19 and 20 April 2010—a meeting originally scheduled for a week earlier but delayed as prior background negotiations proved difficult. The meeting was also notable in that it was the first time a COAG meeting had stretched over two days—a further indication of the problems the proposal presented to the states, particularly the 'clawback' of GST and the implicit rupture of the Intergovernmental Agreement.

The views of the states were put by the NSW Premier and Chair of the Council for the Federation, Kristina Keneally: 'We certainly want to protect our GST revenue from further clawback…We signed an intergovernmental agreement 18 months ago, and we see that as fundamental to maintaining the integrity of our budget' (Maher and Rout 2010). In the lead-up to the meeting, it was not altogether clear whether the Prime Minister would prevail, particularly given the strong opposition from New South Wales and the vociferous rejection of the proposal by Victorian Premier, John Brumby. Significant injections of extra funding, however, a commitment to entrenching safeguards against any further change to the GST arrangements and— crucially—a continuing role for the states as 'system managers for public hospitals' saw all of the states with the exception of Western Australia sign up to the new scheme (COAG 2010a).

Kevin Rudd called it a 'historic agreement for better health and better hospitals' (Hartcher 2010), but the Leader of the Opposition, Tony Abbott, countered that 'Mr Rudd hadn't fixed the health system and hadn't taken it over from the states' (Dodson 2010). Whatever the merits of Abbott's first observation (and at least the 'local network' basis will necessitate some significant administrative changes), Abbott was certainly right with his second point. The COAG agreement was absolutely clear that the states would remain system managers for public hospitals responsible for a range of system-wide functions and that Local Hospital Networks would be established by state governments as separate legal entities under state legislation (COAG 2010b:5).

The Liberal Premier of Western Australia held out, on the grounds that the agreement regarding the GST was one compromise too far regardless of the retained state management oversight and the generosity of the Commonwealth in committing to increases in immediate and future funding of the health system. At the traditional post-COAG media conference, he reminded the Prime Minister that the GST was barely 10 years old, that it was introduced as a substitute for other state taxes that had been either forgone or transferred to the Commonwealth, and that had been presented then as the long-term growth tax and solution to state finances. 'I am not,' he said, 'about to compromise the integrity or the importance of the GST to my state of Western Australia' (Barnett 2010).

Education

Fundamental questions about the degree to which the Rudd government wanted to influence the direction of schooling arose soon after the election. Certainly, previous commonwealth governments had utilised SPPs or direct commonwealth payments to schools in pursuit of their own policy agendas, but these had typically been directed at promoting specific pet programs. The Rudd government, in contrast, advanced a new and potentially more encompassing and more penetrating approach.

In an address in August 2008, the Prime Minister set out three central pillars of reform in schools: improving the quality of teaching, making school reporting properly transparent and lifting achievement in disadvantaged school communities. The states and territories were 'important partners in this process', he conceded, but the Commonwealth's challenge was to get them 'to commit to concrete tangible reforms'. In an echo of the strategy also pursued by the Howard government, Rudd announced that this commitment would be gained by making agreement on individual school performance reporting a condition of the new national education agreement, and of course funding to the states (Rudd 2008c).

This marked the first time that the Prime Minister—facing a situation in which agreement was likely to be difficult—embellished the rhetoric of cooperation with a threat of fiscal coercion. As the veteran commentator Paul Kelly noted, this was not just about schools; it was also a test for Rudd of 'whether his governing model of cooperative federalism is viable' (Kelly 2008).

Source: David Pope, *The Canberra Times*, 28 August 2008

The introduction by the Commonwealth of the My School web site (ACARA 2010) was equally significant in assessing how cooperative the Rudd government would be in practice. The web site describes its purpose in terms of providing information, enabling meaningful evaluation of test results and providing opportunities to improve performance and learn from other schools (ACARA 2010). Behind this apparently innocent prose, however, is the story of a substantial and largely successful imposition by the Commonwealth—

prominently led by Deputy Prime Minister, Julia Gillard—of a transparent national regime of student competency testing on to reluctant states and over the opposition of a hostile teachers' union. Because this approaches the heart of the actual practices and accountability of schools, this could turn out to be the most penetrating intervention yet by the Commonwealth into a policy domain otherwise unambiguously within the jurisdiction of the states. (The Rudd government's education policy is further discussed in Chapter 9 of this volume.)

The Murray–Darling: still state versus state

Negotiations over the management of the Murray–Darling Basin during the term of the Rudd government provide a stark reminder that federalism involves more than relations between the Commonwealth and the states, but also between individual states.

The cooperative federalism promoted by Kevin Rudd showed early signs of promise when at the first COAG meeting after the November 2007 election 'water reform' featured in the brief given to the working parties of commonwealth ministers and state officials (COAG 2007). This promise appeared to be moving closer to fulfilment when at the COAG meeting in March the Commonwealth and the states agreed in principle to a memorandum of understanding on reform of the management of the Murray–Darling Basin (COAG 2008a; Wong 2008). The Prime Minister called the deal 'historic' and declared an end to the 'blame game' on water (Franklin 2008). SA Premier, Mike Rann, agreed, adding that 'more has been achieved in 11-and-a-half weeks of talks over the River Murray than in the [previous] 11-and-a-half years' (ABC 2008a), while Victorian Premier, John Brumby, described it as a 'great step forward' (Wiseman 2008a).

At the next meeting of COAG, in July, it appeared that a century of federal disharmony over the basin might finally be laid to rest when the states and the Commonwealth agreed to sign an intergovernmental agreement under which the states would refer their powers to the Commonwealth and agree to the establishment of an independent Murray–Darling Basin Authority as the single body responsible for the overarching management of the basin. It appeared, however, that action to address the critical condition of the Murray would not immediately follow the agreement, because significant changes in the amount of water that could be traded across the catchment were delayed as 'COAG stated its ambition to increase the cap from four per cent to six per cent by the end of 2009' (COAG 2008b). Media commentators denounced the delay as a 'classic COAG cop out' (Steketee 2008) and it certainly appeared to be a classic stand-off between individual states. Behind this formulation in the communiqué was the determination of Premier Brumby to resist the transfer of water entitlements held by Victorian irrigators. He was unapologetic about this parochial stance: 'If that cap were lifted immediately, it would have a devastating effect on Victorian irrigators', he said, warning that as soon as the cap was lifted 'everyone is going to be after high security Victorian water' (Wiseman 2008b). The response of South Australia's Premier, Mike Rann, was to publicly rebuke his Labor colleague, accusing Victoria of having 'frustrated this process for the past 18 months or more' (Wiseman 2008b).

Eight months after the signing of the Murray Darling Intergovernmental Agreement, and a few weeks short of the first anniversary of the 'historic' agreement at the March 2008 COAG meeting, Premier Rann announced in the SA Parliament that having 'exhausted all diplomatic channels', his government was assembling a legal team to mount a constitutional challenge to the upstream states to protect South Australia's rights to the River Murray and 'to return sufficient permanent fresh water to the river to restore its health'. The Premier particularly highlighted Victoria's refusal to lift the cap on trading as a barrier to long-term reform (Rann 2009). The critical problem of the Murray, and in particular the impact of drought and over-allocation of water on the health of the lower lakes and The Coorong, had become a major political issue in South Australia in what was the lead-up to an election year. The court challenge, however, and the determination of Premier Brumby to protect Victorian irrigators, which brought it about, indicated the extent to which local politics can drive a state's response to 'cooperative federalism'.

Local government

The reform of the federation that Labor promoted during the 2007 election campaign focused largely on developing cooperation between the Commonwealth and the states rather than any major structural change by way of constitutional amendment. Inserting a constitutionally recognised role for local government was, however, an exception, with Rudd committing himself to pursue the process of gaining constitutional recognition for this third tier of government in Australia (Lundy 2007a). Labor also proposed to involve local governments in discussion of issues of national importance and ensure that it had a more effective voice at COAG through the creation of an Australian Council of Local Governments (ACLG) (Lundy 2007b).

In November 2008, the Prime Minister sought to make good on both these commitments when he invited the mayors of all of Australia's councils to meet with him in Canberra at what was to become the inaugural meeting of the ACLG. Addressing the meeting, he said that, in addition to creating a stronger and more coherent relationship between local government and the Commonwealth, he sought their input on his election commitment to its constitutional recognition. Reminding the meeting of the failure to gain bipartisan support for Labor's referenda proposals of 1974 and 1988, he said that this time he wanted to 'get it right', looking for local government to forge a consensus among councils on the nature of any change (Rudd 2008d). Later, the Commonwealth moved to assist this process with a grant of $250 000 to the Australian Local Government Association (ALGA) 'to raise the profile of constitutional recognition of local government' (AAP 2010). Similar initiatives to support the capacity of local government to play a more significant role came with the establishment of a $25 million Local Government Reform Fund, which was focused on improving infrastructure asset management and planning (Albanese 2009a), and the contribution of $8 million towards the establishment of the Australian Centre of Excellence for Local Government to promote best practice and encourage innovation and professionalism within the sector (Albanese 2009b).

It would be easy to dismiss these initiatives as merely symbolic. The specific role of local government in the federation was not mentioned in any communiqué from the 10 COAG meetings held during the period that Rudd was Prime Minister, and a broader examination of the roles and responsibilities of different levels of government was referred to only in regard to reports from officials on specific programs (COAG 2008c, 2008d). Two further meetings of the ACLG were held before Rudd was removed as Prime Minister; however, its large size meant that it could never become the negotiating forum represented by COAG, its meetings instead being 'conducted in the style of community cabinet meetings' with ministers and parliamentary secretaries taking questions from the floor (ACLG 2010).

Symbolism or not, the commitment and the establishment of the council were warmly welcomed by local government (ALGA 2008). Moreover, the issue of constitutional recognition became more real than symbolic for local government following the High Court's decision in *Pape v Commissioner of Taxation* (HCA 2009). This case concerned a challenge to the constitutional validity of the cash payments made by the Rudd government as part of its GFC stimulus package. While the validity of the payments was upheld by a four–three majority, the court was unanimous that the Commonwealth may not spend in areas in which it has no constitutional authority (Saunders 2009:250). Constitutional lawyer Professor George Williams argued that the court's decision confirmed that the Commonwealth did not have any general power to regulate or fund local government and that, as a consequence, a number of programs, such as the National Building Roads to Recovery, could be invalid. He suggested an amendment to Section 96 of the Constitution that would specifically include the power to make grants to local government (Williams 2009).

The broader implications for federalism of the decision did not receive much attention outside local government. As a former Labor Attorney-General in the Keating government commented, no 'state has grasped, or looks remotely likely to want to grasp, the potential Pape offers them to recontest the spending ground earlier claimed by the Commonwealth' (Kerr 2009:319). In many respects, the preference on the part of the Commonwealth for direct funding to local government represents a continuation of the approach of the Howard government. The point of differentiation was the willingness of the Rudd government to take the next step towards a more formal and constitutionally based relationship. While the Prime Minister reaffirmed his support for a referendum on a number of occasions, it was clearly a matter for a second term, but nonetheless a matter now firmly on the agenda.

Global financial crisis

On the eve of the November COAG meeting, the Prime Minister explained to Parliament that there was no point in 'sugar coating' what was happening, with the economies of the major developed nations 'like dominoes…falling one by one into recession' (Rudd 2008b). COAG, however, was to play its part with a 'substantial but responsible' $11 billion to be offered to the states over four years as the third tranche of the government's plan to invest in stimulating the economy, alongside payments to pensioners and carers, families and home owners (Rudd 2008b).

Just more than two months later, COAG met again in a special meeting called to consider the Prime Minister's 'Nation Building and Jobs Plan'—the second stage of the Rudd government's economic stimulus (Rudd 2009a). Following the meeting, the Prime Minister was generous in his public praise for the states and territories for reaching agreement at such short notice (Rudd 2009b). Behind the scenes, however, he was reportedly 'obsessed' with ensuring that his plan be rolled out on time and not 'thwarted by problems with the states' (Taylor and Uren 2010:146). As a result, the National Partnership Agreement established an 'Oversight Group' within the Department of the Prime Minister and Cabinet chaired by a coordinator-general who in turn would work with coordinators-general in each state and territory. To ensure that the states did not cut back their own funding, they were to report against 'expenditure and output benchmarks' with the heads of treasuries charged with analysing these data 'to ensure that existing effort by all jurisdictions is maintained', with final oversight by the Ministerial Council for Financial Relations (COAG 2009). The pressure of the international crisis had seen commonwealth–state relations revert to more familiar territory and the COAG process slip from the heady heights of March 2008.

Conclusion

When Kevin Rudd became Labor leader in December 2006, he declared that, after 10 years of the Howard government, Australia had reached a 'fork in the road'. He placed 'the actual fabric of our federation' at this intersection, with the choice before the country needing to go beyond 'fiddling at the margins' in the direction of 'fundamental reform' (Rudd 2006). Beyond the terrible mixed metaphors, the intention to strike out in a significantly new direction seemed clear. What eventuated?

The Rudd government began by sponsoring a significant and interesting set of reforms that made genuine progress in not only respecting the role of the states in the Australian federation but also leveraging cooperative commonwealth–state relations to achieve worthwhile reforms. But the period ended with a dispute about hospitals that, while leaving the states with continuing key healthcare delivery responsibilities, did so after a pathway that threatened to undermine key foundational elements underpinning the role of the states.

An overall perspective would allow a positive view of Rudd's contribution to Australian federalism, particularly in the further development of COAG as an institution of Australian governance. The consolidation and re-conceptualisation of SPPs formed a remarkable breakthrough. This was, however, tempered by the creation of the NPPs and the later overturning of the financial agreement on the GST. And it is also the case that even COAG—however strong the voices of the states within it—is itself an instrument of cooperative centralism that, in the end, reinforces the dominant role of the Commonwealth at least as an instigator and coordinator and frequently as a policy driver.

There has for many years been a frequent temptation for commentators to foreshadow the demise of the states as effective and autonomous actors within the federal system. Such commentary has always been premature at best and probably naive. Whatever the financial, economic and legal forces that promote centralism, the states remain powerful political entities. As one observer of the health debate commented, had the Prime Minister not made significant concessions to the states and had so many premiers not shared an overriding loyalty to the Labor Party, the premiers of New South Wales and Victoria could well have been able to force the Prime Minister into a humiliating backdown (Savva 2010). The premiers of Western Australia, Queensland and South Australia also played a significant part in the RSPT debate—a key element in Rudd's downfall from office. Many years ago, Liberal premiers were influential in the toppling of an incumbent Liberal Prime Minister, John Gorton (Hughes 1976; Nixon 2002). While not quite so visibly, the three 'mining-state' premiers probably contributed to the toppling of Kevin Rudd.

Thus, as always, Australian federalism—a governmental construction defined via the Commonwealth-dominated legalisms of the Constitution and lubricated via the Commonwealth-dominated public finance system—can only fully be understood as, first and foremost, a realm of politics. So, likewise, the Australian Labor Party's multi-layered engagement with federalism at the Commonwealth and state levels. The politics of 2007, and the need to counter John Howard's warnings of the consequences of wall-to-wall Labor governments, brought a reformist version of cooperative federalism to the fore. The politics of 2010 found federalism still at centre stage but under very different circumstances. Politics will continue to shape the Australian federation for all of Kevin Rudd's successors, both in the prime ministership and in the Labor leadership.

Geoff Anderson *is a senior lecturer in the Department of Politics and Public Policy at the Flinders University of South Australia.*

Andrew Parkin *is the Deputy Vice-Chancellor (Academic) and a Professor in the Department of Politics and Public Policy, Flinders University, South Australia.*

References

Albanese, A. 2009a. Rudd government moves ahead with $25 million local government reform fund, Media release, 9 October, Parliament House, Canberra, <http://www.minister.infrastructure.gov.au/aa/releases/2009/October/aa416_2009.htm>

Albanese, A. 2009b. Centre of Excellence for Local Government officially open, Media release, 14 December, Parliament House, Canberra, <http://www.minister.infrastructure.gov.au/aa/releases/2009/December/aa538_2009.htm>

Anderson, G. 2008. 'The Council of Australian Governments: a new institution of governance for Australia's conditional federalism', *The University of New South Wales Law Journal*, vol. 31, no. 2, pp. 493–508.

Australian Associated Press (AAP) 2010. 'Local government given federal leg up', *AAP Bulletin*, 15 June.

Australian Broadcasting Corporation (ABC) 2006. 'New Labor leader outlines plan: Kerry O'Brien speaks with Kevin Rudd', Transcript, *7.30 Report*, ABC TV, 4 December, <http://global.factiva.com>

Australian Broadcasting Corporation (ABC) 2008a. 'COAG agreements on Murray–Darling system and health', Transcript, *PM*, ABC Radio, 26 March, <http://www.abc.net.au/pm/content/2008/s2200029.htm>

Australian Broadcasting Corporation (ABC) 2008b. 'The cost of federalism a pipe dream', Transcript, *The World Today*, ABC Radio, 10 October, <http://www.abc.net.au/worldtoday/content/2008/s2387704.htm>

Australian Broadcasting Corporation (ABC) 2009. 'Decide on hospital takeover: Mr Rudd's self-imposed deadline has arrived', Transcript, *ABC News*, 30 June, <http://global.factiva.com>.

Australian Council of Local Governments (ACLG) 2010. Australian Council of Local Governments meeting, Canberra, 8 June, <http://www.aclg.gov.au/>

Australian Curriculum, Assessment and Reporting Authority (ACARA) 2010. *My School*, Web site, Australian Curriculum, Assessment and Reporting Authority, Sydney, <http://www.myschool.edu.au/>

Australian Institute of Health and Welfare (AIHW) 2009. *Australian hospital statistics 2007–08*, Health Services Series No. 33, Cat. No. HSE 71, June, Australian Institute of Health and Welfare, Canberra.

Australian Local Government Association (ALGA) 2008. New Australian Council of Local Government, Media release, Australian Local Government Association, Deakin, ACT.

Barnett, C. 2010. COAG joint press conference, Transcript, Prime Minister of Australia Media Centre, Canberra, <http://pandora.nla.gov.au/pan/79983/20100624-1429/www.pm.gov.au/node/6689.html>

Council of Australian Governments (COAG) 2007. *Communiqué*, Council of Australian Governments meeting, Canberra, 10 December, <http://www.coag.gov.au/coag_meeting_outcomes/2007-12-20/index.cfm>

Council of Australian Governments (COAG) 2008a. *Communiqué*, Council of Australian Governments meeting, Adelaide, 26 March, <http://www.coag.gov.au/coag_meeting_outcomes/2008-03-26/index.cfm#reform_agenda>

Council of Australian Governments (COAG) 2008b. *Communiqué*, Council of Australian Governments meeting, Sydney, 3 July, <http://www.coag.gov.au/coag_meeting_outcomes/2008-07-03/index.cfm#water>

Council of Australian Governments (COAG) 2008c. *Communiqué*, Council of Australian Governments meeting, Perth, 2 October, <http://www.coag.gov.au/coag_meeting_outcomes/2008-10-02/index.cfm#aged>

Council of Australian Governments (COAG) 2008d. *Communiqué*, Council of Australian Governments meeting, Canberra, 29 November, <http://www. coag.gov.au/coag_meeting_outcomes/2008-11-29/index.cfm#reform>

Council of Australian Governments (COAG) 2008e. *Intergovernmental Agreement on Federal Financial Relations*, December 2008, Council of Australian Governments, Canberra, <http://www.coag.gov.au/intergov_agreements/ federal_financial_relations/index.cfm>

Council of Australian Governments (COAG) 2009. *Communiqué*, Nation Building and Jobs Plan, Special Council of Australian Governments meeting, 5 February 2009, <http://www.coag.gov.au/coag_meeting_outcomes/2009-02-05/index. cfm>

Council of Australian Governments (COAG) 2010a. *Communiqué*, Council of Australian Governments meeting, 19–20 April, <http://www.coag.gov. au/coag_meeting_outcomes/2010-04-19/index.cfm?CFID=465751&CFTOK EN=81186534>

Council of Australian Governments (COAG) 2010b. *National Health and Hospitals Network Agreement*, Council of Australian Governments, Canberra, <http:// www.coag.gov.au/coag_meeting_outcomes/2010-04-19/index.cfm?CFID=46 5751&CFTOKEN=81186534#reforms>

Dodson, L. 2010. 'Rudd faces Senate row on health', *Australian Financial Review*, 22 April.

Franklin, M. 2008. 'Rudd delivers on new federalism', *The Australian*, 27 March, p. 1.

Galligan, B. and Mardiste, D. 1992. 'Labor's reconciliation with federalism', *Australian Journal of Political Science*, vol. 27 (special issue), pp. 71–86.

Gillard, J. 2008. Priorities for the new Australian government, Speech at the Australian and New Zealand Leadership Forum, 13 June, <http://www. pm.gov.au/node/5740>

Hartcher, P. 2010. 'Confident PM sets the stage for election', *Sydney Morning Herald*, 21 April.

High Court of Australia (HCA) 2009. *Pape v Federal Commissioner of Taxation* (2009) 257 ALR 1, 83 ALJR 765.

Hughes, C. A. 1976. *Mr Prime Minister. Australian Prime Ministers 1901–1972*, Oxford University Press, Melbourne.

Keating, M., Anderson, G., Edwards, M. and Williams, G. 2007. *A framework to guide future development of Specific Purpose Payments*, Discussion Paper by the ALP Advisory Group on Federal State Relations, July, Sydney.

Kelly, P. 2008. 'The PM's courageous gamble', *The Australian*, 30 August, p. 21.

Kerr, D. 2009. '*Pape v Commissioner of Taxation*: fresh fields for federalism?', *Law and Justice Journal*, vol. 9, no. 2, pp. 311–23.

Lundy, K. 2007a. Labor to drive constitutional recognition of local government, Media release, 27 August, Parliament House, Canberra, <http://pandora.nla.gov.au/pan/22093/20071022-1405/www.alp.org.au/media/0807/mslg270.html>

Lundy, K. 2007b. Labor to establish Council of Australian Local Governments, Media release, 29 August, Parliament House, Canberra, <http://pandora.nla.gov.au/pan/22093/20071022-1405/www.alp.org.au/media/0807/msfsrlg290.html>

Maher, S. and Rout, M. 2010. 'Hospital talks deadlocked over GST—Rudd stares down states on health', *The Australian*, 19 April, p. 1.

National Health and Hospitals Reform Commission (NHHRC) 2008a. *Beyond the Blame Game: Accountability and performance benchmarks for the next Australian Health Care Agreements*, National Health and Hospitals Reform Commission, Woden, ACT, <http://www.health.gov.au/internet/nhhrc/publishing.nsf/Content/commission-1lp>

National Health and Hospitals Reform Commission (NHHRC) 2008b. *A Healthier Future for all Australians Interim Report*, December, National Health and Hospitals Reform Commission, Woden, ACT, <http://www.health.gov.au/internet/nhhrc/publishing.nsf/Content/interim-report-december-2008>

Nixon, P. 2002. 'A man for the good of his nation—a Prime Minister's life', *The Australian*, 21 May, p. 11.

Parkin, A. and Anderson, G. 2007. 'The Howard government, regulatory federalism and the transformation of commonwealth–state relations', *Australian Journal of Political Science*, vol. 42, pp. 295–6.

Parkin, A. and Anderson, G. 2008. 'Reconfiguring the federation?', in C. Aulich and R. Wettenhall (eds), *Howard's Fourth Government: Australian Commonwealth Administration 2004–2007*, UNSW Press, Sydney, pp. 93–113.

Parkin, A. and Marshall, V. 1994. 'Frustrated, reconciled or divided? The Australian Labor Party and federalism', *Australian Journal of Political Science*, vol. 29, no. 1, pp. 18–39.

Rann, M. 2009. Ministerial statement, *House of Assembly Hansard*, 5 March 2009, p. 1881.

Rudd, K. 2005. The case for cooperative federalism, Address to the Don Dunstan Foundation, Queensland Chapter, 14 July, <http://www.dunstan.org.au/resources/lectures.html>

Rudd, K. 2006. New Labor leadership team, Transcript, Press conference, 4 December, Parliament House, Canberra, <http://pandora.nla.gov.au/pan/22093/20061206-0000/www.alp.org.au/media/1206/pcloo040.htm>

Rudd, K. 2007a. Meeting of the Council of Australian Governments, effective federalism for the future: practical steps towards ending the blame game and boosting productivity growth, Media release, 10 December, Parliament House, Canberra, <http://www.pm.gov.au>

Rudd, K. 2007b. Joint press conference with Premiers Brumby, Iemma, Bligh, Carpenter, Lennon, Acting Premier Foley, and Chief Ministers Stanhope and Henderson, following the Council of Australian Governments meeting, Transcript, Government House, Melbourne, <http://www.pm.gov.au/node/6000>

Rudd, K. 2008a. Preparing Australia for global competitiveness in the 21st century, Address to the 2008 Future Summit, 11 May, <http://www.pm.gov.au/node/5803>

Rudd, K. 2008b. House of Representatives, *Debates*, 27 November, p. 11 721.

Rudd, K. 2008c. Quality education: the case for an education revolution in our schools, Address to the National Press Club, Canberra, 27 August, <http://pandora.nla.gov.au/pan/79983/20081112-0133/www.pm.gov.au/media/Speech/2008/speech_0443.html>

Rudd, K. 2008d. Address at the Australian Council of Local Government meeting, <http://www.aclg.gov.au/media_centre/speeches2008.aspx>

Rudd, K. 2009a. Prime Minister's address to the nation, Transcript, Parliament House, Canberra, 3 February, <http://pandora.nla.gov.au/pan/79983/20090212-0444/www.pm.gov.au/media/Speech/2009/speech_0786.html>

Rudd, K. 2009b. Joint press conference of COAG meeting, Transcript, Main Committee Room, Parliament House, Canberra, 9 February, <http://pandora.nla.gov.au/pan/79983/20090212-0444/www.pm.gov.au/media/Interview/2009/interview_0795.html>

Rudd, K. 2010. Better health, better hospitals: the national health and hospitals network, Speech to the National Press Club, Canberra, 3 March, <http://pandora.nla.gov.au/pan/79983/20100624-1429/www.pm.gov.au/node/6534.html>

Saunders, C. 2009. 'The sources and scope of Commonwealth power to spend', *Public Law Review*, vol. 20, no. 4 (December), pp. 256–63.

Savva, N. 2010. 'Rudd revenge on ALP agenda', *The Australian*, 27 April, p. 10.

Shanahan, D. 2007. 'Politically correct will stay in the doghouse', *The Australian*, 23 November.

Steketee, M. 2008. 'Deferred decision a classic cop out', *The Australian*, 4 July, p. 5.

Swan, W. 2008a. *Australian federal relations*, Budget Paper No. 3, *Commonwealth of Australia Budget 2008–09*, Commonwealth of Australia, Canberra, <www.budget.gov.au>

Swan, W. 2008b. House of Representatives, *Debates*, 27 November, p. 11 729.

Swan, W. 2009. *Australian federal relations*, Budget Paper No. 3, *Commonwealth of Australia Budget 2009–10*, Commonwealth of Australia, Canberra, <www.budget.gov.au>

Taylor, L. 2008. 'States demand $23bn as price of backing Rudd reform', *The Australian*, 10 October, p. 1.

Taylor, L. and Uren, D. 2010. *Shitstorm*, Melbourne University Press, Carlton, Vic.

Wanna, J. 2009. 'Political chronicles, Commonwealth of Australia July to December 2008', *Australian Journal of Politics and History*, vol. 55, no. 2, pp. 261–315.

Williams, G. 2009. Advice to the Australian Local Government Association: Re: *Pape v Commissioner of Taxation* and direct funding of local government, 12 August, <http://www.councilreferendum.com.au/>

Williams, G. 2010. 'Too rich, too weak to succeed seceding', *The Age*, 11 May.

Wiseman, J. 2008a. 'History making deal shares rivers—Rudd's new federalism', *The Australian*, 27 March, p. 4.

Wiseman, J. 2008b. 'Premier's spray taps Murray frustration', *The Australian*, 5 July, p. 2.

Wong, P. 2008. Murray Darling deal delivered, Media release, 26 March, Parliament House, Canberra, <http://www.climatechange.gov.au/~/media/Files/minister/wong/2008/Media%20Releases/March/mr20080326.ashx>

7. The opposition

GWYNNETH SINGLETON

In a two-party unicameral parliament, the official opposition is deemed to be the largest majority party that is able to assume office if the government should resign (McKay 2004:247–8). In Australia's bicameral system, where the government is formed by the majority party in the House of Representatives, the official opposition is 'the main non-government party in that chamber' (Parliamentary Education Office 2010:17.1). After the 2007 federal election, when the Australian Labor Party (ALP) won government, the Coalition parties, being the significant minority grouping in the House of Representatives, formed the official opposition.

A government–opposition relationship is determined by the relative party numbers in the House of Representatives and reflected in the physical seating pattern of the parties facing each other across the House (Michaud 2000:74). The relationship has, however, a significant broader political meaning because it maintains and reinforces the competitive and adversarial environment implicit in Australia's majoritarian form of democracy. The adversarial status of the parties is contextualised by the fact that the opposition does not have the numbers to defeat the government, it cannot influence the legislative program, its function is to oppose (Birch 1978:167) and the job of the Leader of the Opposition is to contest government policy (Hawker 2008:11). This is certainly true given that an opposition predominantly responds to government legislation and government policy (Birch 1978:167), and its critical scrutiny of government performance is mostly negative because its activities are directed towards the electorate with the primary intent of destroying the credibility and the electoral prospects of the government (Bach 2003:243).

These factors could imply the relative powerlessness of an opposition vis-a-vis the government, with little opportunity for an opposition to influence government policy. An opposition can, however, hold a government to account by raising issues and exposing government policy to criticism in the Parliament; matters that are then taken up by the media can force a government to reappraise its approach to a particular policy. For example, the opposition's use of Question Time to probe the Rudd government about critical problems with its roof insulation installation scheme and media coverage of related fires and deaths largely contributed to the cessation of the program. The bicameral nature of the Australian Parliament—with its powerful senate elected by proportional voting—means the government of the day is less likely to have a majority. This can offset the apparent powerlessness of the opposition (Kaiser 2008:33) because it has the capacity to block or amend government legislation.

The question of whether an opposition is limited to opposing the government is investigated in this chapter by assessing the capacity of the opposition to influence government policy during the legislative process, particularly in relation to the Senate. It is beyond the scope of the chapter to examine every bill that has passed through the Parliament, so relevant examples have been used to draw out the arguments.

First, however, the significance of the leader in the contest between the opposition and the government requires an examination of the reasons for the three leadership changes that occurred during the period of the Rudd government between November 2007 and 24 November 2009.

The opposition: significance of the leader

The media focus on the leaders of the parties contending for office in Australian federal elections means that how a leader performs, either as prime minister or as opposition leader, can affect the result of a federal election (Senior and van Onselen 2008:226). The significance of the performance of the leader as a determinant of electoral success is indicated by the inclusion in regular political polling of questions asking respondents to identify whether the incumbent Prime Minister or the Leader of the Opposition is their preference for prime minister. This poll has been used by political analysts and the media to judge the performance of the respective leaders, and a leader of the opposition who fails to make headway against the government is unlikely to survive (Hawker 2008:5–6). It will be seen below that poor showings in the preferred prime minister polls and the indicative or notional two-party preferred result for the major parties led to the replacement of two leaders of the opposition during the period under review. The existence of potential rivals and a lack of cohesion brought about by internal division between conservative and moderate members of the Liberal Party were also factors in that process.

When John Howard lost his seat of Bennelong at the October 2007 election, the parliamentary Liberal Party had to select a new leader. Heir apparent, Peter Costello, surprisingly announced that he would 'not seek' nor 'would he accept' a nomination to be opposition leader (Costello 2008), and former Howard government senior ministers Alexander Downer and Philip Ruddock also decided not to contest the leadership. The ballot on 29 November 2007 between Brendan Nelson and Malcolm Turnbull (Tony Abbott withdrew because he did not have sufficient support) was won by Nelson with 45 votes to 42 (Wanna 2008a:294). Costello's presence on the backbench, however, fuelled continuing speculation about his leadership aspirations.

Brendan Nelson

Brendan Nelson, a 'small-c' conservative considered progressive on social issues (ABC 2007), was elected Leader of the Opposition as the result of a backroom deal brokered by conservative Liberal senate leader, Nick Minchin, with six West Australian members to give Nelson the numbers to win. Minchin and other conservatives gave their support to Nelson because they were intent on blocking moderate Malcolm Turnbull, whom some in the party considered to be 'a dangerous leftie' (MacCallum 2008:15), and, in particular, because of Turnbull's declaration that Howard should have said 'sorry' to Indigenous Australians over the Stolen Generations issue (Wright 2007). As leader, Nelson's approach to policy became wedged between his need to shore up his support with the conservative right to preserve his leadership against a potential challenge from Turnbull and to remain electorally relevant on social policy (Milne 2008a).

No opposition leader elected directly after a federal election had stayed in the office long enough to win a federal election (MacCallum 2008:12). Nelson was handed the 'poisoned chalice' (Wright 2007) of taking on the job of renewal and revitalisation of a party that had suffered defeat after 12 years in office and faced a popular, newly elected government. His inability to create a strong profile, his failure to lift the Coalition in the polls, and mixed responses to policy issues gave his conservative critics within the party the ammunition to attack his leadership.

The difficulties Nelson experienced in managing this situation are evident in his response to the Rudd government's apology to the Stolen Generations. Conservatives within the party opposed the apology because they considered the current government was not responsible for the actions of previous generations, although more moderate members were more supportive. Nelson approached the issue by seconding the government's apology yet including statements in his speech that the present generation did not own the actions nor should it feel guilty for what was done in the past, often with the best of intentions (Nelson 2008a:174–5). His statement caused people in the Parliament and thousands watching on television to turn their backs and 'people booed, hissed and shouted' during his speech (The Age 2008a). He was criticised publicly and from within his own party for diffidence in dealing with the issue and displaying a lack of leadership (MacCallum 2008:12; Wanna 2008b:611). His popularity as preferred prime minister slumped to 7 per cent and the Coalition's notional two-party preferred vote dropped to 37 per cent (see Table 7.1), leading to speculation about a possible leadership challenge (Wanna 2008b:615).

Nelson's approval rating as preferred prime minister peaked at a low 17 per cent at the beginning of June 2008 (Table 7.1), but this reflected public discontent with the government over rising petrol prices rather than increased support for Nelson (Shanahan 2008a). His propensity to 'flip-flop' on policy issues (Wanna 2009a:262) including climate change evoked 'enormous unhappiness' in the shadow cabinet (Shanahan 2008b). When Nelson withdrew the Coalition's support for the government's emissions trading scheme, the government responded that he could not be taken seriously as he had 'already changed his position seven times' (McManus 2008).

Nelson's muddled performance on policy, his poor standing as preferred prime minister and the relative weakness of the opposition compared with the government in two-party polling created the conditions for a leadership spill.

Table 7.1 Brendan Nelson's performance in the polls (per cent).

Date of poll	29 February – 2 March 2008	30 May – 1 June 2008	22–24 August 2008
Preferred prime minister	7	17	14
Notional two-party preferred vote, Coalition	37	43	44

Source: Newspoll/The Australian (2010).

Potential rivals for the Liberal leadership were Malcolm Turnbull, who reportedly had not readily accepted his loss to Nelson (Wanna 2008a:295), and Peter Costello, 'the leader-who-might-have-been-or-still-might-be' (Hawker 2008:10). As Shadow Treasurer, Turnbull was constrained by the convention of cabinet collective responsibility from publicly criticising Nelson, but this did not prevent him from doing so in private. A leaked email from Turnbull to Nelson opposing the opposition leader's proposal for a reduction in the fuel excise by five cents a litre fuelled speculation about a leadership challenge. Costello's refusal to challenge Nelson unless others put themselves forward (Wanna 2009a:264) inhibited Turnbull from standing against Nelson because it would draw Costello into the contest and he was likely to win any ballot between them (Grattan 2008). The way was cleared for Turnbull when Costello announced his departure from federal politics on 10 September (Sydney Morning

Herald 2008). Nelson's tenure as Leader of the Opposition came to an end on 15 September 2008 when he lost a pre-emptive spill he had brought on to resolve the leadership issue; Turnbull won by 45 to 41 votes (Wanna 2009a:264).

Malcolm Turnbull

Turnbull, a moderate, 'small-l' liberal, had lost his 2007 challenge to Nelson because a group of conservatives who considered him too far to the left had blocked his run for the leadership. At the time of his 2008 challenge, only about one-third of Liberal party-room MPs were considered moderates (Kerr 2008), which indicates that Turnbull had won the leadership with the support of sufficient conservative Liberal MPs to secure him the victory. Those who did so considered he could do a better job than Nelson by better articulating the party's policies and principles and would 'take the fight up to Labor' (AAP 2008). Internal party politics, however, was also a factor, as members of the NSW right are believed to have supported Turnbull because Nelson supported changes to the NSW party's constitution that would have diminished the conservatives' dominance in that division.

Turnbull's leadership created the paradox of a substantively conservative party with a small-l liberal leader (Kerr 2008). Many pro-Howard conservative MPs had difficulty accepting Turnbull because of his moderate stance and his personality (Kelly 2008). He 'bulldozed his way into the leadership' (Kelly 2008) with a 'crash through or crash' approach to politics (Barns 2010) and lacked the consultative, team-bonding skills deemed necessary to unite the philosophically divided party (Kelly 2008). His leadership was characterised by poor people skills, a 'tremendous ego', 'withering contempt' (Waterford 2008) and 'arrogance' (Milne 2008b). These factors sowed the seeds of his later destruction.

Turnbull's leadership began on a promising note with a small lift in the polls (Table 7.2), but the onset of the global financial crisis (GFC) in September 2008, the government's restorative stimulus package and tensions between conservative and liberal factions within the parliamentary Liberal Party made it difficult for him to make further headway. He upset the party's right-wing conservative faction when he appointed moderates to key positions in the parliamentary party (Franklin and Taylor 2009; Shanahan and Kenny 2009), sacked conservative Senator Cory Bernardi from the shadow cabinet for making derogatory remarks about opposition frontbencher Christopher Pyne (Karvelas 2009) and publicly contradicted statements by Tony Abbott on opposition pension policy and Andrew Robb on climate change policy (Franklin and Taylor

2009). The Liberal party room became unruly, members and senators criticised Turnbull's domineering leadership style and divisions emerged over policy (Wanna 2009b:587).

Turnbull's political standing deteriorated after his mishandling of the 'OzCar affair'. OzCar was established by the Rudd government to provide funding assistance to car dealers unable to access credit as a result of the GFC. On 4 June 2009, Turnbull questioned the Prime Minister in Parliament on whether he or the Treasurer had made representations for OzCar assistance on behalf of Queensland car dealer John Grant Motors (Turnbull 2009a:5756). The issue was dubbed 'Utegate' because John Grant had lent the Prime Minister a utility to use within his electorate (Senate Privileges Committee 2009:1.8). When Godwin Grech, a Treasury public servant responsible for OzCar, told a Senate Economics Legislation Committee inquiry that the initial contact he had received regarding John Grant had come in an email from the Prime Minister's office (Grech 2009:E17, E38), Turnbull accused Rudd and Treasurer, Wayne Swan, of 'cronyism, patronage and abandonment of ethical standards' and the Treasurer of misleading Parliament (Turnbull 2009b:6665).

An Australian National Audit Office (ANAO 2009:14–15) inquiry found there 'was no evidence that either the Prime Minister or his office' had played a role in any representations made to Treasury, nor had the 'Treasurer or his office applied any pressure on Treasury' to give the dealer preference over other applicants. Grech, a 'Liberal sympathiser' who had provided information to Turnbull and Liberal Senator Eric Abetz on a number of issues (Maley 2010), had fabricated the email upon which the opposition based its attack on the Prime Minister and the Treasurer (Senate Privileges Committee 2009:1.4, 1.8, 2.4, 2.63, 2.10). Turnbull's poor handling of this issue weakened his leadership (Eltham 2009), as both his standing as preferred prime minister and support for the Coalition fell (see Table 7.2).

Differences between conservatives and moderates over the opposition's response to the Rudd government's carbon pollution reduction scheme (CPRS), discussed below, caused a schism in the party room that brought about the challenge that toppled Turnbull. One Liberal MP commented that politics 'isn't a winner-take-all business deal. When you lead a political party you have to take people with you and you have to accept compromise. That's part of the job—not to divide and rule' (Franklin 2009a). When Turnbull refused to adopt a compromise position proposed by conservatives Tony Abbott and Nick Minchin to refer the CPRS bills to a senate committee, a number of shadow ministers, including Abbott and Minchin, resigned (Kelly 2009a; Prasser 2009). Turnbull persisted in upholding the deal he had made with the government despite a deluge of emails and protests from the grassroots of the Liberal Party calling for the CPRS legislation to be delayed (Berkovic 2009) and a similar statement by climate change spokesman, Andrew Robb (Franklin and Taylor 2009). Turnbull's prospects for holding on to the leadership were undermined by polling showing 60 per cent of Australians were against the government rushing the CPRS (Milne 2009). Turnbull's approach and the hostility of conservatives within the party to his moderate views finally caused his unmaking.

Source: David Pope, *The Canberra Times*, 26 June 2009

Costello, who had continued to be promoted as a contender for the leadership, ceased to be a 'weapon of mass distraction' (Wanna 2009a:287) when he announced on 7 October 2009 that he was retiring from Parliament (Costello 2009). The leadership challenge came from conservative anti-Turnbull forces concerned that he was taking the party too far to the left and climate change sceptics. It was described as 'a factional war between conservatives and small-l liberals' (Grattan 2009) and 'an ambush on the leader' (Murphy 2009). The move was supported by Liberal MPs who were sympathetic to an emissions trading scheme but were doubtful about the government's rush to proceed before the outcomes of the Copenhagen conference were known. Members were also concerned at what many perceived to be Turnbull's ego-driven leadership style. Conservative Kevin Andrews, a central player in the leadership crisis (Murphy 2009), challenged Turnbull for the leadership on 24 November, but lost by 35 votes to 48. Some members of the parliamentary party, however, still wanted Turnbull out of the leadership (Turnbull 2009c). His standing in the polls declined (Table 7.2), with more Liberal Party supporters disapproving than approving of his leadership (Colebatch 2009). Conservative Tony Abbott moved a spill motion (Franklin 2009b) and put himself forward as a candidate, as did Joe Hockey, a moderate supporter of the emissions trading scheme. In the ballot held on 1 December, Hockey was eliminated and the final ballot between Turnbull and Abbott was won by Abbott 42 to 41 (Sharp 2009). On 6 April 2010, Turnbull announced he would resign from the House of Representatives, but on 1 May 2010 he changed his mind and announced that he had decided to stay.

Table 7.2 Malcolm Turnbull's performance in the polls (per cent)

Date of poll	10–12 October 2008	26–28 June 2009	24–26 July 2009	27–29 November 2009
Preferred prime minister	26	18	16	14
Notional two-party preferred vote, Coalition	45	44	43	43

Source: Newspoll/The Australian (2010).

Tony Abbott

Even though Tony Abbott won the leadership ballot by only one vote, his accession to the leadership brought the conservatives back into ascendancy within the party, and he replaced moderates in the shadow ministry with the hardline conservatives who had worked to topple Turnbull (Coorey 2009). He has been described as a 'conviction' politician, clever and populist, a 'social conservative', a 'natural pugilist', a 'fitness fanatic', and 'unable to conceal his beliefs or blunders with spin' (Kelly 2009b). His Catholic conservativism, strongly influenced by B. A. Santamaria, a prominent activist with the Catholic National Civic Council (Abbott 2009:11), was considered likely to prove a disincentive for women voters (Kelly 2009b).

Abbott's keen approach to physical sporting pursuits became front-page news when he was photographed just days after taking over the leadership emerging from the surf in a pair of red Speedo swimming trunks, commonly known as 'budgie-smugglers'—an image caricatured by the nation's cartoonists and comedians ever since. In March, reporters followed the progress of 'Iron Man Abbott' in a triathlon and, in April, a Lycra-clad Abbott was again in the news when he participated in a Melbourne–Sydney bike ride.

According to Abbott, political parties need some 'hard men' and he developed a reputation as the 'attack dog' of the Howard government (Abbott 2009:21). Not surprisingly, he took a more aggressive approach in opposing the Rudd government than his two predecessors (Daley 2010). The fact that his leadership opened up a wider divide in the political debate between the government and the Coalition was a function of this approach and it was also in keeping with Abbott's view that philosophical arguments assume more significance because the opposition's job is 'to clarify its own thinking rather than govern the country' (Abbott 2009:53). He recognised that the necessity to be viewed as a valid alternative government must be a constraint on unfettered political comment (Dusevic 2010a). His leadership came under critical scrutiny in May 2010 when he stated on the ABC's *7.30 Report* that sometimes in the heat of discussion he went 'a little bit further than you would if it was an absolutely calm, considered, prepared, scripted remark, which is one of the reasons why the statements that need to be taken absolutely as gospel truth are those carefully prepared scripted remarks' (ABC 2010a). In a critical editorial, *The Australian* (2010) commented that Abbott too often offered 'flippancy rather than gravitas', that he had 'the grit' and 'an ironman certificate to prove it' but, it was pointed out, 'politics is not a bike ride, and energy alone will not get Mr Abbott across the line'.

Abbott's aggressive style and his view that an election could not be won without a fight, with the opposition providing an alternative and not an echo to the government (Rodgers 2009), contextualised his attacks on the performance of both the Rudd and the Gillard governments. One of Abbott's first moves as leader was to vote down the CPRS bills in the Senate (with the support of the Greens and Senators Steve Fielding and Nick Xenophon). The Coalition's policy became direct action to reduce carbon dioxide emissions 'without the need for a great big new tax' (Liberal Party of Australia 2010a). Abbott pledged to restore the budget to surplus through cuts to government expenditure rather than higher taxes, with a commitment to reject Labor's 'massive new mining tax' (Abbott 2010). The Coalition rejected Rudd's population target of 36 million and promised that their migration program would be 'consistent with a sustainable population growth path' (Liberal Party of Australia 2010b).

The opposition and the Rudd–Gillard governments advanced many similar policies although there were differences in the detail. These included support for Australia's commitment to Afghanistan, paid parental leave, and offshore processing and detention of asylum-seekers (although the

Liberals would have restored temporary protection visas and would have 'returned boats and/or their passengers to their point of departure or an alternative third country destination') (Liberal Party of Australia 2010c).

Abbott's performance in the polls was better than his predecessors'. In May 2010, the Coalition was in a winning position with 50 per cent of the two-party preferred results, and Abbott had improved his preferred prime ministerial rating to 37 per cent (Table 7.3). Some of this improvement was due to the penetration of Abbott's attacks on Labor's spin and Rudd's poor performance (Dusevic 2010b). More significant was the poor performance of the Rudd government, including policy reversals on climate change and childcare centres, an increase in tobacco tax, problems with the insulation installation and the Building the Education Revolution (BER) building programs, interest rate rises, and a heated campaign from the mining industry against the mining resources profits tax. After Julia Gillard became Prime Minister, Abbott fell back in the preferred prime minister polls, to 27 per cent, in the two days leading up to the announcement of the federal election and in the two-party preferred poll, to 45 per cent. Once the campaign got under way, however, his support as preferred prime minister in polling undertaken on 23–25 July increased to 34 per cent and the Coalition's two-party preferred vote also increased, to 48 per cent. A Herald/Nielsen poll published on 31 July saw Labor leading the two-party preferred vote by 52 per cent to 48 per cent and Abbott's approval rating as preferred prime minister reducing the gap at 41 per cent, with Julia Gillard on 49 per cent. Immediately prior to the election Abbott's rating as preferred prime minister stood at 37 per cent. At no time had he surpassed either Rudd or Gillard in this regard.

The 2010 election resulted in a hung parliament and even though Abbott failed to form government, his performance in bringing the Coalition so close was a significant achievement. He ran a disciplined campaign with a united team and benefitted from Labor's policy mishaps. He is credited with pressuring Labor to the point where it ruthlessly dumped Rudd in favour of Gillard. He responded to criticism that he ran a negative campaign by pointing to his 'strong, positive agenda' to 'end the waste', 'pay back the debt', 'stop the big new taxes' and 'stop the boats' (Hartcher 2010). He was returned as Leader of the Opposition unopposed.

Table 7.3 Tony Abbott's performance in the polls (per cent)

Date of poll	26–28 March 2010*	14–16 May 2010*	18–20 June 2010*	16–18 July 2010*	23–25 July 2010*	31 July 2010**	17–19 August 2010*
Preferred prime minister	27	33	37	27	34	41	37
Coalition notional two-party preferred vote	44	50	48	45	48	52	49.8

Sources: * Newspoll/The Australian (2010); ** AAP (2010).

Opposition influence over government policy

Because the government had a majority in the House of Representatives, the opposition in that house was restricted to raising issues and probing government performance through Question Time and debate. The opposition did not oppose all legislation because there were many issues on which there was bipartisan agreement. For example, until 1 April 2010, of the 438 bills that had passed the House of Representatives, only 80 (or about 18 per cent) required a division (Department of the House of Representatives 2010). This does not necessarily mean that the opposition agreed entirely with those uncontested bills, but it let the bills pass through the House of Representatives without a division. Bills relating to run-of-the-mill machinery-of-government issues usually have bipartisan support.

The situation in the Senate was different because the opposition's majority in that house until 30 June 2008 meant it could amend or vote down government legislation. Even so, the Senate passed 84 government bills and only five were negatived or discharged from the *Notice Paper* (Senate 2008a). This pattern continued after 1 July 2008 when the opposition required the support of one of the crossbench senators to vote down government bills and two to pass amendments or pass its own bills. For the remainder of 2008, 80 bills were agreed to and only eight were negatived or discharged from the *Notice Paper* (Senate 2008a). Not all the bills passed, however, were uncontested by the opposition; five were passed when the Greens and the two independent senators voted with the government (Senate 2008b). As an example, the government's bill to lift the luxury car tax to 33 per cent was defeated in the Senate in 2008 when Family First Senator, Steve Fielding, voted with the opposition against the bill. It passed, however, after Senators Fielding and Xenophon negotiated amendments with the government (The Age 2008b).

Despite having a senate majority, the opposition's capacity to have any real influence on the policy agenda was constrained by government control of the legislative program. For example, Liberal MHR Petro Georgiou's Private Member's Bill to establish an independent reviewer of the Terrorism Laws Bill 2008 was defeated in the House of Representatives, passed the Senate on 13 November 2008 with the support of Senators Fielding and Xenophon, but was not listed for consideration after it was reintroduced into the House of Representatives on 24 November 2008.

In 2009, Rudd government ministers complained that they were dealing with 'the most obstructionist opposition in 30 years' (ABC 2010b) because the Senate voted down 41 bills. The actual outcome, however, was not significantly different from the previous years of the Rudd government because some of those bills subsequently passed and 11 bills relating to the CPRS scheme were voted down twice (Senate 2009a). Harry Evans makes this same point in Chapter 5 of this volume.

Negative influence: blocking bills

Voting down government bills in the Senate is a negative action because it denies the government its preferred policy but does not necessarily influence government policy. The government's bill to means test the private health insurance rebate was defeated in the Senate on the combined vote of the opposition, the Greens and the two independents (Senate 2009b:6184). The government threatened a double dissolution if the bill was defeated in the Senate a second time (Breusch 2009), but the threat of an early election did not dissuade the opposition from defeating the legislation in the Senate a second time with the support of Family First Senator, Steve Fielding (Senate 2010:1384).

Positive influence: amending bills

The opposition had the opportunity to make a positive contribution to policy by passing amendments to government bills using its senate majority until 30 June 2008 or with the support of two crossbench senators after 1 July 2008. The Broadcasting Legislation Amendment (Digital Television Switch-Over) Bill 2008 was amended in the House of Representatives to delete a clause inserted by the opposition and Senators Fielding and Xenophon that would have required the government to report to each House of the Parliament the action taken to identify and rectify digital transmission black spots. The Senate did not agree to the government's amendment and, as the government did not insist on its amendment, the opposition's amended policy was retained.

Nevertheless, opposition influence is marginal if limited to minor amendments. When the opposition used its senate majority to include a review process in the legislation to establish a teen dental plan and a new dental benefits schedule, the government did not think that the amendment moved in the Senate added sufficient value but was happy to concede if the opposition insisted it be included in the bill (Roxon 2008).

If the government refuses to accept opposition-derived senate amendments, the opportunity for any positive influence is lost because the options are to let the legislation pass through the Parliament without those amendments or to vote down the bill in the Senate. The Families, Housing, Community Services and Indigenous Affairs and Other Legislation Amendment (2008 Budget and Other Measures) Bill 2008 is a good example. It included, amongst other measures, the introduction of a means test for Family Tax Benefit Part B and the baby bonus; the requirement that claimants of the Commonwealth Seniors Health Card provide their tax file numbers (TFNs) (Schedule 3); and an increase in the Partner Service Pension qualifying age for males from fifty to sixty years and for females from fifty years to fifty-eight years and six months (Schedule 5). The opposition used its majority in the Senate to amend the bill to introduce a tapered rate for the baby bonus for incomes in excess of $150 000, to express concern at the imposition of a means test on the Family Tax Benefit, and to negate Schedules 3 and 5 (Senate 2008c:3252).

After aggressive lobbying of senior ministers by the not-for-profit sector (ABC 2008a), the government introduced its own amendment to the bill to reverse changes to the Fringe Benefit Tax rules implemented by the Howard government in 2006 that had reduced the incomes of charity and community-sector workers. The opposition supported the amendment in order to provide certainty to workers in the charity sector (Senate 2008c:3260). An opposition amendment for a review of operations of the amendments to the act was also passed and the bill was referred back to the House of Representatives.

The government accepted the Senate's amendments criticising the baby bonus and the Family Tax Benefit Part B and the inclusion of the review mechanism. These were marginal changes that did not affect the substance of the bill. It refused, however, to exclude Schedules 3 and 5 relating to the TFN and the Partner Service Pension. Despite its vehement disagreement with these two proposals, the opposition in the Senate did not insist on these amendments for the politically pragmatic reason that it would have meant that charity and community workers would have lost up to $100 a week from 1 July if the bill was not passed before the Senate rose for its winter break (Abbott 2008:5958).

The opposition also did not persist with its senate amendments to the Nation-Building Funds Bill 2008 after they were rejected by the government despite significant disagreement within Coalition ranks. The bill had been vehemently opposed by the Coalition, particularly the Nationals, because it removed the Communications Fund set up by the Howard government in 2005. An opposition amendment to delete this provision passed by the Senate with the support of Senators Fielding and Xenophon was rejected by the government. When the bill returned to the Senate, despite vigorous and angry debate from Liberal and National senators, the Liberal leadership did not insist on its amendments for the politically strategic reason that if it had done so the government would 'spend the next two months falsely asserting all over the country that we are responsible for denying infrastructure funding to every road, bridge and port in the country' (Minchin 2008:8336). Many Coalition senators, including Liberal Leader in the Senate, Nick Minchin, vented their displeasure at this about-face by not being present in the Chamber when the vote was taken, and four National senators and two Liberals crossed the floor in protest. Only five Liberal senators voted with the government. This discord within Coalition ranks—regarded as 'open rebellion' against Leader of the Opposition, Malcolm Turnbull (ABC 2008b)—was a forerunner to the more significant split over climate change that led to the downfall of Turnbull's leadership, discussed above.

Influence through cooperation or compromise

Meaningful input to government policy occurred when the government, having failed to get the support of the crossbenchers, turned to the opposition to pass its bills through the Senate. Again, practical politics was a reason for its decision to pass the bill. The opposition had voted with Senator Fielding to prevent the exclusion of part-time work as eligibility for independence status under the Youth Allowance (Social Security and Other Legislation) Amendment (Income Support for Students) Bill 2009 (No. 2) on the basis that it disadvantaged rural and regional families and students who had done this type of work in the previous year when it was allowable. The government negotiated changes to the bill with the Greens and Senator Xenophon to get their support, but was not able to secure the critical vote of Senator Fielding. The failure to pass the bill meant that 150 000 students entering university in first semester 2010 would not receive scholarships. The government then negotiated with the opposition and agreed to amend the bill so that students who lived in very remote, remote or outer regional centres who had to move away from home to study would be eligible for the Youth Allowance under the existing independence test. The bill then passed the Senate with the opposition's support (Gillard 2010). When Senator Fielding berated the Coalition for selling out on inner rural students (Sydney Morning Herald 2010), Senator Mason reminded him that the Coalition was in opposition and, although the deal was not perfect and a lot of his colleagues were not happy about it, it was worth hundreds of millions of dollars over the next 10 years or so to enable rural students to go to university. 'I think the Coalition overall has done a very good job in securing what it can for rural students', he said (Mason 2010:2056).

Conclusion

The significance of political polling as a central factor in maintaining or losing the Liberal leadership is evident from the way in which the Liberals brutally disposed of Brendan Nelson and Malcolm Turnbull when they failed to make headway against the government in the two-party preferred vote and preferred prime minister poll results. In Turnbull's case, poll results provided justification for the spill, but it was underpinned by the ideological split between the conservatives and moderates in the party that came to a head over Turnbull's support for the government's CPRS legislation. The driving force of electoralism as a critical factor in maintaining the leadership is captured in Abbott's statement that 'the only really happy opposition is one that's convinced it's on the verge of winning government' (Abbott 2009:54).[1]

The proposition that an opposition in a two-party system in the Westminster tradition is powerless to influence government policy, apart from raising issues in the Parliament and the media, has to be reconsidered in the context of Australia's bicameral system. During the term of the Rudd government, the opposition in the Senate was able to influence government policy by blocking or amending legislation, but the distinction has to be drawn between negative influence where the government refuses to accept the outcome and positive input where opposition amendments are accepted. Positive input was achieved when the government, for various reasons, accepted opposition amendments, although these were primarily of a minor nature. More substantive input was achieved when the government negotiated an agreed outcome with the opposition in order to get its bills through the Parliament after it failed to get the support of the Greens and Senators Fielding and Xenophon.

Brendan Nelson held the view that an opposition should not just oppose everything and that if a government was doing the right thing, the opposition

---

1   The same adage probably applies to the government, as we saw when Prime Minister, Kevin Rudd, was ousted when falling public support for his leadership and the party was seen to be a threat to the re-election of the Labor government.

needed to say so (Nelson 2008b). In the Australian system, however, an opposition is in an adversarial relationship with the governing party. In this context, the opposition attacked the performance of the Rudd government at every opportunity in Question Time, in parliamentary debate and in the public arena through the media. It blocked and amended government bills in the Senate with which it disagreed. The opposition also has to provide voters with a choice by differentiating its policies from those of the government. In Abbott's words, the job of the opposition is 'to be an alternative, not an echo' (Rodgers 2009). This contextual framework of the relationship is captured by Abbott's stated determination to draw the battlelines between the opposition and the Labor government (Abbott 2009:182) and Gillard's incitement to Abbott when she became Prime Minister for him 'to bring it on'.

Gwynneth Singleton *is an Adjunct Associate Professor at the University of Canberra.*

References

Abbott, A. 2008. House of Representatives, *Debates*, 25 June.

Abbott, A. 2009. *Battlelines*, Melbourne University Press, Carlton, Vic.

Abbott, A. 2010. Leader of the Opposition Address to the Liberal Party Federal Council, 26 June, Liberal Party of Australia, Barton, ACT, <www.liberal.org.au/Latest-News/2010/06/26/Leader-of-the-Opposition-Address-to-the-Liberal-party-Federal-Council.aspx>

Australian Associated Press (AAP) 2008. *Australian National News Wire*, 16 September, Australian Associated Press, accessed through EBSCOhost, Australia/New Zealand Reference Centre, Accession No. 74C429459612.

Australian Associated Press (AAP) 2010. 'Abbott leads Gillard in latest poll', *Australian Associated Press*, 31 July, <http://www.news.com.au/breaking-news/abbott-leads-gillard-in-latest-poll/story-e6frfku0-1225899282954#ixzz0vK7BTuZl>

Australian Broadcasting Corporation (ABC) 2007. 'Brendan Nelson elected as opposition leader', *PM*, ABC Radio, 29 November, <http://www.abc.net.au/pm/conent/2007/s2105607.htm>

Australian Broadcasting Corporation (ABC) 2008a. 'Fringe benefits changes to hit low paid workers', *ABC News*, 17 June 2008, <http://www.abc.net.au/news/stories/2008/06/12/2276703.htm>

Australian Broadcasting Corporation (ABC) 2008b. 'Opposition disarray over dumping of Telstra fund', *PM*, ABC Radio, 5 December, <http://www.abc.net.au/pm/content/2008/s2439346>

Australian Broadcasting Corporation (ABC) 2010a. 'Abbott quizzed on mixed messages', *7.30 Report*, ABC TV, 17 May, <www.abc.net.au/7.30/content/2010/s2901996.htm>

Australian Broadcasting Corporation (ABC) 2010b. 'Ministers savage "just say no Abbott"', *ABC News*, 10 March, <http://www.abc.net.au/news/stroies/2010/03/10/2841751.htm>

Australian National Audit Office (ANAO) 2009. *Representations to the Department of the Treasury in relation to motor dealer financing assistance*, Audit Report No. 1 2009–10, Australian National Audit Office, Barton, ACT, <http://www.anao.gov.au/uploads/documents/2009-10_Audit_Report_1.pdf>

Bach, S. 2003. *Platypus and Parliament: The Australian Senate in theory and practice*, Department of the Senate, Canberra.

Barns, G. 2010. 'Malcolm Turnbull's small "l" liberalism leaves big legacy', *The Drum Unleashed*, ABC TV, 6 April, <http://www.abc.net.au/unleashed/stores/s2865144.htm>

Berkovic, N. 2009. 'Climate deal sparks a new wave of Coalition frontbench resignations', *The Australian*, 27 November, <http://www.theaustralian.com.au/politics/climate-deal-sparks-a-wave-of-coalition-frontbench-resignations/story-e6frgczf-1225804365829>

Birch, A. 1978. *The British System of Government*, (Revised edition), George Allen & Unwin, London.

Breusch, J. 2009. 'PM puts poll pressure on Turnbull', *Australian Financial Review*, 14 September.

Colebatch, T. 2009. 'Poll numbers turn against leader', *The Age*, 30 November, <http://www.theage.com.au/natioal/poll-numbers-turn-against-leader-20091129-jywi.htm>

Coorey, P. 2009. 'Climate change sceptics triumph', *Sydney Morning Herald*, 9 December, <http://www.smh.com.au/national/climate-change-sceptics-triumph-20091208-khqb.html>

Costello, P. (with Coleman, P.) 2008. *The Costello Memoirs*, Melbourne University Press, Carlton, Vic.

Costello, P. 2009. Statement concerning Higgins electorate, Official web site of Peter Costello, 7 October, <http://www.petercostello.com.au/press/statement-concerning-higgins-electorate>

Daley, P. 2010. 'Abbott takes aim at a PM all at sea', *National Times*, 4 January, <http://www.nationaltimes.com.au/opinion/politics/abbott-takes-aim-at-a-pm-all-at-sea-20100201-1mgg.html>

Department of the House of Representatives 2010. List of bills passed by the House of Representatives in the 42nd Parliament, showing the bills on which the House divided, Email to G. Singleton, 1 April 2010, from Chamber Research Office, Department of the House of Representatives, Canberra.

Dusevic, T. 2010a. 'The battle within', *The Weekend Australian*, 20–21 March.

Dusevic, T. 2010b. 'Rudd on the slide', *The Weekend Australian*, 8–9 May.

Eltham, B. 2009. 'The political rip snorter that was 2009', *newmatilda.com*, 17 December, <http://newmatilda.com/2009/12/17/political-rip-snorter-2009>

Franklin, M. 2009a. 'Malcolm Turnbull unmoved as support dives', *The Australian*, 28 November, <http://www.theaustralian.com.au/news/nation/malcolm-turnbull-unmoved-as-support-dives/story-e6frg6nf-1225804755606>

Franklin, M. 2009b. 'Joe Hockey set to take on Malcolm Turnbull', *The Australian*, 30 November, <http://www.theaustralian.com.au/news/joe-hockey-set-to-take-on-malcolm-turnbull/story-e6frg6n6-1225805155171?from=public_rss>

Franklin, M. and Taylor, L. 2009. 'Pressure builds on Malcolm Turnbull as Liberal infighting erupts', *The Australian*, 20 February, <http://www.theaustralian.com.au/news/nation/pressure-builds-on-turnbull/story-e6frg6nf-111111889099072>

Gillard, J. 2010. Government delivers on youth allowance, Media release, 16 March 2010, Parliament House, Canberra, <http://www.deewr.gov.au/Ministers/Guillard/Media/Releases/Pages/Article_100316_175824.aspx>

Grattan, M. 2008. 'No challenge by Turnbull, but wriggle room aplenty', *The Age*, 22 May, <http://www.theage.com.au/news/national/no-turnbull-challenge-but-wriggle-room-aplenty/2008/05/21?1211182895814.htm>

Grattan, M. 2009. 'Minchin's emissions opposition a direct challenge to Turnbull', *National Times*, 20 November, <http://www.nationaltimes.com.au/opinion/politics/minchins-emissions-opposition-a-direct-challenge-to-turnbull-20091119-iotb.html>

Grech, G. 2009. Senate Economics Legislation Committee, Reference: Car Dealership Financing Guarantee Appropriation Bill 2009, *CPD Official Committee Hansard*, 19 June, <http://www.aph.gov.au/hansard/senate/committee/S12204.pdf>

Hawker, G. 2008. 'Between somewhere & nowhere: Brendan Nelson as federal Liberal leader', *Australian Quadrant*, vol. 80, no. 2 (March–April), pp. 4–12.

Kaiser, A. 2008. 'Parliamentary opposition in Westminster democracies: Britain, Canada, Australia and New Zealand', *The Journal of Legislative Studies*, vol. 14, no. 1, pp. 20–45.

Karvelas, P. 2009. 'Turnbull sacks SA senator Cory Bernardi over Pyne claim', *The Australian*, 19 February, <http://www.theaustralian.com.au/news/turnbull-sacks-senator-over-pyne-claim/story-01111118903519>

Kelly, P. 2008. 'A Liberal dose of hope', *The Australian*, 17 September, <http://www.search.ebscohost.com>, Accession No. 200809171016549011.

Kelly, P. 2009a. 'Rebels with a lost cause', *The Australian*, 28 November, <http://www.theaustralian.com.au/news/opinion/rebels-with-a-lost-cause/story-e6frg6zo-1225804740400>

Kelly, P. 2009b. 'The great conservative revolt', *The Australian*, 2 December, <http://www.theaustralian.com.au/news/opinion/the-great-conservative-revolt/story-e6frg74x-1225805945617>

Kerr, C. 2008. 'The man most likely to succeed', *The Australian*, 27 September.

Liberal Party of Australia 2010a. The Coalition's direct action plan: environment and climate change, Liberal Party of Australia, Barton, ACT, <http://www.liberal.org.au>

Liberal Party of Australia 2010b. Coalition rejects Prime Minister's 36 million population target, 29 April, Liberal Party of Australia, Barton, ACT, <http://www.liberal.org.au/Latest-News/2010/04/29/Coalition-rejects-PMs-population-target.aspx>

Liberal Party of Australia 2010c. Restoring sovereignty and control to our borders: policy direction statement, 27 May, Liberal Party of Australia, Barton, ACT, <http://www.liberal.org.au >

MacCallum, M. 2008. 'The nation reviewed', *The Monthly*, no. 33 (April), pp. 12–15.

McKay, W. 2004. *Erskine May Parliamentary Practice*, (23rd edition), LexisNexis Butterworths, London.

McManus, G. 2008. 'Brendan Nelson warns of climate change economic doom', *Herald Sun*, 8 July, <http://www.heraldsun.com.au/news/liberals-warn-of-doom/story-0-1111116850500>

Maley, P. 2010. 'Abetz admits Turnbull fed him Grech leaks', *The Australian*, 26 March.

Mason, B. 2010. Senate, *Debates*, 17 March.

Michaud, N. 2000. 'Designating the official opposition in a Westminster parliamentary system', *The Journal of Legislative Studies*, vol. 6, no. 4.

Milne, G. 2008a. 'Nelson wedges himself trying to please all', *The Australian*, 16 June.

Milne, G. 2008b. 'Malcolm Turnbull wins public support', *Sunday Mail* [Brisbane], 21 September, <http://www.couriermail.com.u\au/news/national/public-warms-to-turnbull/story-e6freooo-1111117541090>

Milne, G. 2009. 'Malcolm Turnbull stance cops a poll axing', *Sunday Telegraph*, 29 November, <http://www.dailytelegraph.com.au/news/sunday-telegraph/malcolm-turnbull-stance-cops-a-poll-axing/story-e6frewx0-1225804931826>

Minchin, N. 2008. Senate, *Debates*, 4 December.

Murphy, K. 2009. 'Nationals maverick sets course for lower house', *The Age*, 4 December, <http://www.theage.com.au/national/nationals-maverick-sets-course-for-lower-house-20091203k8tu-html>

Nelson, B. 2008a. House of Representatives, *Debates*, 13 February.

Nelson, B. 2008b. Transcript of interview with Geoff Hutchison, ABC 720 Perth, ABC Radio, <http://www.parlinfo/download/media/radioprm/M21Q6/upoand_binary/m2161.pdf>

Newspoll/The Australian 2010. 'Political and issues trends', *Newspoll/The Australian*, <http://www.newspoll.com.au/cgi-bin/polling/display_poll_data.pl>

Parliamentary Education Office 2010. 'Alternative government—the opposition', *Our Government*, no. 17, Parliamentary Education Office, Canberra, <http://www.peo.gov.au/faq/faq_17.html>

Prasser, S. 2009. 'Peter Costello's to blame for the leadership crisis tearing the party apart', *The Australian*, 1 December, <http://www.theaustralian.com.au/news/opinion/peter-costellos-to-blame-for-the-leadership-crisis-tearing-the-party-apart/story-e6frg620-1225805523074>

Rodgers, E. 2009. 'Abbott comes out fighting after leadership coup', *ABC News Online*, 1 December, <http://www.abc.net.au/news/stories/2009/12/01/2758345>

Roxon, N. 2008. House of Representatives, *Debates*, 23 June.

Senate 2008a. *Senate Statistical Summary*, Parliament of Australia, Canberra, <http://www.aph.gov.au/Senate/work/statistics/stats_sum/2008/s06.htm>

Senate 2008b. Senate, *Debates*, 26 August to 4 December.

Senate 2008c. Senate, *Debates*, 24 June.

Senate 2009a. *Legislation Statistics 2009*, Parliament of Australia, Canberra, <http://www.aph.gov.au/Senate/work/statistics/bus_senate/2009/legislation/legis_stats.html>

Senate 2009b. Senate, *Debates*, 9 September.

Senate 2010. Senate, *Debates*, 9 March.

Senate Privileges Committee 2009. *Matters arising from the Economics Legislation Committee Hearing on 19 June 2009 (referred 24 June and 12 August 2009)*, 142nd Report, 25 November, Senate Privileges Committee, Canberra, <http://www.aph.gov.au/senate/committee/priv_ctte/report_142/index.htm>

Senior, P. and van Onselen, P. 2008. 'Re-examining leader effects: have leader effects grown in Australian federal elections 1990–2004?', *Australian Journal of Political Science*, vol. 43, no. 2 (June).

Shanahan, D. 2008a. 'Brendan Nelson's vision lost in carbon fog', *The Australian*, July 30, <http://www.theaustralian.com.au/news/brendans-vision-lost-in-cargon-fog/story-e6frg6no-1111117054261>

Shanahan, D. 2008b. 'Rudd pays personal toll for anger about petrol prices', *The Australian*, 3 June, <http://www.theaustralian.com.au/news/national/rudd-pays-personal-toll-newspoll/story-e6frg6nf-1111116519902>

Shanahan, D. and Kenny, M. 2009. 'Liberal Senator Cory Bernardi demoted over Christopher Pyne', *Adelaide Now*, 19 February, <http://www.adelaidenow.com.au/news/sa-libs-sacking-sets-up-leadership-fight/story-0-1111118902643>

Sharp, A. 2009. 'Abbott wins Liberal leadership—by one vote', *The Age*, 1 December, <http://www.theage.com.au/national/abbott-wins-liberal-leadership-by-one-vote-20091201-klva.html>

Sydney Morning Herald 2008. 'Costello says he is leaving politics', *Sydney Morning Herald*, 10 September, <http://news.shm.com.au/national/costello-says-he-is-leaving-politics-20080910-4d5h.html>

Sydney Morning Herald 2010. 'Youth allowance reforms all but passed', *Sydney Morning Herald*, 17 March, <http://www.smh.com.au/breaking-news-national/youth-allowance-reforms/all-but-passed-20100317>

The Age 2008a. 'Liberal leader provoked outrage', *The Age*, 13 February, <http://www.theage.com.au/articles/2008/02/13/1202760367682.html>

The Age 2008b. 'Luxury car tax bill passes Senate', *The Age*, 24 September, <http://www.theage.com.au/business/luxury-car-tax-bill-passes-senate-20080924-4mqu.html>

The Australian 2010. 'Editorial', *The Australian*, 21 May.

Turnbull, M. 2009a. House of Representatives, *Debates*, 4 June, p. 5756.

Turnbull, M. 2009b. House of Representatives, *Debates*, 22 June, p. 6665.

Turnbull, M. 2009c. Doorstop interview, Rose Bay, NSW, 28 November, <http://malcolmturnbull.com.au/Media/LatestNews/tabid/articleType/ArticleView/articleId/695/Doorstop-Interview-Rose-Bay.aspx>

Wanna, J. 2008a. 'Commonwealth of Australia July to December 2007', *Australian Journal of Politics and History*, vol. 54, no. 2, pp. 289–341.

Wanna, J. 2008b. 'Commonwealth of Australia January to June 2008', *Australian Journal of Politics and History*, vol. 54, no. 4, pp. 609–62.

Wanna, J. 2009a. 'Commonwealth of Australia July to December 2008', *Australian Journal of Politics and History*, vol. 55, no. 2, pp. 261–315.

Wanna, J. 2009b. 'Commonwealth of Australia January to June 2009', *Australian Journal of Politics and History*, vol. 55, no. 4, pp. 584–92.

Waterford, J. 2008. 'Turnbull the great contradiction', *Australian Policy Online*, 18 September, <http://www.apo.org.au>

Wright, T. 2007. 'Backroom deal seals Nelson bid', *The Age*, 30 November.

Part III. Policy Issues

8. Citizen-centred policy making under Rudd: network governance in the shadow of hierarchy?

DAVID MARSH, CHRIS LEWIS AND PAUL FAWCETT

The 2007 Policy Platform of the Australian Labor Party (ALP) asserted that 'Labor will pursue new and innovative measures designed to foster greater participation and engagement of the Australian population in the political process' (cited in Manwaring 2010). It seemed that Labor was following a trend that many authors have identified as a move from government to governance—more specifically to 'network governance',[1] in which governments encourage greater participation, especially by 'expert citizens' (see Bang 2005), in policy making, recognising that they can at best steer, not row (see Osborne and Gaebler 1992). Indeed, as Martinetto (2003:593) contends, this idea has taken on a 'semblance of orthodoxy'. In this chapter, we examine two major initiatives taken by the Rudd government that were designed to deliver on this platform promise: the 2020 Summit and the Community Cabinets initiative. Our aim is to assess both the extent to which these initiatives marked a genuine move towards greater participation and, more broadly, whether they reflect a move towards network governance. We begin, however, with a brief discussion of the literature on governance that we use to frame this chapter.

Models of governance

Rhodes (1997), among many others, distinguishes between three modes of governance—hierarchy, markets and networks—arguing that networks have become the dominant mode.[2] Newman (2005:11) outlines this view:

---

1 The network governance literature is only loosely related to the literature on policy networks (see Marsh and Rhodes 1992), and owes much more to the European literature on modes of governance (see, for example, Kickert et al. 1997). For a more detailed discussion of these issues, which pays particular attention to Rhodes' works, see Marsh (forthcoming).

2 Actually, Rhodes' view has changed to a significant extent over time as he has embraced interpretativism and a 'decentred' approach to polity. He still, however, sees the network governance 'narrative', and the related differentiated polity narrative, as superior to the more hierarchical perspective of the Westminster

It is argued that the capacity of governments to control events within the nation state has been influenced by the flow of power away from traditional government institutions, upwards to transnational bodies and downwards to regions and sub-regions. The old mechanisms of 'control through hierarchy', it is suggested, have been superseded by the rise of markets during the 1980s and early 1990s, and by the increasing importance of networks and partnerships from the mid-1990s onwards.[3]

Many do not accept the blanket claim about the rise of network governance. In particular, it is argued that the distinction between government, based on hierarchy and markets, and governance, based on networks, creates a dualism, when it is better seen as a duality. From this perspective, governments oversee the various modes of governance through a process of meta-governance: 'they get involved in redesigning markets, in constitutional change and the juridical re-regulation of organizational forms and objectives, in organizing the conditions for self-organization' (Jessop 2004:70–1).

As such, Fawcett (2009:24) contends that, while hierarchies, markets and networks are distinct modes of governing, hierarchy and control remain

> an important, if not the most important, form of coordination and governance, whether it is actively imposed on others from above or used as a latent threat to ensure compliance. This is because the state is typically understood to have retained its capacity to intervene in the activities of self-regulating markets and networks.

As such, meta-governance involves attempts by the state to coordinate modes of governing. For Jessop (2004:65), these 'different forms of coordination (markets, hierarchies, networks, and solidarities) and the different forms of self-organization characteristic of governance take place in the shadow of hierarchy'. In our view, in Westminster systems particularly, one aspect of such meta-governance is the way in which the discourse of network governance and increased participation in the policymaking process is used as a means of legitimising decisions that have already been taken. It is therefore not only a discourse that serves to mask the continued role of hierarchy but also a political system that is itself underpinned by a hierarchical conception of democracy.

---

model (see Marsh forthcoming; Rhodes et al. 2009).

3   Within the literature on network governance there is considerable focus on the role of experts, but in our view there is a tension within the literature between those who see network governance as largely involving experts and those who see it as more broadly participatory (for a fuller discussion of this issue, see Fawcett and Marsh 2010). As we shall see, this is a tension evident in our case studies; so, for example, the 2020 Summit was promoted as a participatory initiative, but it largely involved expert citizens.

Rudd's mode of governance: towards network governance?

Glyn Davis, co-convenor with Rudd of the 2020 Summit, argued that '[d]uring his first weeks in office, Kevin Rudd evaluated various ways to gather voices outside the usual channels' (Davis 2008:379). The idea to supplement the formal political process and incorporate experts and, to a lesser extent, ordinary citizens, into the policymaking process was therefore at the core of both the 2020 Summit and the Community Cabinet initiative.

The 2020 Summit[4]

The 2020 Summit was held on 19 and 20 April 2008, six months after the Rudd government took office. It claimed that the Summit would

* harness the best ideas across the nation
* apply those ideas to the 10 core challenges that the government has identified for Australia—to secure our long-term future through to 2020
* provide a forum for free and open public debate in which there are no predetermined right or wrong answers
* produce options for consideration by government in each of the Summit's 10 areas[5]
* stimulate a government response to these option papers by the end of 2008 with a view to shaping the nation's long-term direction.

So, the Rudd government seemed to view the Summit as an exercise in network governance, drawing together the best minds in Australia to address some of the most crucial, difficult and complex public policy problems facing the country. As Glyn Davis (2008:381) argued:

> The Australia 2020 Summit can be understood as a new government addressing a demand for public participation by an articulate and vocal citizenry. The Summit offered a new way to communicate directly with people, outside the standard pattern of policy debates, political institutions and the media selection of issues.

---

4   The analysis here is based upon the information published by the government on the 2020 Summit, interviews with 20 participants in the Summit, including two area chairs, and a wide variety of secondary material, most of it from the press, but some of it from the academy.

5   The 10 areas were: the productivity agenda; the future of the Australian economy; sustainability and climate change; rural Australia; health; communities and families; Indigenous Australia; creative Australia; Australian governance; and Australia's future in the world.

Similarly, the government's post-Summit report (see <http://www.australia2020.gov.au/about/index.cfm>) asserted: 'Government, irrespective of its political persuasion, does not have a monopoly of policy wisdom. To thrive and prosper in the future we need to draw on the range of talents, ideas and energy across the Australian community.'

Many of the Summit participants whom we talked to acknowledged that the government was stressing the need to incorporate expert citizens, and others, into a process designed to produce the best policy solutions to complex problems, outside the normal parliamentary system. As one participant in the governance stream put it:

> One of the things that [was] going on [was] Rudd's attempt to use the media to re-engage people with the centre of the polity, and, by putting himself up there and inviting people in, he [was] actually attempting to use the media to make these communicative links, which would have once been done by parties.

The Summit's initial report was published quickly, while the final report was published on 3] May. Individuals were subsequently able 'to contribute their ideas and be part of this conversation about Australia's future by making a submission on line' (<http://www.australia2020.gov.au>). The government's response to the 900 'ideas' in the final report was published in April 2009.

Here, we focus on three key questions (for a more extended discussion, see Fawcett and Marsh 2010).

1. Who was involved in the Summit?
2. How were the recommendations of the Summit developed?
3. What effect has the Summit had on subsequent public policy?

Who was involved in the Summit?

Of course, considerable efforts were made to make the Summit broadly representative. As Davis (2008:382) pointed out: 'Planning for the 2020 Summit reflected [the] atomisation of society. It would be a gathering of individuals not representatives.' In demographic terms, 51 per cent of the participants were women, while the Australian Capital Territory and the Northern Territory, as well as people in the forty-five to fifty-four-year age group were over-represented, compared with the general population (Nethercote 2008).

A number of our respondents, without prompting, used the phrase 'the usual suspects'.[6] Similarly, Carson (2008:1) argues that the governance stream 'was

---

6 Certainly, many participants were known to each other and a socio-metric analysis of the membership would be interesting.

heavily weighted with academics (including constitutional lawyers), former and current politicians, journalists, people from think tanks and non-governmental organisations, students and a few members of the public...This then was primarily a gathering of *specialists*'.[7]

At the same time, some participants who were not among the usual suspects felt marginalised. As one young member of the security stream put it: 'We students felt a lot of the time that, because we didn't have the experience and perhaps eloquence, and the detailed knowledge that most others had, we found it a little frustrating, we were kind of jumping up and down with our hands in the air, and not being listened to.'

Particular attention was paid to ensuring a gender balance and to including adequate Indigenous representation. That was not, however, always welcomed; indeed, it was, perhaps, not always appropriate. In this vein, another man in the security stream echoed the views of the earlier participant in arguing that

> at least in my panel, which was the security and foreign affairs one, there were actually very few people with genuine expertise invited. I would classify myself as someone with some expertise, but a lot of the people invited, well, first of all, over 50 per cent of them had to be women, and it's not an area in which there are that many women professionals for a whole range of reasons.

Relatedly, Twomey (2008:15) argues that there was a tension because of the nature of the participants; they were neither one thing (experts who had knowledge) nor another (representatives of the community/general public who could have been informed).

How were the recommendations of the Summit developed?

A number of issues were raised about the process. First, many were sceptical about the celebrity aspect of the Summit. One participant in the security stream argued: 'I became quite cynical about the whole thing. The balance was very much weighted towards these sort of set-piece public events, which were pretty vacuous to be honest, very vacuous in some cases, and there was a relatively short time for discussion and negotiation' (see also Twomey 2008:17).

Certainly, there was a clear element of celebrity politics involved in the operation of the Summit, with much of the media coverage of the event concentrating on

---

7   In contrast, a participant in the security stream emphasised: 'I have to say I was quite surprised at...the lack of heavy hitters in there.'

celebrities, leading some participants to speak cynically about that aspect of the process. Most dramatically, a participant in the creative Australia area, co-chaired by Cate Blanchett, staged a walkout in protest against this celebritisation.

A number of participants were also concerned about the way the process of arriving at the key theme ideas was managed (see also Manne 2008a, 2008b). As Guest (2008:9) argues:

> It became clear on day two that the aim was to produce a Final Statement of Outcomes that represented a consensus among the group on a given topic, rather than a statement capturing the range of ideas that were discussed. It was to be a political document, and that rendered it banal and virtually meaningless.

For many participants, this meant that much discussion was within existing parameters. A security-stream participant claimed:

> One of the things I knew, having done the ACT [preliminary] one, was that truly new ideas didn't have a shot in hell, because you've got, at best case, 36 hours and you don't have enough time in 36 hours to get something from unknown to acceptance, so walking in with a truly new idea you're out of luck, don't even start it.

In addition, the fact that complex issues and discussions had to be reduced to a number of bullet points concerned participants. Here, Twomey (2008:17) recalled: 'At one stage the governance group facilitator said that what was being proposed had to be reduced to a T-shirt slogan by 4 pm. He was half joking.' A participant in the productivity theme made the point more forcefully:

> There was always this sensitivity about being too prescriptive until the very end of the Summit when, of course, all the bureaucrats disappeared into the cabinet room and they crunched all the ideas into the ones that I think the government thought well, okay, these are at least palatable.

> The process had a great impact on what came out in terms of the substance; it really was designed for big ideas that could be quickly captured in a PowerPoint line; this meant that some of the more innovative ideas didn't fair very well, as they weren't able to rely on established concepts or ideas.

In a similar vein, a security-theme participant emphasised:

> The draft communiqué that came back on the Sunday morning after it had been through Rudd and Glyn Davis had eliminated all the suggestions we had put forward from our group and replaced them with language that wasn't ours and didn't come from the group at all. We then

had to rework our suggestions, put them into a more politically palatable language, send them back up, along with various pointed comments that the media would be very interested to hear about the way this had been handled, if we got rolled again and they did find their way into the final communiqué. I didn't think it was necessarily a top-down process but it was certainly a very managed process—highly managed.

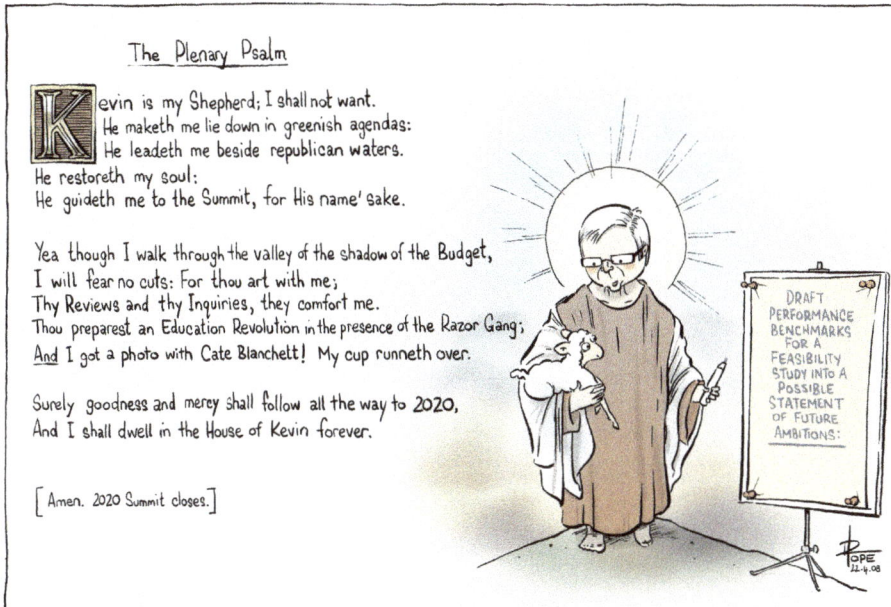

The Plenary Psalm

Kevin is my Shepherd; I shall not want.
He maketh me lie down in greenish agendas:
He leadeth me beside republican waters.
He restoreth my soul:
He guideth me to the Summit, for His name' sake.

Yea though I walk through the valley of the shadow of the Budget,
I will fear no cuts: For thou art with me;
Thy Reviews and thy Inquiries, they comfort me.
Thou preparest an Education Revolution in the presence of the Razor Gang;
And I got a photo with Cate Blanchett! My cup runneth over.

Surely goodness and mercy shall follow all the way to 2020,
And I shall dwell in the House of Kevin forever.

[Amen. 2020 Summit closes.]

DRAFT PERFORMANCE BENCHMARKS FOR A FEASIBILITY STUDY INTO A POSSIBLE STATEMENT OF FUTURE AMBITIONS:

Source: David Pope, *The Canberra Times*, 22 April 2008

What effect has the Summit had on subsequent public policy?

Measuring influence is noticeably difficult and that is particularly the case when 900 recommendations emerged from the Summit; clearly, no government could act on all these recommendations. The government did, however, respond to all 900 recommendations in April 2009.

The government claimed that it wanted the Summit to have influence, so it is unsurprising that it subsequently claimed that it did. Of course, if there is limited evidence of the Summit having broad influence then that could be because the government did not really want it to have influence—a conclusion that would throw more doubt on the network governance model and fit much more happily with a meta-governance argument.

Of course, we have not examined all 900 of the government's responses to the Summit recommendations. Rather, we highlight two areas in which the government itself claimed that the Summit had an effect, before turning to our respondents' assessments (see Fawcett and Marsh 2010 for a broader treatment; and see Manwaring 2010 for a similarly sceptical assessment of the effect of the governance stream's proposals).

In the foreword to the government's response, Rudd began by highlighting two crucial areas in which the Summit had influenced policy:

> The government has already acted on many of these ideas. We have commenced a major review of Australia's future tax system. We have implemented a broad program of reform of our collaboration with the states and territories, culminating in new national agreements and national partnerships in critical policy areas, including health and education, in November last year. (<http://www.australia2020.gov.au/ docs/government_response/2020_summit_response_foreword.doc>; see also Foster 2008:6)

There is certainly no doubt that these are two areas where there were new directions. So, the government set up the Henry Tax Review in May 2008 and it reported in May 2011. In addition, there is no doubt that such a tax review was widely discussed in the 'Role of Government in the Economy' subgroup—one of five in the economy theme. The real question concerns the extent to which the idea was novel and had not previously been considered by the government. In our view—and this was shared by a number of participants in the economy stream whom we interviewed—the government was already committed to such a review.

Here, we would point to a number of factors in support of our argument. First, in the run-up to the 2007 election, Labor was widely accused of not having a tax policy, although Wayne Swan, as Shadow Treasurer, claimed during the election campaign: 'We've been talking tax reform for a long time. And if you care to go through the record, you'll see many speeches from me about tax reform, about the need to streamline the tax system' (*The 7.30 Report*, ABC TV, 22 October 2007). As such, tax policy was something Labor needed to address on coming to power and a review was an obvious solution for a party that could have been short of its own ideas. Second, the government was particularly active in the subgroup arguing for a review. As Foster (2008:5) emphasises: 'The group was the source of one of the key ideas—tax reform—and it was one in which both the Prime Minister and the Treasurer actively participated.' Third, the review was announced with terms of reference some three weeks after the Summit, so, it is likely that plans for a tax review were already in train. The words used when the review was announced are also interesting: 'The review *follows* the recent 2020 Summit, which proposed a comprehensive review of State and Federal taxes' (our italics). Note it does not say 'emerged from' or 'was suggested by', rather the more passive 'follows'.

An even clearer picture emerges on regulatory harmonisation. This was a policy change that occurred before the Summit. Indeed, the first Council of Australian Governments (COAG) meeting after the Labor victory in 2007 established a Business Regulation and Competition Group and the COAG meeting of 26 March 2008 developed an agenda for reform in 27 areas of business regulation. So, while the Summit clearly endorsed this development, it hardly initiated it.

In general, our respondents—all interviewed at least nine months after the Summit—were sceptical about its influence, although most acknowledged its symbolic importance. One participant in the governance stream claimed:

> It was obviously a clever political exercise; you're going to get a massive list of suggestions; you're free to cherry pick any of them you want, some of which you might have done anyway and then you can hold up your head high saying 'I have listened to the people'. So, it was a bit cynical in that regard but, at the same time, I really felt that there was the sense of renewal, that it was a chance for us to move in new directions and that of the millions of ideas that had been put out there if there were just one or two ideas that had traction and that made Australia a better place or that made lives easier or better for people then that would have been worthwhile.

Some participants were also sceptical about the government's motives. So, Guest (2008:11) argues: 'Was there a net national benefit from the Summit? I doubt it. There was definitely net benefit for the government—it gave the impression that the government was listening and it was a worthwhile investment in galvanising support from opinion-makers and community leaders.'

Others, however, while acknowledging the absence of a clear effect on policy, were much less sceptical of the government's motives and saw the very process of consultation as crucial. Here, another participant in the governance stream argued:

> It was clear from the beginning that the government would like to use this Summit to break down the kind of distrust that had [existed] between reform-minded public intellectuals, etc., and government. [It was a] better experience, and a positive thing, but not something that was really geared towards getting a coherent, ordered list of public policy priorities.

Overall, then, the 2020 Summit seems better viewed as an exercise to strengthen the legitimacy of government than as a genuine move towards network governance or a more participatory democracy.

Community Cabinets

Community Cabinets were introduced by the Queensland Labor government in 1998 (see Reddel and Woolcock 2004) and involved ministers visiting various locations to receive delegations and meet with anyone who attended to discuss local issues. In that context, Reddel and Woolcock (2004:79) claim that '[t]he Community Cabinet process has extended the reach of executive government to Queensland citizens'. Certainly, to date, there have been 132 Community Cabinets in Queensland and, following a recent Community Cabinet in Roma, in which the number of delegations had almost doubled since the previous one 10 years earlier (from 67 to 129), the state's current Premier, Anna Bligh, optimistically concluded that 'far from the community tiring of those sort of events, their enthusiasm and appetite for them are increasing' (Barry 2010). As Barry also notes, however, the delegations that have attended have typically represented commercial interestsand the number of people involved has been very limited.

Subsequently, Community Cabinets have been a feature of state governance in Victoria since 2003, South Australia since 2001 and New South Wales from 2007—all, unsurprisingly, under Labor governments. All of these governments claim that Community Cabinets have extended consultation and participation, as the annual report of the NSW Department of Premier and Cabinet (2008–09) asserts: 'Community Cabinet visits give local community groups and individuals an opportunity to discuss local issues directly with the Premier, Ministers and senior leaders of the public service.'

Given this context, and Rudd's experience with Community Cabinets in Queensland, it was perhaps unsurprising that the federal Labor government introduced Community Cabinets shortly after it came to office. It claimed that 'Community Cabinet meetings are part of the Prime Minister's commitment to ensure close consultation with the Australian people on the things that concern them, whether they are national or local matters' (PM&C 2010). Echoing this theme at the first Community Cabinet meeting in January 2008, which was attended by 600 people in Perth, Rudd asserted that ministers had come to listen, arguing that governments that did not remain in touch were not worth 'a pinch of salt' (The Age 2008). In the end, a total of 23 federal Community Cabinets were held before the 2010 election.[8]

Offering her impressions of that first meeting in Perth, Peatling (2008) has argued that:

---

8   For a list, see: <http://www.dpmc.gov.au/community_cabinet/meetings/index.cfm>

Part parent-teacher interview, part political rally and part old-time revivalist meeting, the event boasted an hour-long general question-and-answer session where people selected to attend could ask questions.

Some people read their questions to make sure they didn't miss anything; others were clear about what to ask.

Health, home ownership, the environment and whether the Chinese government was harvesting the organs of Falun Gong supporters were all on people's minds.

The ministers sat at individual desks and conducted six 10-minute interviews. If they or their staff or public servants could not answer, they promised to send the information to the person as quickly as possible.

Peatling's first impressions were positive, but the question of what influence, if any, the Community Cabinets would have was never far away. To address this issue, we focus upon two issues widely discussed in Community Cabinet meetings to date: home ownership and disability services (for a more extended treatment, see Lewis and Marsh 2010).

Home ownership

Labor had identified the issue of housing as a key policy area in opposition and had hosted a Housing Affordability Summit on the issue in July 2007. The unanimous opinion of the 150 experts who attended was that increasing the first-home-owners' grant would simply result in higher house prices, and Labor accepted that view. So, at the 2007 election, Labor promised reform in this area, including: a dedicated housing minister; the introduction of First Home Saver Accounts to assist first-time home buyers to save for a deposit, which it subsequently implemented in February 2008; a $600 million National Rental Affordability Scheme (NRAS), which it launched in May 2008, with the aim of boosting the supply of rental housing for poorer households through the construction of an extra 50 000 homes; and a $500 million Housing Affordability Fund, which was introduced by the government in September 2008, with the aim of lowering the cost of building new homes (Barrymore 2008; Irvine 2009b). Importantly, therefore, several of the government's most important policies on home ownership had been announced before any Community Cabinets had actually taken place and many of these policies were launched after only a handful of these meetings had been held, suggesting that their influence was limited at best.

It was also clear that both Rudd and his ministerial team often used Community Cabinet meetings as an opportunity to promote current government policy. For example, Rudd often used the meetings to promote aspects of the government's $10.4 billion stimulus package, which was announced on 14 October 2008. This included provisions to help with housing construction—more specifically, a trebling of the first-home-owners' grant for newly constructed homes and a doubling of the same grant for established properties.

Specific examples of Rudd's use of Community Cabinet meetings as a means of promoting the government's stimulus package were evident at the meeting held at Geelong, Victoria, on 7 December 2008, where Rudd noted that helping first home buyers supported the housing industry and jobs (<www.dpmc.gov.au/ community_cabinet/docs/corio_comcab_transcript.pdf>). Similar sentiments to these were expressed at a subsequent meeting held on 22 April 2009 at Ballajura, Western Australia, where Rudd noted that the government had provided $62.5 million for 4200 first-home owners in Western Australia between October 2008 and February 2009. He also used this meeting to argue that the boom in Australia's housing sector and construction industry contrasted with 'the devastation in developing economies elsewhere in the world' (<www.dpmc. gov.au/community_cabinet/meetings/ballajura.cfm>). In Elizabeth, South Australia, Rudd also used the Community Cabinet meeting, on 28 July 2009, to argue that assistance to help first-home buyers was essential to prevent retail sales from collapsing and to ensure continued economic growth (<www.dpmc. gov.au/community_cabinet/meetings/elizabeth.cfm>).

Promotion of government policies was also evident after the announcement, in February 2009, that the government would provide $6.6 billion to build 20 000 new social housing dwellings and 802 new defence homes (Hudson 2009). Rudd noted at a Community Cabinet meeting held in Townsville, Queensland, on 8 December 2009, that the government had provided $84.9 million to create affordable housing in north Queensland, and that such spending was helping small businesses to survive and employ apprentices (<www.dpmc. gov.au/community_cabinet/meetings/townsville.cfm>). Similarly, when asked about social housing in Tasmania at the meeting held in Hobart on 13 October 2009, Jenny Macklin, Minister for Families, Housing, Community Services and Indigenous Affairs, spoke of the $5 billion invested in additional social housing and asserted that Tasmania 'is getting its fair share' (<www.dpmc.gov.au/ community_cabinet/meetings/hobart.cfm>).

By April 2009, however, signs of a worsening housing situation were clear. Many corporations were taking advantage of the government's NRAS, which allowed investors a tax break of $8000 per annum, per dwelling, for a decade, at a time when rental vacancy rates in Melbourne, Perth, Adelaide and Darwin were only 2 per cent (Franklin 2008). In this context, the Managing Director of SQM Research, Louis Christopher, warned that the scheme was contributing to spiralling house prices under $500 000, making home purchase more expensive, yet benefiting investors (Irvine 2009a:5). Craig James, Chief Economist at CommSec, also noted that the housing market needed many more investors and developers as a housing shortage and surge in buyer interest would result only in higher prices (Cummins 2009).

Perhaps unsurprisingly, Community Cabinet meetings did not resolve the housing crisis, which only became worse both for renters and for aspiring first-time home buyers. To take just one example, while it was predicted that 220 000 First Home Saver Accounts would be opened in their first year, by 30 June 2009, there were just 13 946 (Chancellor 2009). We would argue that, overall, the Community Cabinets were worried less with listening to the concerns of people and more about promoting the government's policy positions, although it is clear that this did change in response to both the global financial crisis and a deepening housing crisis.

Disability services

Disability services were a frequent topic at Community Cabinet meetings. In our view, however, they again had little, if any, influence on policy and served more as a forum for promoting government policy than as a genuine consultation process.

Policies to assist Australians with disabilities were announced by the Rudd government early in its term, although there was ongoing pressure for further assistance. In July 2008, the government ratified the UN Convention on the Rights of Persons with Disabilities. More specifically, in May 2008, the government announced an extra $1.9 billion for a new commonwealth–state–territory agreement to help fund 2300 additional supported-accommodation places, a similar number of home-support packages and 10 000 respite places (The Advertiser 2008). The new National Disability Agreement (2009–13) between the Commonwealth and the states and territories meant that the Australian government would contribute $5.3 billion to state and territory-run disability services over the next five years. This included an extra $408 million to fund services and reforms to the disability services system. The Commonwealth's contribution was to be indexed at more than 6 per cent over the life of the five-year agreement, compared with a previous arrangement of 1.8 per cent (Lunn 2008).

There was no doubt that these early measures were appreciated and this was reflected in the Community Cabinets. So, the mother of an autistic daughter acknowledged at the Beenleigh, Queensland, meeting, which was held on 30 June 2009, 'the tremendous things that have happened under this government in the disability employment sector and in disability advocacy. Bill Shorten is the breath of fresh air that has been missing for a long time.'

As with our earlier example, however, the government also used Community Cabinet meetings as a forum to promote its own policies; a few specific examples should help to make this point (for a more extended treatment, see Lewis and Marsh 2010). The first example can be seen in the Community Cabinet meeting that was held in Launceston on 5 November 2008, where the government once again promoted its policy, by noting the number of disability pensioners who would benefit from its stimulus package (<www.dpmc.gov.au/community_cabinet/meetings/launceston.cfm>).

At the Geelong meeting held on 7 December 2008 and the Townsville meeting held on 8 December 2009, Rudd again spoke of the assistance that one-off payments had given carers and people with disabilities (<www.dpmc.gov.au/community_cabinet/meetings/corio.cfm>). Similarly, at the Ballajura meeting, the Health Minister, Nicola Roxon, emphasised Labor's efforts to establish six early childhood centres to 'support children very early in their life with autism', and argued that '[i]t's new for the Federal Government to have taken any sort of steps' (<www.dpmc.gov.au/community_cabinet/meetings/ballajura.cfm>). At the meeting at Elizabeth, Bill Shorten, Parliamentary Secretary for Disabilities and Children's Services, was asked what action the Commonwealth was taking with regards to accessibility for people with disabilities. He noted that some of the social housing being built 'will be governed under the principals of universal design', emphasised that the Howard government did nothing from 2004, and claimed 'that there is a lot more to be done but I would say that the Rudd government has put issues of access to the physical premises well and truly on the map' (<www.dpmc.gov.au/community_cabinet/meetings/elizabeth.cfm>).

What all of these examples suggest is that—as was the case in relation to housing issues—Community Cabinet meetings did not appear to make any substantive difference to existing government policy. One final example—the fate of the proposal for a national disability insurance scheme for Australia—will help to further reinforce this point.

The Disability Investment Group (DIG) was commissioned by the Rudd government in 2008 to investigate funding for the sector and called for major structural reform 'to move the care and support for people with disabilities out of the dark ages and into the 21st century', including support for a no-fault, government-funded national disability insurance scheme funded by general revenue or a Medicare-style levy (Lunn 2009b). Concerns about disability services were raised at a number of Community Cabinet meetings from April to November 2009 (<http://www.pm.gov.au/PM_Connect/Community_Cabinet/Previous_Meetings>).

After nearly two years of debate about a national disability insurance scheme for Australia, the Treasurer, Wayne Swan (2009), indicated that the Productivity Commission 'will undertake a feasibility study into long-term care and support for people with disability in Australia, including investigating the feasibility for a no-fault social insurance scheme to cover people's disability and mental service needs', but only 'if it proves feasible' and 'the economy gives us the means to afford them'.

The commission is due to report in July 2011 with the result that the issue has effectively been 'put on the backburner', despite the fact that the cost of maintaining disability services has been rising at 5 per cent more than inflation (Steketee 2009), and the Australian Institute of Health and Welfare biennial report predicts that almost 2.3 million Australians will be living with a severe disability by 2030, compared with 1.5 million today (Lunn 2009a).

Based on the evidence that we have presented, it is hard to argue that Community Cabinets are genuine participatory forums. As one Labor MP argued, while most participating ministers and parliamentary secretaries were committed to these meetings because Rudd constantly emphasised the need to stay in touch at a local level, 'you really have to wonder what actually results, besides getting a hearing for the people who come' (Daley 2009). At the same time, Chalmers (2009) estimates that the cost of Community Cabinets has blown out to about $3.5 million a year.

Conclusion

In our view, these two cases clearly indicate the limitations of the network governance argument, at least as it applies to Australia. Neither the 2020 Summit nor the federal Community Cabinet initiative seems to mark a turn towards a more participatory mode of governance, despite the Rudd government's rhetoric. Rather, we would argue that they both represent examples of meta-governance. This is because, in both cases, the Rudd government used the discourse of network governance and increased participation in the policymaking process largely as means of legitimising or promoting decisions that had already been taken. The discourse of increased participation therefore masked the continued role of hierarchy in a political system that essentially remains underpinned by a top-down conception of democracy in which network governance occurs in the 'shadow of hierarchy'.

David Marsh *is a Professor in the School of Sociology, Research School of Social Science, The Australian National University.*

Chris Lewis *is a Research Fellow at the Centre for Policy Innovation, Research School of Social Science, The Australian National University.*

Paul Fawcett *is a Lecturer, Department of Government and International Relations, University of Sydney.*

References

Bang, H. 2005. 'Among everyday makers and expert citizens', in J. Newman (ed.), *Remaking Governance: Peoples, politics and the public sphere*, The Policy Press, Bristol, pp. 159–79.

Barry, D. 2010. 'Should community cabinets be part of democracy's furniture', 5 August, <http://nebuchadnezzarwoollyd.blogspot.com/2010/08/should-community-cabinets-be-part-of.html>

Barrymore, K. 2008. 'A budget to build on', *Herald Sun*, 19 May, p. 29.

Carson, L. 2008. '2020 Summit: meetings in the foothills', *Australian Review of Public Affairs*, April, <http://www.australianreview.net/digest/2008/04/carson.html>

Chalmers, E. 2009. 'Cabinet proves a costly traveller', *The Courier-Mail*, 20 May, p. 10.

Chancellor, J. 2009. 'Public shuns government's home saver accounts', *Sydney Morning Herald*, 21 November, p. 5.

Cummins, C. 2009. 'First purchase grant gives market a fillip', *Sydney Morning Herald*, 10 April, p. 13.

Daley, P. 2009. 'Little more than one-sided chat', *Sun Herald*, 24 May, p. 14.

Davis, G. 2008. 'One big conversation: the Australian 2020 Summit', *Australian Journal of Public Administration*, vol. 67, no. 4, pp. 379–89.

Department of the Prime Minister and Cabinet (PM&C) 2010. *Community Cabinet*, Department of the Prime Minister and Cabinet, Commonwealth of Australia, Canberra, <http://www.dpmc.gov.au/community_cabinet/index.cfm>

Fawcett, P. 2009. Government, governance and metagovernance in the British core executive, Unpublished PhD thesis, The University of Birmingham, Birmingham.

Fawcett, P. and Marsh, D. 2010. Network governance and the 2020 Summit, available from <david.marsh@anu.edu.au>

Foster, J. 2008. 'The 2020 Summit: the future of the economy', *Agenda*, vol. 15, no. 2, pp. 5–7.

Franklin, M. 2008. 'Tax deal rush for low-rent housing', *The Australian*, 13 September.

Guest, R. 2008. 'The 2020 Summit: population, sustainability, climate change and water', *Agenda*, vol. 15, no. 2, pp. 9–11.

Hudson, P. 2009. 'New stimulus worth $42bn', *The Canberra Times*, 3 February.

Irvine, J. 2009a. 'Cheap rent tax break is pushing up house prices', *Sydney Morning Herald*, 13 April, p. 5.

Irvine, J. 2009b. 'It's bricks and slaughter out there', *Sydney Morning Herald*, 22 April, p. 11.

Jessop, B. 2004. 'Multi-level governance and multi-level meta-governance', in I. Bache and M. Flinders (eds), *Multi-Level Governance*, Oxford University Press, Oxford, pp. 49–75.

Kickert, W. J. M., Klijn, E.-H. and Koppenjan, J. F. M. (eds) 1997. *Managing Complex Networks: Strategies for the public sector*, Sage, London.

Lewis, C. and Marsh, D. 2010. Network governance, metagovernance and the federal Community Cabinets in Australia, available from <david.marsh@anu. edu.au>

Lunn, S. 2008. 'New deal at COAG for the disabled', *The Australian*, 29 November, p. 6.

Lunn, S. 2009a. 'Disability to hit 2.3m as nation grows grey', *The Australian*, 18 November, p. 5.

Lunn, S. 2009b. 'Care of disabled "national disgrace"', *The Australian*, 3 December, p. 7.

Manne, R. 2008a. 'Comment', *The Monthly*, May, pp. 10–13.

Manne, R. 2008b. 'What is Rudd's agenda', *The Monthly*, November, pp. 22–32.

Manwaring, R. 2010. As good as it gets?: the 2020 Summit and Labor's democratic renewal agenda, Paper delivered at the Australian Political Science Association Conference, Melbourne, September.

Marsh, D. (forthcoming). 'The new orthodoxy: the differentiated polity model', *Public Administration*.

Marsh, D. and Rhodes, R. A. W. 1992. *Policy Networks in British Politics*, Clarendon Press, Oxford.

Martinetto, M. 2003. 'Governing beyond the centre: a critique of the Anglo-governance school', *Political Studies*, vol. 51, no. 3, pp. 592–608.

Nethercote, J. 2008. '2020 Summit snubs over-75s and Queenslanders', *Crikey Online*, 1 April, <http://www.crikey.com.au/2008/04/01/2020-summit-snubs-over-75s-and-queenslanders/>

Newman, J. 2005 'Introduction', in J. Newman (ed.), *Remaking Governance: Peoples, politics and the public sphere*, The Polity Press, Bristol, pp. 1–15.

NSW Department of Premier and Cabinet (NSW DPC) 2008–09. *Annual Report 2008–2009*, NSW Department of Premier and Cabinet, Sydney.

Osborne, D. E. and Gaebler, T. 1992. *Reinventing Government: How the entrepreneurial spirit is transforming government*, Addison-Wesley, Reading.

Peatling, S. 2008. 'Rudd in touch with tea talk', *Sydney Morning Herald*, 21 January.

Reddel, T. and Woolcock, G. 2004. 'From consultation to participatory governance? A critical review of citizen engagement strategies in Queensland', *Australian Journal of Public Administration*, vol. 63, no. 3, pp. 76–87.

Rhodes, R. A. W. 1997. *Understanding Governance: Policy networks, governance, reflexivity and accountability*, Open University Press, London.

Rhodes, R. A. W., Wanna, J. and Weller, P. 2009. *Westminster Compared*, Oxford University Press, Oxford.

Steketee, M. 2009. 'Disability insurance a real reform', *The Australian*, 12 September, p. 2.

Swan, W. 2009. Making every Australian count, Launch of Endeavour Foundation Endowment Challenge Fund, Brisbane, 11 December, <http://www.treasurer.gov.au/DisplayDocs.aspx?doc=speeches/2009/034.htm&pageID=005&min=wms&Year=&DocType>

The Advertiser 2008. 'Editorial: $2bn new funding for the disabled', *The Advertiser*, 31 May, p. 17.

The Age, 2008. 'Community cabinets a worthwhile exercise', Editorial, *The Age*, 22 January 2008, <http://www.theage.com.au/news/editorial/community-cabinets-a-worthwhile-exercise/2008/01/21/1200764167390.html>

Twomey, A. 2008. 'The 2020 Summit: the future of governance', *Agenda*, vol. 15, no. 2, pp. 15–20.

9. The education revolutionary road: paved with good intentions

CAROLE KAYROOZ AND STEPHEN PARKER

Kevin Rudd promised an 'education revolution', to widespread acclaim and almost no opposition. In this analysis, we argue that Rudd's education policy was paved with good intentions to redress long-term deficiencies inherited largely from the Howard years. In many respects, however, the policy lacked the strategic and structural blueprint needed to realise its underlying ideals. The lack of a coherent educational framework informed by a deep knowledge of the Australian educational sector created conflicting policy agendas, some confused objectives and a lack of focus. The unexpected advent of the global financial crisis (GFC) precipitated one of the fastest surges of spending on education in Australia's recent history, but hurried and uncoordinated consultation and implementation processes led to some publicly damaging outcomes. These ultimately played a role in undermining the confidence of the Australian public and also Rudd's own party. As we enter a new administration headed by Julia Gillard, the former Minister for Education, it remains to be seen whether the education revolution will lead to the fundamental systemic transformation implicit in the word 'revolution'.

Rudd's intentions for prosperity, productivity growth and human capital investment

In the Labor Party's educational election platform, *The Australian Economy Needs an Education Revolution*, Kevin Rudd and Stephen Smith (then Shadow Minister for Education and Training) continued Howard's framing of education as an economic good; however, they raised and vehemently challenged the Howard government's under-investment. In 2007, Australia's overall investment in education was 5.8 per cent of GDP—behind 17 other leading economies, including the United States, Britain, New Zealand and Poland. They argued that with the rise of China and India, Australia's 'only future was in a long-run national strategy that enshrined education as the driver of productivity and prosperity'. This would require a 'revolution in the quantity of our investment in human capital and in the quality of outcomes that the education system delivers'. Aiming to make Australia a 'competitive, innovative, knowledge based economy', the intent was to overhaul the entire national education system from early childhood to mature-age learning. The unifying theme would be education as the engine of the economy. Education would drive productivity, and productivity would bring prosperity (Rudd and Smith 2007:27). This logic was strongly reflected in the creation of a mega-ministry under the deputy leader of the government, Julia Gillard, which comprised education, employment and workplace relations. Gillard was informally referred to as the 'Minister for Productivity', and under the program of the Council of Australian Governments (COAG) an expansive agenda was established under a Productivity Working Group chaired by Gillard.

In examining Rudd's first-term legacy, this analysis focuses in turn on the school and tertiary sectors where significant reform was initiated. In the vocational education sector, reform through COAG was attempted but only modest changes were realised, and then largely in the context of an imploding overseas student market, which had followed a number of violent attacks against Indian students in Australia. The chapter tracks progress against the objectives for the education revolution, drawing comparisons with the educational achievements of Blair's first term in the United Kingdom and, to a lesser extent, with the United States. Both countries informed much of the thinking underpinning Labor policy. It will be argued that contrary to Labor's insistence on local, evidence-based policy, these sources show that much Labor policy was derivative and largely unsupported by any Australian-based research.

The school sector: revolution or evolution?

The GFC precipitated one of the fastest spending sprees on education in the nation's recent history. In 2009–10, the states received $19.4 billion in Specific Purpose Payments from the Commonwealth to support state education services— an increase of 64.4 per cent compared with the $11.8 billion the states received in 2008–09. In addition, further funding was allocated as part of the federal finances reform package agreed by COAG in November 2008, the Commonwealth and states/territories reform based on National Partnership Agreements relating to the Smarter Schools Program for Quality Teaching ($550 million), Low SES (socio-economic status) School Communities ($1.5 billion), literacy and numeracy, and the Productive Places programs (Australian Government 2010). It included the funding announced under the 'computers in schools' Digital Education Revolution (DER) program.

The school infrastructure programs were massive, comprising: Building the Education Revolution (BER), Trade Training in Schools and the DER. The government committed to spending $16.2 billion for building or upgrading all of Australia's government and non-government schools (DEEWR 2010a) as part of the $42 billion Nation Building Economic Stimulus package. As part of the DER, it provided $2.2 billion over six years for new information technology (IT) equipment for all secondary schools with students in years nine to 12 (the National Secondary School Computer Fund); the deployment of high-speed broadband connections to Australian schools; new and continuing teacher training in the use of information and communications technology (ICT) (DEEWR 2010b); and online curriculum tools and resources. The Trade Training Centres in Schools provided $2.5 billion over 10 years to enable all secondary schools to apply for funding up to $1.5m for Trade Training Centres (DEEWR 2010c). Other system-wide initiatives included the development of the national curriculum for kindergarten to year 12 by means of the Australian Curriculum, Assessment and Reporting Authority (ACARA) and the development of the 'My School' web site (ACARA 2010) to encourage transparency in school performance data, reporting and assessment.

The first of these, and by far the biggest, the BER, was a rushed response, in part to avert the collapse of the building industry following the GFC. The pace was extraordinary. Within six months of the announcement, the Department of Employment, Education and Workplace Relations (DEEWR) had approved projects for about 8000 schools (DEEWR 2010d; O'Keefe 2010). By 2010, all BER funding was allocated for each of its three elements: $14.1 billion for 7961 primary schools covering 10 665 projects including new libraries, classrooms and refurbishment; $821.8 million for Science and Language Centres (SLCs) in 537 schools for the construction or refurbishment of existing science laboratories or language learning centres; and $1.28 billion for the National School Pride (NSP) program to 9497 schools for 13 047 projects including refurbishment or construction of buildings and sporting grounds. By 2010, the Minister for Education, Julia Gillard, had also released the BER *National Coordinator's Implementation Report* that outlined the progress of these initiatives in the first eight months of the program (DEEWR 2009).

Hasty consultation and implementation, spurred by the GFC, led to damaging public claims of rorts by unscrupulous providers creating perceptions that could have played a part in Rudd's declining popularity and subsequently his demise as Prime Minister. By early 2010, complaints about the BER had intensified in the popular press, leading eventually to polarised views in the professional press. To counter what the government perceived to be a media 'beat-up' led by *The Australian* newspaper and whilst claiming there were only 100 complaints about the BER despite 2400 projects under way, the Education Minister established an implementation task force to investigate claims of overcharging and excessive project management fees. The task force was allocated $13.2 million in the 2010 budget, redirected from the administrative costs of the BER and taken on a proportionate basis from the states, territories and private school authorities according to the investigations held in each sector.

Whilst a Commonwealth Auditor-General's report into the $14.1 billion primary school building program found that spending was slower than anticipated, there were far more damaging claims of rorting by those involved in the building industry. An independent inquiry into the BER claimed that government schools were being charged nearly double the standard commercial rates (Hannaford 2010). Craig Mayne, a former civil engineering design draughtsman, conducted an analysis over a 15-month period of the building conducted under the BER banner in New South Wales and found projects were significantly more expensive than they needed to be. He claimed Catholic and independent schools achieved good value for money but that costs had been higher in government schools. Based on Rawlinson's *Australian Construction Handbook*, Mayne argued that half the cost could have achieved a credible project with a profit margin. Even the signage was criticised, and the whole affair proved to be disappointing for a government that, as some saw it, had had 'the prescience and bold action to save the nation from the experience of other advanced countries in the Global Financial Crisis' (Taylor and Uren 2010:229).

Certainly, the infrastructure expenditure involved some waste of public monies due to poor implementation by some state government school systems (notably in New South Wales) compared with other parts of the school sector. Increased local autonomy in determining priorities for the school sector might have led to more effective outcomes, and appears to have done so in the non-government sector. Certainly, greater efficiencies were possible. A hasty stimulus response led to unmonitored implementation and attracted unscrupulous providers. Some cited faulty implementation as a necessary feature of the circumstances in which the stimulus spending arose. Others highlighted Rudd's centrist disorganisation emanating outwards (Taylor and Uren 2010:147). Still others pointed to the lack of coordination between state and federal regulatory frameworks, laying blame on the tendering process and excessive administration. Overall, the criticism was damaging but Julia Gillard overrode claims of incompetence by launching investigations—a tactic that had eluded her environment ministerial colleague.

The DER, entailing the commitment of a computer or laptop for every year nine– 12 student in the nation, also sustained heavy criticism. Some commentators asked if schools had the educational capacity to make the best use of this technology (Moyle 2010). Like the BER, for the DER, infrastructure spending alone on improved technology would not necessarily make a revolution. New breakthroughs in technology and greater connectivity required more than a massive spend; they required a fundamental shift in the approach to learning. In addition, a roll-out of the infrastructure targeted to those areas with the greatest need would have enabled funds to be diverted to other pressing local problems within the school sector. But of course, more time would have been needed to delineate local problems, consult widely and enable timely solutions—and time was something that the government felt it could not afford.

The complexity of commonwealth–state school arrangements no doubt created complications. By September 2009, the states and territories had taken different approaches to the computers for schools program. In New South Wales, for example, year nine students would be able to keep their laptops if they completed year 12. Under the Commonwealth model, there would be a need to equip every state high school with new technology every year. This would likely be a costly and short-term exercise if some states chose to allow their students to keep computers.

Transparent accountability was perhaps the only intervention that had the potential to transform the educational landscape. This feature of Labor's educational policy was informed in part by Gillard's visits to the United States and, to a lesser extent, to the United Kingdom. Two programs were cited as making schools transparent and accountable: the National Assessment Program for Literacy and Numeracy and the My School web site.

The Rudd government had argued that school standards were not high enough and that failing schools had to be held accountable. Rudd urged parents unhappy with an under-performing school to vote with their feet and move to a more successful one. After many years of planning and at times inaction under the Howard government, the National Assessment Program—Literacy and Numeracy (NAPLAN) commenced in schools in 2008 with all students in years three, five, seven and nine nationally assessed in reading, writing, language conventions and numeracy. The My School web site developed by ACARA was launched on 28 January 2010 and had more than nine million hits on the first day. The web site included a report card for almost 10 000 Australian schools, with each report card providing 'rich' performance and contextual information about individual schools. The web site listed statistically similar schools as the point of comparison. Each school had a grading on the Index of Community Socio-Educational Advantage (ICSEA), calculated using students' residential addresses and information from the Australian Bureau of Statistics.

On 7 February 2010, the Minister for Education announced an additional $11 million for 110 schools identified through the My School web site as needing help to ensure students improved their literacy and numeracy. By this stage, there was a divided response to the intention and method of NAPLAN and the My School web site. The main arguments supporting the process were based on the principle that national assessments represented crucial accountability features of high-performing education systems and the transparent comparison of school performance was needed for resource allocation to help reduce inequality (see Jensen 2010).

Source: David Pope, *The Canberra Times*, 7 May 2010

The rhetoric was to make every school transparently accountable for its literacy and numeracy performance. There was, however, little critical analysis of this concept. Accountability—a key concept in quality assurance amongst professional bodies—usually involves a blend of internal (self-review) and external (inspection) indicators. If quality is high, public resources would be wasted on a massive bureaucratic exercise with little risk for high-performing schools. The policy also lacked a rigorous evidence base, with little sustained research showing long-term outcomes for schools—ironic given that evidence-based policy was Labor's strong motif in the early days of government.

Labor policy was not particularly innovative or tailored to the Australian context. It was derived largely from the United Kingdom and, to a lesser extent, the United States. Reports on the effectiveness of similar schemes in the United Kingdom and the United States were mixed. In the United Kingdom, an analysis of the effectiveness of the similar National Literacy Strategy implemented in 1998 showed that too much testing narrowed the curriculum, robbing students from lower socioeconomic backgrounds of the broad-based education needed to break cultural barriers to disadvantage. Adam Curtis (2008), in an influential series of BBC documentaries, *The Trap*, maintained rich parents moved to areas with the best schools, pushing up house prices and exacerbating social segregation.

In the United States, there were similar views on the 'No Child Left Behind' (NCLB) legislation, and Joel Klein's New York State program setting targets for schools and consequences for failure (US Department of Education 2001). Diane Ravitch (2010), Research Professor of Education at New York State University and once a proponent of the scheme, cited the perverse effects of focusing on the test. Since the law permitted every state to define 'proficiency' as it chose, many states announced impressive gains. But the states' claims of improvement were contradicted by the federally sponsored *National Assessment of Educational Progress* (*NAEP*). The states responded to NCLB by dumbing down their standards so that they could claim to be making progress. Because the law demanded progress only in reading and maths, schools had an incentive to show gains only in those subjects. Meanwhile, there was no incentive to teach the arts, science, history, literature, geography, civics, foreign languages or physical education. Transparent accountability had seemingly produced graduates who had been drilled regularly on the basic skills yet complaints continued about the poor preparation of university entrants (Bamford 2010; Boston 2009).

Despite the huge outlay on infrastructure, the Rudd government avoided addressing the underlying structural inequities in the educational system. Reform of the funding model was intentionally deferred until the assumed second term of a Labor government to avoid the backlash that Mark Latham's policy reform of school funding had suffered at the previous election. According to commentators in the school sector, whilst 'equity and excellence' had been superficially tackled, the sector lacked the reforms needed to address the complex and inconsistent forms of funding and governance arrangements that entrenched sectoral division. The burden of educating those with the greatest need fell on a relatively small proportion of schools (Keating 2010). The policy setting also failed to address the inequities set up by the funding of private schools (Caldwell 2009). Some argued that public funding needed to be limited for those schools that practised religious training and/or restricted access on social or economic grounds. The different resourcing patterns for state and private schools also entrenched further inconsistencies and inequities in school resourcing arrangements in Australia.

The tertiary sector: transformation or tinkering?

A failure to address structural fault lines could also be found in the Rudd government's approach to reforming the tertiary sector. As a result, incompletely thought-through policy, conflicting agendas and confused objectives were evident, creating a lack of focus for many policy initiatives. Hurried and uncoordinated consultation and implementation also undermined the attainment of objectives for many initiatives.

The higher education sector

In March 2008, Julia Gillard commissioned Professor Denise Bradley, former Vice-Chancellor of the University of South Australia, to conduct a broad-ranging review of higher education and its fitness for purpose in meeting the needs of the Australian community and economy. The report's 46 recommendations were released in December 2008, underpinned by a predominantly economic rationale that tied higher education to workforce productivity and skills shortages (DEEWR 2008).

In the lead-up to the Bradley Review, Gillard had criticised the higher education sector's participation rates, particularly of those from disadvantaged backgrounds, and also unacceptably low completion rates, estimated later by Bradley to be 72 per cent. Further justification for change was provided by the nation's slippage in degree attainment from seventh to ninth in the previous 10 years amongst twenty-five to thirty-four-year-olds. The academic workforce was ageing and the nation's best were being lured overseas, it was said. Student–staff ratios had climbed from 13:1 in 1990 to 20:1 in 2006; student satisfaction with higher education teaching was static, and seemingly lower than in the United Kingdom and the United States. Public investment in higher education—as distinct from student fees and contributions through the Higher Education Contribution Scheme (HECS)—was said to be amongst the lowest of the members of the Organisation for Economic Cooperation and Development (OECD) (DEEWR 2008). The Bradley recommendations promised improved indexation and infrastructure upgrade funding, leading to optimism in the sector that higher education would at last receive the funding needed to maintain facilities and quality.

The government responded in May 2009 with its twin platform of equity and excellence in higher education, detailed in the policy document *Transforming Australia's Higher Education System*. Expansion of the sector was the order of the day; the sector would move to a demand-driven funding system for domestic higher education students, worth $491 million over three years, to be phased in through transitional raising of the volume cap on places in 2010 and 2011.

Recognised providers could enrol as many eligible students as they wished. The government set the national attainment target at 40 per cent of twenty-five to thirty-four-year-olds educated to bachelor-level degree or above by 2025. Social inclusion was another key agenda with at least 20 per cent of higher education enrolments to be from low socioeconomic backgrounds by 2020. Equity funding was to constitute about 2 per cent of teaching and learning grants, increasing to 3 per cent in 2011 and 4 per cent directed to outreach and retention by 2012.

Courtesy of the GFC, university infrastructure was the biggest winner with a nearly $3 billion capital injection over three years in the form of the Education Investment Fund. Recurrent funding was to be adequately indexed with revised indexation, totalling $578 million, to be introduced from 2012 (departmental officials euphemistically referred to 2010 as a 'gap' year for funding). An extra $80 million a year—and possibly a new national university for regional areas—was promised to improve higher education provision in remote regions, including through collaboration with TAFE.

Gillard claimed that the government was supporting the higher education and research sectors at a cost of an additional $5.4 billion over four years and would commit further resources over the next 10 years. This included funding of $1.5 billion for teaching and learning, $700 million for university research, $1.1 billion for the Super Science initiative and $2.1 billion from the Education Investment Fund for education and research infrastructure.

Quality was to be paramount, and would certainly be an essential element in a demand-driven higher education world. A new national super-regulator would be set up to oversee accreditation and quality assurance, based on standards and outcomes, of public and private institutions by 2010. Universities as institutions would become, for the first time, subject to accreditation standards set by the regulator but would still accredit their own courses. The promise was that regulation would be one step removed from government, but applied more evenly and objectively across both public and private providers, including international universities establishing an Australian presence and TAFE providers seeking to offer degree-level qualifications. Significant funding for structural change would be introduced to a total of $402 million, which could potentially include new models of education. The Sustainable Research Excellence in Universities was to be introduced with a $512 million increase in funding for the indirect costs of research.

The sector's initial enthusiasm for the governmental agenda gradually palled. For example, the Vice-Chancellor of the University of Canberra, one of the authors, questioned the attainment target, arguing that the sector had already been on track for 40 per cent well before 2025. Simply by raising the cap on places and providing more funded places under the existing system, the sector would easily achieve the target, effectively removing the need for partial deregulation of the system. Parker (2009) argued for an easy achievement of targets by addressing the higher education and vocational education and training interface, targeting those with diplomas and advanced diplomas.

Many criticised the ensuing consultation and implementation process (see Slattery 2010a). Four ministers—Julia Gillard (Education), Kim Carr (Science and Research), Simon Crean (Trade) and Nicola Roxon (Health)—had significant reform agendas, some of which conflicted with the recommendations and direction of the Bradley Review. At the institutional level, Labor's reforms were to be negotiated in individualised mission-based compacts with each university. Mission-based compacts would take effect from 2011 as agreements between universities and the Australian government, detailing public funding commitments and reciprocal institutional commitments. They would support universities 'to pursue their distinctive missions and to contribute to the Australian government's aspirations for the higher education sector as a whole' (DIISR 2010).

Besides conflicting agendas, there were confused objectives. Whilst compacts would be an individual exercise, the sector would respond uniformly to the government's proposed indicator framework for funding teaching and learning. A standardised suite of measures was proposed to assess all universities. Participation and inclusion indicators specified agreed increases. There were to be student experience, student attainment, and quality of outcome measures. Whilst the government claimed the sector was responsive to the reform agenda, some suggested a contradiction between the proposed indicator framework and the compact discussions with individual institutions, wondering how standardised indicators could be used across the sector, yet individual compacts foster institutional diversity. If institutions were to achieve their unique missions, they needed institutionally determined indicators, tailored to unique circumstances. To add to the complexity, the Commonwealth had also emphasised partnerships in the funding provisions to address low SES numbers. Yet, there was little encouragement of linked compacts or any collaborative activity beyond forming partnerships in various grant-getting exercises.

Vice-chancellors interpreted this sense of dissonance as being the product of the Rudd government's split of responsibility for education (DEEWR, under Gillard) and research (DIISR, under Carr), with the two ministers happening to have different views about the relative priorities of sectoral performance and individualised missions for institutions.

In tandem, the highly prescribed draft guidelines from the Tertiary Education Quality and Standards Agency (TEQSA) were released for comment. The guidelines comprised nine 'hard to argue' standards concerning mainly sound financial management, quality student standards, teacher quality and the like. The 87 requirements accompanying them, however, were at a level of detail likely to require intensified reporting and bureaucratic process in universities. The standards and requirements showed little regard for the distinction between the existing self-accrediting and non self-accrediting institutions. Some felt they infringed institutional autonomy too much. Although departmental officials claimed the standards were not intended for use against existing universities, there was a growing sense of unease about their very existence. A regulatory zeal was found in some recommendations that prescribed process rather than outcomes—akin to the process-driven approach said to be associated with the Australian Universities Quality Agency (AUQA), which TEQSA was replacing (Email correspondence, DVCA Executive).

Overall, the sector responded well to the underlying sentiments of the government's response to Bradley, but as time wore on it became concerned about the internal contradictions and complexity of the reforms, as well as being sceptical about whether the Public Service could actually keep up with and implement them. But a more fundamental concern also began to take hold—namely, whether higher education policy was actually being developed consistently with vocational education policy, despite the prevalence of words such as 'convergence', 'integration' and 'alignment'.

The vocational education and training sector

The COAG skills target agreed from 1 January 2009 was to halve the proportion of twenty to sixty-four-year-olds without qualifications at Certificate III level by 2020, and double the number of higher vocational education and training (VET) qualification completions by 2020. Although these targets for VET qualifications were described by the government as complementing higher education attainment goals, they could not obviously be meshed with them, if only because the population groups differed, with the VET targets related to twenty to sixty-four-year-olds and the higher education (HE) targets related to twenty-five to thirty-four-year-olds (Parker 2009)

It was widely understood that smooth transitions from VET to HE would be needed for the government's participation agenda to succeed. Appropriate regulation between the two sectors would also be needed to ensure quality educational provision, but there were many hurdles of history, practice, culture and jurisdiction to overcome. Some called for a unified set of national tertiary education protocols for eligibility, approval and transition. They suggested a focus on non-VET diplomas and advanced diplomas to resolve the tension between the competency (VET) and knowledge (HE) basis of the two sectors (Ross 2010). A milestone statement of agreement from Universities Australia and

TAFE Directors Australia (TDA) proposed unified protocols covering the new tertiary sector. At the same time, a study showed that TAFE had only 12 per cent low SES students from 2008 figures—significantly behind the 17 per cent found in higher education (Hare 2010). Low SES students were more likely to be found in Certificate I, II and III levels, making the transition less likely to be accessible to university entrance.

The quality agenda for VET was also unlikely to mesh with higher education. Pam Caven, CEO of TDA, stated that the separate evolution of national regulators for the TAFE and university sectors could lead to incompatible models (Ross 2010b:8). A joint statement by TDA and Universities Australia proposed diploma and above as a marker of tertiary institutions in line with the OECD's International Standard Classification of Education. This would make clear the operating boundaries and protocols for the tertiary sector particularly if non-competency-based diplomas were included in VET provision. The TAFE sector argued for overlapping board membership, compatible statutory objectives and consistent conditions of service. The TDA–UA statement asserted that opportunities should be made for students to move in both directions. The Education Minister expressed a wish for TEQSA and the VET regulator to merge in 2013 but COAG and the Ministerial Council for Tertiary Education and Employment had not agreed. Others queried how seamless this approach could be with VET required to have a standards council as well as a regulator, unlike the university sector.

A key thread in the VET–HE meshing was the Australian Qualifications Framework Council (AQFC). In 2009, the government commissioned the AQFC to improve the articulation and connectivity between the university and VET sectors to enable competency-based and merit-based systems to become more student focused. Yet there seemed to be little coordination with standards set by TEQSA, and the proposed performance indicator framework. To add to the mix, the Commonwealth minister announced that the ambit of Skills Australia would expand to encompass the full scope of Australia's labour-market needs, to give advice to the Commonwealth about the effectiveness of both the university and the VET systems in meeting the broad range of Australia's skill needs.

Despite extensive policy work under the remit of COAG's Productivity Working Party, reforms in the VET sector were hard fought, and achievements fairly limited. In part this related to the attempt by the Commonwealth to adopt the reforms in the Victorian VET sector and apply them nationally despite the unwillingness of other states to do so. As a consequence, big spending reform packages that had occurred in schools and higher education were not undertaken in VET. Prior to the 2010 federal budget, funding for VET had not been as generous as for the school and higher education sectors. The 2010 budget redressed, to some extent, the lack of new spending on the VET sector by the

Labor government since taking office despite their often stated 'productivity' mantra. The Minister for Education, in a speech to the Big Skills Conference (Gillard 2009), claimed the government had made a strong start to improvements in the VET system by opening the multibillion-dollar Education Investment Fund to universities and VET institutions alike, so as to invest in the capital requirements of further education providers generally. In December 2008, the government launched the $500 million capital fund for VET and community education in order to improve the quality of teaching and learning right across the system. It also funded the Trade Training Centres in Schools Program by $2.5 billion over 10 years to enable all secondary schools to access new trade facilities in traditional and emerging fields. These initiatives were, however, shared with the school and university sectors.

In the 2010 budget, the government announced a suite of measures totalling $660 million aimed at expanding and improving VET to address skills shortages (Slattery 2010b). Vocational education and training would create 39 000 training places in high-demand skills ($200 million) and 22 500 apprenticeship start-ups ($120 million) to tackle language and literacy difficulties for 140 000 Australians. The greatest beneficiaries were those seeking diplomas and those apprentices and adults with poor literacy and numeracy. This funding would be dependent on the sector improving quality and transparency. A new My Skills web site would be created as well as a new regulator for VET at a cost of $93.3 million.

The funding was seen to come largely at the expense of the university sector, though sparing The Australian National University—a commonwealth university and the alma mater of Prime Minister, Kevin Rudd—which benefited by $112 million over four years to establish public policy, national security and China initiatives. In a statement provided by Universities Australia, the 2010–11 budget increased the official level of higher education from $7.5 billion to $8.1 billion—broadly in line with 2009 commitments. The Education Investment Fund provision was, however, reduced by $130 million from the previous budget provisions. Universities Australia declared that the 2010–11 provision 'begins the decline in public higher education funding as a share in GDP, taking Australia's provision further below OECD norms' (Withers 2010).

A comparison with the United Kingdom and the United States

Rudd's legacy needs to be referenced not only to his considerable achievements but also to Howard's and Blair's performances on education in their (longer) first terms. It is hard not to conclude there were honourable intentions for education by the Rudd government but administrative shortcomings and a lack of public relations know-how gave its critics ammunition and undermined public confidence.

For the most part, Labor's education funding addressed the long-term neglect of the Howard years (1996–2007). Howard, in his first term, used a budget shortfall, which he blamed on the previous government, to implement a series of massive cuts to education. Whilst known for its middle-class welfare, the Coalition increased university fees (under the HECS loan system), and introduced full 'up-front' fees for some students. In following years, when the budget surplus reappeared, the money was applied to other purposes, such as a private health insurance rebate or income tax cuts for people on high salaries. This represented a reduction in real terms of education funding. The hallmark of Howard's full term was an increased emphasis on private delivery of what had previously been public services.[1] In 1995, Australia was already at the lower end compared with other OECD countries in terms of the public share of tertiary education spending—13 points below the average. After another decade, though, the public share had dropped to less than half—48 per cent—and Australia was then 26 points below the average. In 2005, Australia spent 0.8 per cent of GDP on tertiary education compared with an average of 1.1 per cent. In other words, Australian expenditure would have had to increase by about 35 per cent to bring it up to the OECD average. In the other countries for which we have data, public spending on tertiary education was up by 30 per cent in real terms over the decade 1995–2005. Only in Australia did it decrease.

Claims of a lack of coherence and confused objectives are shared with Tony Blair's first term in government. In the lead-up to the election, Blair stated that his top three priorities were 'education, education, education'. During the first two terms of the Blair government, there were massive changes in almost every aspect of education. The most important initiatives in Blair's first term included the National Literacy and Numeracy Strategies to ensure that all primary children met agreed targets, the establishment of a Social Exclusion Unit within the Cabinet Office and the creation of the General Teaching Councils. The structure and funding of schools and education for fourteen to nineteen-year-olds were also targeted (Walford 2005).

Focus in the first half of the Blair government was on the schools standards agenda, the rationale being that general improvement in student attainment would significantly improve the economy. There was evidence that it had

---

1 This comment has also been made in relation to a range of services across health, education, employment support and child care, where publicly provided services were increasingly being delivered through private mechanisms (see, for example, Aulich 2010).

worked in the first term. But during the second term the rise in attainment had plateaued, with commentators stating that much of it was due to teachers teaching to the test.

Blair's second term promised increased investment in higher education, and the expansion to 50 per cent of the proportion of people under thirty with a higher education experience. It also stressed the government's desire for diversity of mission within higher education, emphasising teacher quality, the raising of top-up fees and the introduction of an independent regulator to negotiate contracts with universities.

There is a striking similarity with Australia in the continuing debate in the United Kingdom about contradictions between different elements of Blair's policy. Some aspects of Blair's policy were aimed at reducing inequity and others were aimed at the opposite. Some policies led to centralisation, some to localisation. Like Rudd's policies, in the United Kingdom, the sheer variety and number of separate initiatives have led to a sense of overall incoherence (referred to as 'initiativitis' in Chapter 1 or 'a government of announcements' in Chapter 2 of this volume).

To a lesser extent, specific US initiatives, mostly in New York State, were also a source of Labor's education initiatives. 'Teach for Australia' was a program based on the 'Teach for America' program; NAPLAN and the My School web site (<http://inside.org.au/my-school-and-your-school/>) have already been cited as programs introduced in New York by Joel Klein; and Minister Gillard based the leadership development program for school principals on the leadership academy created by Klein. Whilst the United States provided ideas for specific initiatives, it was not, however, as extensively influential as the United Kingdom.

Conclusion

A massive spend on infrastructure does not make a revolution. Geoffrey Blainey (ABC 2009) has argued that the real education revolution began in 1873 when Victoria mandated compulsory education for all, lasting until age thirteen or fourteen (soon followed by South Australia and New South Wales). Primary schools needed to be built throughout the states and, at the time, this was progressive when compared with nations in Europe, in that it was a radical law against child labour. Rudd's education revolution is hardly a revolution in comparison with these initiatives. Similarly, secondary education experienced great growth after World War II, as did the university sector, which grew substantially when the sector opened its doors to returning servicemen and women, effectively beginning the tertiary trajectory from elite to mass education in Australia.

The education revolution was a missed opportunity for structural reform in and across all sectors covered in this chapter. Conflicting economic, educational and equity agendas led to confused objectives and hasty implementation and, ultimately, publicly damaging outcomes. Conflation of the education and economic goals from investment in education led to a situation in which neither was addressed adequately. Considering the expense of the programs relative to possible outcomes, there has been considerable wastage. Greater engagement with local issues by the Rudd government coupled with increased local autonomy for spending might have allowed greater effectiveness and certainly greater efficiencies.

There was not a long-term vision for the sector in the education revolution. In the school sector, the state–private funding conundrum was not addressed. In the tertiary education sector, the VET–HE transition zone remained unclear, as did the relationship of private providers to a national quality system. Overall, confused agendas and conflicting objectives left an awkward experience for students traversing institutional settings that do not mesh and with poor integration between targets, standards and regulation.

There is likely to be greater 'transparent accountability' in the repetitive motifs of the Labor government—My School, My University, My Skills— together with their perverse effects related to the inaccurate use of statistics for funding, further cultural impoverishment for disadvantaged students and the entrenchment of social segregation. An expensive and bureaucratic system will be needed to gather a huge variety of data.

The main focus on infrastructure and transparent accountability in the education revolution missed an important opportunity to address all of the above issues, which remain unaddressed. The various reviews conducted also missed the opportunity to examine the radical transformation of learning in the future created by the rapid acquisition of knowledge and the incredible pace of technological development. Further, the failure to come to grips with international education—one of Australia's greatest exports—has done little to stimulate expenditure on aspects of the education system that are likely to generate more income.

By necessity, haste in the policy process meant a diminution of consultation and implementation. It is unlikely that, when conceived in haste, all buildings were 'fit for purpose' or even needed. The stipulation of infrastructure to address perceived need might have meant real need was not addressed elsewhere.

In his tearful farewell address as Prime Minister, Kevin Rudd indicated that, under his leadership, the education revolution topped a litany of his achievements. Although paved with good intentions, the education revolution was not a revolution and was likely to be a missed opportunity to significantly advance student learning outcomes in the Australian educational sector.

Carole Kayrooz *is Deputy Vice-Chancellor (Education) at the University of Canberra.*

Stephen Parker *is Vice-Chancellor at the University of Canberra.*

References

Aulich, C. 2010. 'Privatization in service delivery: lessons from Australia', in T. Moon Joong (ed.), *The Service Sector Advancement: Issues and implications for the Korean economy*, Korean Development Institute, Seoul, pp. 155–71.

Australian Broadcasting Corporation (ABC) 2009. 'Education Revolution?', *Counterpoint*, 28 September, <http://www.abc.net.au/rn/counterpoint/stories/2009/2698310.htm>

Australian Curriculum, Assessment and Reporting Authority (ACARA) 2010. *My School*, Australian Curriculum, Assessment and Reporting Authority, Sydney, <http://www.myschool.edu.au/>

Australian Government 2010. *Budget Paper No. 3*, Commonwealth of Australia, Canberra, <http://www.aph.gov.au/budget/2010-11/content/bp3/html/index.htm>

Bamford, P. 2010. 'Teaching to the test', *Inside Story*, 7 April, <http://inside.org.au/teaching-to-the-test/>

Boston, K. 2009. 'Lesson from England on league tables', *Education Review*, September, p. 7.

Caldwell, B. 2009. 'Education revolution fails grade', *The Age*, 2 November, <http://www.theage.com.au/national/education/education-revolution-fails-grade-20091101-hrjv.html>

Curtis, A. 2008. *The Trap*, BBC documentary, <http://video.google.com/videoplay?docid=404227395387111085#>

Department of Education, Employment and Workplace Relations (DEEWR) 2008. *Review of Australian Higher Education*, Department of Education,

Employment and Workplace Relations, Commonwealth of Australia, Canberra, <http://www.deewr.gov.au/highereducation/review/pages/reviewofaustralianhighereducationreport.aspx>

Department of Education, Employment and Workplace Relations (DEEWR) 2009. *National Coordinator's Implementation Report*, Department of Education, Employment and Workplace Relations, Commonwealth of Australia, Canberra, <http://www.deewr.gov.au/Schooling/BuildingTheEducationRevolution/Documents/NCIReport.pdf>

Department of Education, Employment and Workplace Relations (DEEWR) 2010a. *Nation Building: Economic stimulus plan*, Department of Education, Employment and Workplace Relations, Commonwealth of Australia, Canberra, <http://www.deewr.gov.au/Schooling/BuildingTheEducationRevolution/Pages/default.aspx>

Department of Education, Employment and Workplace Relations (DEEWR) 2010b. *Digital Education Revolution*, Department of Education, Employment and Workplace Relations, Commonwealth of Australia, Canberra, <http://www.deewr.gov.au/Schooling/DigitalEducationRevolution/HighSpeedBroadband/Pages/HighSpeedBroadbandToSchools.aspx>

Department of Education, Employment and Workplace Relations (DEEWR) 2010c. *Trade Training Centres in Schools Program*, Department of Education, Employment and Workplace Relations, Commonwealth of Australia, Canberra, <http://www.deewr.gov.au/Schooling/TradeTrainingCentres/Pages/default.aspx>

Department of Education, Employment and Workplace Relations (DEEWR) 2010d. *Building the Education Revolution*, Department of Education, Employment and Workplace Relations, Commonwealth of Australia, Canberra, <http://www.deewr.gov.au/Schooling/BuildingTheEducationRevolution/Documents/BERsustainabilityFactSheet.pdf>

Department of Innovation, Industry, Science and Research (DIISR) 2010. *Mission-based compacts for universities*, Fact sheet, Department of Innovation, Industry, Science and Research, Commonwealth of Australia, Canberra, <http://www.innovation.gov.au/Section/AboutDIISR/FactSheets/Pages/Mission-BasedCompactsforUniversitiesFactSheet.aspx>

Gillard, J. 2009. Speech at the Big Skills Conference, Darling Harbour, NSW, 5 March.

Hannaford, S. 2010. 'Inquiry told of education building program rip-off', *The Canberra Times*, 20 May, p. 1.

Hare, J. 2010. 'TAFE no haven for low-SES students', *Campus Review*, vol. 20, no. 7 (April), p. 1.

Jensen, B. 2010. 'NAPLAN tests help champion equality in the classroom', *The Age*, 15 April, <http://grattan.edu.au/publications/025_jensen_oped_age_education.pdf>

Keating, J. 2010. *Resourcing for Schools. A proposal for the restructure of public funding*, The Foundation for Young Australians, Melbourne, <http://www.fya.org.au/what-we-do/research/research-publications/>

Moyle, K. 2010. 'So you want a revolution', *Education Review*, May, pp. 23–25.

O'Keeffe, D. 2010. 'Building capacity, but slowly', *Education Review*, May, p. 1.

Parker, S. 2009. 'The Bradley review: unfinished business', *Australian Financial Review* Higher Education Conference, Sydney, 9–10 March.

Ravitch, D. 2010. *The Death and Life of the Great American School System: How testing and choice are undermining education*, Basic Books, New York.

Ross, J. 2010a. 'It's time for unified protocols', *Campus Review*, vol. 20, no. 8 (27 April), p. 1.

Ross, J. 2010b. 'Fractured regulation threatens tertiary integration', *Campus Review*, vol. 20, no. 8 (27 April), p. 8.

Rudd, K. and Smith, S. 2007. *The Australian Economy Needs an Education Revolution*, Australian Labor Party, Barton, ACT.

Slattery, L. 2010a. 'Reforms recipe for mediocrity, not excellence', *The Australian*, 10 May, p. 39.

Slattery, L. 2010b. '$660m will benefit Gillard's battlers', *The Australian*, 12 May, p. 8.

Taylor, L. and Uren, D. 2010. *Shitstorm*, Melbourne University Press, Carlton, Vic.

US Department of Education, 2001. *No Child Left Behind*, US Department of Education, Washington, DC, <http://www2.ed.gov/nclb/landing.jhtml>

Walford, G. 2005. 'Education and the Labour government: an evaluation of two terms', *Oxford Review of Education*, vol. 31, no. 1 (March), pp. 3–9.

Withers, G. 2010. 2010/11 higher education budget analysis, Universities Australia email communication to Australian university executive.

10. The economy

ANNE GARNETT AND PHIL LEWIS

Kevin Rudd claimed to be an economic conservative—a younger version of John Howard—during his campaign to win government in 2007. Rudd's government of two-and-a-half years was, however, characterised by high spending, high debts and ill-fated economic policies and there were also a large number of policy about-turns and failures. The period was also dominated by the global financial crisis (GFC), and Australia was not alone in having to recalibrate its economic strategies to respond to what has been a significant, worldwide phenomenon.

The GFC prompted the government to increase spending to cushion the potential effect on Australia. While both major political parties generally supported the idea of stimulus spending, the amount and form of the spending have been the subject of considerable debate. Rudd took office in 2007 with net government saving of almost $45 billion and left office in June 2010 with an estimated net debt of almost $42 billion—forecast to increase to almost $94 billion by 2012, with annual interest repayments of more than $6 billion. During this time, however, Australia did not experience the rise in unemployment rates or the falls in economic growth rates of the same magnitude as many other countries in the industrialised world. The question is whether this was due to policies of the Rudd government, or whether other factors protected Australia, including a stable and well-regulated financial system, strong growth in the mining sector driven by demand in China and India, and the strong economy, budget surplus and net savings it inherited from the previous, Coalition government.

The GFC

The GFC largely dictated the fiscal policy direction of the Rudd government. Concerned that the financial crisis experienced in the United States, Europe and parts of Asia would spread to Australia, the Labor government embarked on a series of large economic stimulus measures.

The GFC originated in the United States, as the result of very poor credit standards, high levels of borrowing—arguably assisted by the low interest rate policy of the Federal Reserve Bank and enabled by China's surplus of funds—and asset price bubbles (shares and real estate priced higher than their underlying value). The lack of financial regulation by both the US government and its financial sector allowed home loans to be made to an enormous number of households that were not in a position to repay them. People were able to buy homes with no deposit, no employment, very low incomes, poor credit histories, and could, in some instances, borrow up to 110 per cent of the value of their properties. The risk associated with these 'sub-prime mortgages' was spread as they were repackaged and sold as financial assets to other financial institutions in many parts of the world. Therefore, when the inevitable loan defaults began to emerge towards the end of 2007, the impact spread throughout much of the world. Australia's financial system had minimal exposure to these 'toxic' debts due to existing prudential regulations, which were tightened by the former Coalition Treasurer Peter Costello, and due to more responsible lending behaviour and low exposure to risky assets by the majority of Australian banks and financial institutions. In fact, in 2010, the Governor of the Reserve Bank of Australia (RBA), Glenn Stevens, referred to the GFC as a North Atlantic financial crisis. The shortage of credit globally, however, did impact on liquidity and interest rates in Australia, with banks claiming that in 2008 credit shortages were forcing them to increase interest rates on loans.

Following the massive financial institution bailouts, which converted much private debt to public debt, a history of deficits by some governments, and the recent large fiscal stimulus measures, the problem of the GFC has now become a problem of public debts of unprecedented proportions, with some European governments in danger of defaulting. Australia's public debt is large by Australian standards, but relatively small as a proportion of GDP especially when compared with the debts of many other major industrialised countries. When the Rudd government came to power in November 2007, the annual rate of economic growth in Australia was about 4 per cent, following more than 16 years of continual economic growth. Annual growth had slowed to 2.8 per cent by June 2008 and then to 0.3 per cent by June 2009 (ABS 2010a). Economic growth in Australia was negative for only one quarter—December 2008—which meant that Australia had avoided a recession (often measured as two consecutive quarters of negative economic growth). When compared with the severe recessions experienced by the United States, the United Kingdom and Europe, and parts of Asia, the Australian experience was remarkable. By 2010, Australia's economic recovery was under way, with an annual economic growth rate of 3.2 per cent by June 2010 (ABS 2010a). When Rudd took office in November 2007, the rate of unemployment was 4.3 per cent (ABS 2010d). It rose far less than in many other countries during the GFC, peaking at 5.8 per cent in 2009, and falling back to 5.2 per cent by the time Rudd was replaced as Prime Minister in June 2010 (ABS 2010d).

Economic stimulus policies

So how did Australia avoid the recessions experienced in so many other parts of the world? The Rudd government claimed that it was due to its quick and strong economic stimulus measures. Other analysts point to Australia's well-regulated financial system, which had very little exposure to the toxic loans being sold around the world, arguing that Australia was never going to experience many of the effects of the GFC. The strength of the mining sector, driven by demand in China and India, is frequently cited as protecting Australia from significant effects of the crisis. The opposition parties claimed that Australia avoided a recession in large part due to the strength of the economy created during their time in government and the flexibility they had introduced into the labour market.

With the onset of the GFC, the Labor government commenced a range of economic stimulus measures that comprised cash handouts and subsidies and infrastructure building as part of the $42 billion Nation Building: Economic Stimulus Plan (Australian Government 2010b). Following the advice from the head of the Commonwealth Treasury, Ken Henry, to 'go hard, go early, go households', Rudd began to implement stimulus measures. In December 2008, cash payments to pensioners and families with children and an increase in the first-home-buyers' grant amounted to $10.4 billion. This was then quickly followed by direct cash payments to the majority of taxpayers of up to $900 a person in 2009 (Australian Government 2010b). There is no doubt that the large cash handouts and government spending of the Rudd government boosted economic growth and protected some employment during the GFC. The injections increased retail spending, which strengthened during the first half of 2009 (ABS 2010e). Some economists, however, argued that a significant proportion was spent on imported goods and was also saved or used to repay debts, reducing the stimulus effect on the economy. The then Leader of the Opposition, Malcolm Turnbull, argued that the 'cash splash' was 'very little bang for a very big buck' (ABC 2010a).

The other major component of the Labor government's stimulus policy was a series of infrastructure building projects, some of which met with disaster and were subsequently abandoned. These infrastructure and job support programs included new buildings in schools, new public housing and housing upgrades, community infrastructure grants, extra funding for national highway maintenance and rail upgrades, subsidies for households who switched to more energy efficient appliances and a home insulation scheme.

Source: David Pope, *The Canberra Times*, 9 December 2008

One of the most controversial programs was the disastrous $2.4 billion home insulation, or 'pink batts', program, which paid a rebate of $1200 a home for the cost of home insulation. Overseen by the then Minister for the Environment, Heritage and the Arts, Peter Garrett, the program aimed to create jobs and to insulate more than two million homes. Serious breaches of safety, however, due to rushed jobs by poorly trained installers, led to four deaths, a number of injuries, 120 house fires and more than 200 000 homes with faulty or poorly fitted insulation (The Australian 2010a). The Rudd government was criticised for not acting sooner given the many warning letters from businesses within the insulation industry and from state governments regarding the lack of monitoring of workers' qualifications and safety standards. The program began in July 2009 and was axed in February 2010. It was then followed by a long safety inspection program for homes fitted with foil insulation—at an estimated cost of about $1 billion (The Australian 2010a).

The Building the Education Revolution (BER) 'school halls' program was another major component of the Labor government's stimulus policies, implemented by the then Minister for Education, Julia Gillard. It aimed to provide rapid construction of multi-purpose halls and libraries to stimulate the building industry while at the same time providing improved facilities for schools. The largest component of this policy was $12.4 billion of capital works in primary schools, which became $14.1 billion due to cost increases of $1.7 billion (ANAO 2010). The scheme became the subject of significant criticism with claims of rorts and hugely inflated building prices. It was argued by some schools that the scheme lacked flexibility and that they were receiving buildings they did not need. The involvement of state and territory government administration added much to costs, managing contractors were charging more than three times the usual fee, the time frame for construction completion was too short, and some local builders were greatly inflating prices (The Australian 2010b). For example, in March 2010, lobbying by a school principal led the NSW state government to finally reverse a decision to spend $1 million on a shade-cloth structure (originally quoted as costing $400 000), which was valued at market prices at only $250 000 (The Australian 2010b). In Parramatta, a school hall was built in a private school for $170 000, and in a BER-funded public school a similar hall was built for $350 000. In 2009 and 2010 in Queensland, more than 20 per cent of the BER was being absorbed in administration costs (The Australian 2010b). The widespread extent of the apparent price gouging led to audits commencing in 2010, conducted by state governments and the Australian National Audit Office (ANAO). As the BER program was scheduled to run until 2012, serious concerns began to arise that the waste was going to be even greater than in the insulation program. Following much public outcry, in May 2010, Julia Gillard set up the government's own task force to investigate formal claims of waste and rorting in the BER. There were, however, also accusations of waste even within the task force, with more than $1 million spent on consultants within the first two months, and a total budget allocation for the task force of $14 million (ABC 2010b). An additional problem emerged with the sudden and large demand for building materials and labour for the BER flowing through to higher prices in non-school construction, and increasing costs in other industries.

Many schools, however, reported that the building programs were useful, and formal complaints were made by about only 3 per cent of schools (Australian Government 2010a). The building industry also received a boost in profits and employment. The key question is whether or not the BER represented value for money, and whether the stimulus effects justified the waste and government debt. This is, of course, the same question facing the entire Nation Building program. Economists and analysts generally acknowledge that some stimulus was required to help shield Australia from the effects of the GFC, and that the speed of the Rudd government's policy response was instrumental in its early impact on the economy. The debate centres on whether the size of the economic stimulus was appropriate or too big, the way in which the funds were used, the size of the ensuing government debt, and on whether the stimulus measures should have been wound back faster once economic growth returned to healthy levels.

Government spending, budgets and debt

The Rudd government came to office at a time when the Australian economy had achieved its lowest rate of unemployment in more than 30 years and economic growth was strong. The Commonwealth budget was in surplus by about $20 billion and the government was one of the very few in the world that had net savings—about $45 billion—instead of large net debt levels (Australian Government 2010c). As part of Labor's 2007 election campaign, Rudd promised that his government would be fiscally conservative and would keep the budget in surplus. Interestingly, achieving a balanced or surplus budget again became an important objective for both sides of Parliament in the 2010 federal election, indicating that a surplus budget has now become a very important issue with voters. The strong emphasis on a surplus budget is a relatively new objective for Labor, and, as Figure 10.1 shows, from the mid-1970s to the mid-1990s, the budget was more often in deficit than in surplus. It was clear, however, that despite the fiscally conservative pitch, the Rudd government remained less concerned than the Coalition about increasing government spending and the consequent debt, with Rudd arguing in favour of 'classic Keynesianism' spending during the GFC (Rudd 2009).

The Rudd government commenced governing with the intent of balancing budgets, but this aim was no longer possible following the large GFC fiscal stimulus policies, and was further exacerbated by significant policy cost blowouts. In addition to the stimulus policies discussed earlier, a number of other policies exceeded budget forecasts, including the provision of laptop computers in schools; the solar panel rebate—so successful that it exceeded its budget and had to be ended early; the Green Loans Scheme—cancelled in 2010 due to allegations of rorting (The Australian Greens 2010); the Indigenous housing program; and Grocery Choice (axed in 2009). Figure 10.1 shows that the Rudd government's budget deficit is large by historical standards, moving from a surplus of close to $20 billion in June 2007 to a deficit of about $55 billion in June 2010 (Australian Government 2010c). When expressed as a percentage of GDP, the deficit in 2010 is the largest in more than four decades, at 4.4 per cent of GDP.

As indicated earlier in this chapter, there is little doubt that the Rudd government's stimulus spending cushioned Australia from the impact of the GFC, preventing the rate of economic growth from falling as far as it might otherwise have done. By the end of Rudd's term, however, questions were being asked by some economists and analysts as to whether or not Australia was actually going to be significantly affected by the GFC, whether the stimulus spending was appropriate in size and gave value for money, and why the stimulus programs were continuing until 2012 even though the threat of recession was clearly over.

The stimulus spending involved substantial government borrowing, with net government debt forecast to rise to almost $94 billion by 2012, with annual interest repayments of more than $6 billion (Australian Government 2010c). This represents about 6 per cent of GDP, which is substantially lower than the debts incurred by the Labor government in the 1980s and early 1990s, which peaked at 18 per cent of GDP in 1996.

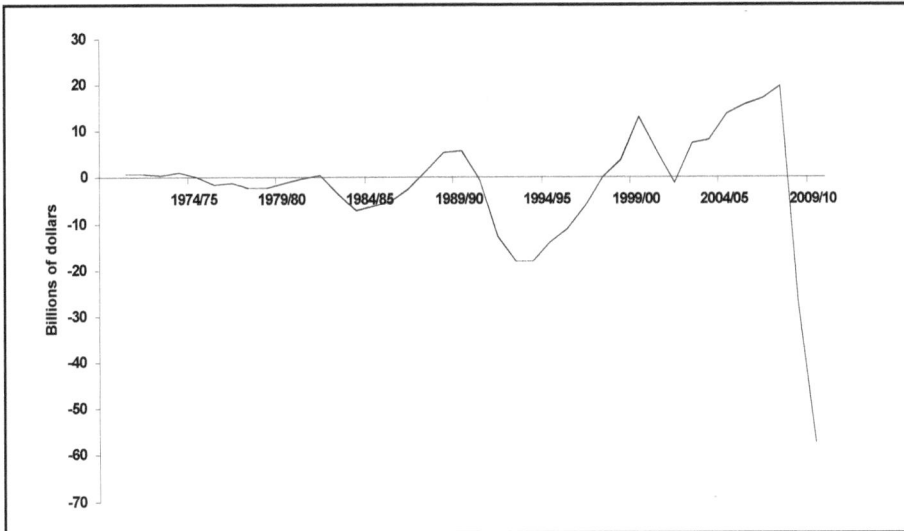

Figure 10.1 Commonwealth government budget: surpluses and deficits, 1970–71 to 2009–10

Source: Australian Government (2010c).

It should be remembered that borrowing during an economic downturn or recession is normal and even expected, as tax receipts are down and spending increases to fund payments for unemployment benefits and pensions. An important economic issue is that government borrowing carries with it a future burden in the form of higher taxes and reduced government services, as the debt must be repaid, with interest. If borrowing is used in ways that will increase the future productivity of the economy, such as a better educated workforce and improved infrastructure, future economic growth will enable the repayment of the debt without imposing a significant burden on the country. If government borrowing is used for non-productive purposes, such as cash handouts and programs dominated by waste, the future burden is much greater. It is likely that the Labor government's debts have led to a mix of both outcomes: some improvements in the productive capacity of the economy, together with a significant amount of waste.

Government borrowing also puts upward pressure on interest rates, and this has effects on the private sector. Prior to the GFC, the RBA was increasing interest rates, believing that the Australian economy was in danger of overheating and that the rate of inflation would then accelerate. During the boom years of the 2000s, the RBA increased the official cash rate (the rate set by the RBA upon which all other interest rates are based) from a low of 4.25 per cent in December 2001 to a high of 7.25 per cent in March 2008 (RBA 2010). When the extent of the GFC was realised, the RBA rapidly reduced the cash rate to a low of 3 per cent in April 2009, with some economists crediting the RBA's rapid and significant action with preventing a recession in Australia. After April 2009, the cash rate was increased on six separate occasions, to 4.5 per cent by the end of the Rudd government's term (RBA 2010). While economic recovery allowed the RBA to begin to return interest rates from an expansionary stance to a more neutral stance, government borrowing also put upward pressure on interest rates. By 2010, the Labor government was borrowing more than $1 million each day and continuing its stimulus programs—even though the economic growth rate had returned to a healthy level and was forecast by the Governor of the RBA to remain healthy (Stevens 2010). The continued stimulus spending put upward pressure on inflation, leading the RBA to raise interest rates by more than it otherwise would need to. This then meant that the private sector faced higher interest rates, which discourages private investment and economic activity—the *crowding-out* effect.

The rush to accumulate debt to finance marginal short-term infrastructure spending contrasted with the pressing need for investment expenditure to improve Australia's wealth-creating activities in response to mining booms, population growth, skills shortages and transport. Unfortunately, these are the direct responsibility of the states and territories (most with Labor governments), although funding is often delivered by the Commonwealth. The failure of most states and territories to keep pace with infrastructure needs—particularly New South Wales—has led to significant price rises for many services, particularly water and electricity, which have mainly fuelled inflation while price rises for most other goods and services in the economy have been relatively modest.

The labour market

The Rudd government inherited one of the best-performing labour markets in the world; in 2007 the unemployment rate reached a 33-year national low of 4.3 per cent, and in some states and territories, particularly Western Australia and the Australian Capital Territory, unemployment rates of approximately 2 per cent were recorded. Despite this relatively rosy picture of the Australian labour market, more than 1.2 million people of working age rely on social security payments as their major means of income, representing a major source of potential labour supply (Lewis 2008). In examining the labour market during the latter years of the Howard government, one of the biggest issues facing the Australian economy was a *shortage* of labour. These shortages arose in both the private and public sectors, in both skilled and unskilled labour. This particularly affected the numbers of professionals such as medical practitioners, nurses, schoolteachers, pilots, economists, tradespeople and engineers through to agricultural workers and shop assistants (Lewis 2008). As an economy nears full employment, bottlenecks in certain parts of the economy are expected, as economic growth and structural change are not evenly spread throughout the economy and some industries can adjust quicker than others. Specific labour shortages continued during Rudd's term, even during the GFC.

One attempt to alleviate this was to increase the intake of migrants and temporary residents. In 2006 the net inflow of new migrants was 134 600—up 23 per cent from 2003—and there was a net addition of more than 200 000 long-stay arrivals over departures (ABS 2007). Under the Rudd government, planned migration rose by 7 per cent and 8 per cent, respectively, in the financial years 2007–08 and 2008–09. In addition, at the peak of 2009 there were 146 600 temporary business, 116 800 working holiday and 434 000 student visa-holders in Australia (DIAC 2009). Overall, workers from overseas made up about 8 per cent of the workforce.

It is rather strange, given the role that immigration played in meeting Australia's labour shortages, that, as the economy resumed its growth path following the GFC, both major political parties went to the 2010 election on a platform of reducing migration! Yet again, issues requiring well thought-out discussion—such as population growth, workforce needs, skills policy and infrastructure requirements—were reduced to a largely nonsensical slanging match about numbers. The perceived excess demand for labour took the policy focus away from unemployment. Indeed Labor's Treasurer, Wayne Swan, boasted in his budget speech of May 2010 that the government was within striking distance of achieving full employment (Swan 2010). He said full employment was consistent with a rate of 4.75 per cent. It seemed to be an indictment on a Labor government that such a large proportion of the population had not found useful work and that, with all the social problems this entails, it could be referred to as 'full employment'. Successive Coalition and Labor governments have failed to bring about reform of social security, education and training, and the labour market (particularly the minimum wage) necessary to get the unemployment rate down to 1970s levels of about 2 per cent, and necessary to move more than 1.2 million people from welfare to work. The more appropriate interpretation of the magic 4.75 per cent is that when the unemployment rate reaches something like this level, bottlenecks in certain labour markets begin to arise and employers find it difficult to recruit labour. This puts pressure on wages to rise and therefore raises fears about inflation. Hence labour market reforms and reforms in other markets are essential if the unemployment rate is to be lowered without leading to wage and price inflation.

Industrial relations

Workplace industrial relations was one of the defining issues in the 2007 federal election. The possibility of the return of WorkChoices—the former Howard government's labour market reforms—was still being played as a major card by Labor in the 2010 election campaign. The Rudd government's Fair Work Australia was set up as an alternative that would wind back many of the most feared parts of WorkChoices. On 1 July 2009, Fair Work Australia began operations as part of a new national workplace relations system underpinned by the *Fair Work Act 2009*. The new system, which also includes the Office of the Fair Work Ombudsman and Fair Work divisions of the Federal Court and Federal Magistrate's Court, was introduced in stages and replaced that which operated under WorkChoices. The key feature of Fair Work Australia was the abolition of the Australian Fair Pay Commission, the Office of the Employment Advocate, the Office of Workplace Services and the Industrial Relations Commission, bringing their functions together under Fair Work Australia. There was also the return of much of the 'unfair' dismissal provisions axed under WorkChoices. The main points contained in the *Fair Work Act 2009* are

- enterprise bargaining and awards to be the main bases of wage determination
- Australian Workplace Agreements (AWAs) abolished and existing AWAs fazed out by 2012
- individuals earning more than $100 000 may negotiate employment contracts without reference to awards
- safety-net minimum conditions expanded from six to 10
- secondary boycotts to remain outlawed
- no pattern bargaining
- restrictions on union officials' right of entry to workplaces to remain
- unfair-dismissal claims may be made after 12 months' employment in firms with fewer than 15 employees and after six months in firms with 15 or more employees.

While Rudd's industrial relations 'reforms' reversed the most hated parts of WorkChoices, they also reversed many of the earlier changes brought in by the Hawke–Keating and Howard–Reith reforms to industrial relations, which had reduced the influence of unions and tribunals in wage setting and dispute resolution. It is still too early to evaluate the impacts of all the workplace changes, but the major complaint by employers, particularly small business, is the reduction in flexibility in employment. The most obvious, and widely publicised, example is the loss of jobs for school students who are no longer able to work after school because under workplace legislation it is illegal to employ anyone for less than a three-hour shift! The benefits of increased labour market flexibility under Hawke–Keating and Howard–Reith were best evidenced by the failure of unemployment to rise as much as predicted after the GFC. Many employers and employees adopted flexible responses to the economic downturn such as taking leave, reducing hours and shifting to part-time work. In effect, employees took wage cuts because the reduction in their hours of work was more than the reduced output, reducing the cost of labour per unit of output. The willingness of workers to accept cuts would not have been expected in the days before labour flexibility, as evidenced by union responses to the recessions of the 1970s. Added worker compliance was probably the result of the experience of employers coming out of a period of labour shortage, not wishing to lose workers only to have to face recruitment difficulties during the recovery. Of great interest will be the impact of the Rudd government's increased labour market regulation when the economy achieves low unemployment rates.

Taxation reform

The Rudd government was forced to implement the reductions in personal income tax of former Coalition Treasurer Peter Costello, due to the promise made during Labor's 2007 election campaign. Labor's Treasurer, Wayne Swan, however, went a long way to reversing the concessions to those who salary sacrificed into superannuation. The biggest news stories on taxation related to the Henry Tax Review, which was completed in December 2009, but the report of which was withheld from the public until May 2010. This was to be the most significant 'root and branch' review of taxation in Australia, at least since the Campbell inquiry. The head of Treasury, Ken Henry, produced a comprehensive report based on sound economic principles. Perhaps inevitably, good economics is not always compatible with popular politics, as Labor adopted only three of the 138 recommendations, the most controversial being the Resource Super Profits Tax (RSPT). The government also proposed one measure opposed by the review: raising the percentage of compulsory superannuation contributions.

There are several criteria generally used by economists to evaluate taxes: *equity, allocative efficiency, simplicity and inability to evade* (Lewis et al. 2010). The argument for resource rent taxes, like many taxes, such as a broad-based goods and services tax (GST), is hard to dispute on the basis of these criteria. As with the GST, however, the details, the response of vested interests and the selling of the tax to the public are all important. The RSPT was to apply a 40 per cent tax on mining profits, in addition to the usual company income tax (Swan 2010). Mining companies would be allowed to subtract a tax-free allowance (normal profit) at the long-term bond rate (approximately 6 per cent) from their existing earnings. The Federal Government would refund the royalties that resource companies have to pay to states and territories. Importantly, the RSPT proposals allowed for 40 per cent of any losses to be either claimed back from the government as a refund or carried over to other projects. In effect, the government was to become an equity partner in resource projects bearing 40 per cent of all costs and 40 per cent of all economic rents.

Several commentators put forward the view that Rudd believed the RSPT to be a sure winner with the electorate. After all, who could argue with sound economics and who would not want the nation to get its fair share of excessive mining profits? The massive anti-tax campaign of the mining companies, which was very damaging to Rudd and the Labor Party, was a lesson in politics. Kevin Rudd and his inner cabinet made a huge mistake in putting forward a major tax change without prior consultation with the industry concerned, without calling for public submissions, and without Rudd even consulting most of his own ministers. As soon as she became Prime Minister, Julia Gillard took on the job of negotiating with the big mining companies and, on 2 July 2010, she announced that the Minerals Resource Rent Tax (MRRT) would replace the RSPT. The new tax would apply only to the iron ore and coal industries; and the tax rate was reduced from 40 per cent in the RSPT to 30 per cent, levied on 75 per cent of net profit. The rate for losses carried forward and used royalty credits was increased to 7 per cent above the long-term government bond rate. The government claimed that only $1.5 billion less revenue would be raised under the MRRT, but many commentators put the revenue loss at more than $4.5 billion, even under extremely conservative assumptions (see, for instance, Knight 2010), with some estimates rising up to $20 billion (Probyn and Wright 2010).

Another tax issue, although it was not described as such, was the emissions trading scheme (ETS)—a defining feature of the Rudd period. The purpose of an ETS is to reduce the use of carbon by households and firms because of the view that burning carbon causes environmental damage—climate change. To reduce carbon use, using carbon needs to be made more costly and the simplest way to do this is through a tax on carbon. This, however, raises the prices of coal, gas and electricity and the price of goods that use these resources as inputs (as the Leader of the Opposition, Tony Abbott, frequently expressed it in 2010: 'A great big new tax on everything'). The Rudd government was not very successful at getting this point across; as with the GST, with an ETS, prices would rise but losers can always be compensated. The ETS as originally proposed was quite economically elegant. The option adopted by Rudd, however, was more complex, containing large amounts of compensation to reduce the effects on costs and prices (which is counter-intuitive to the purpose of reducing carbon emissions), and ensured that few people would understand it. The ETS was ultimately rejected in the Senate and, instead of continuing with his fight for a carbon reduction scheme, in April 2010, Rudd postponed the proposal until at least 2012 or 2013. The electoral backlash for Rudd was intense, and was a major contributing factor in his removal as Prime Minister (van Onselen 2010). (The issue of climate change is discussed in detail in Chapter 11 of this volume.)

International trade and the balance of payments

Australia is a relatively free trading nation, with minimal trade or foreign investment barriers. This differentiates it from most other countries, many of which heavily protect their local industries with subsidies, and with tariffs and quotas on imported goods, making their local industries more inefficient and uncompetitive. As a small economy with insufficient savings to fund investment, Australia relies on foreign investment and loans to provide the funding and capital to enable investment and continued economic growth. The interest repayments on these overseas borrowings are measured as a negative item in Australia's current account of its balance of payments, and make up such a large component that it means that Australia will always operate with a current account deficit. Dividends paid on portfolio investment from overseas also represent an outflow of funds, further increasing the current account deficit. Interestingly, the balance between export earnings and import payments—the balance of trade—even when positive, as it was at times during 2009 and 2010 due to a rise in minerals exports, is never sufficient to bring the current account into a surplus. While the balance of trade was a positive $3.5 billion in June 2010, the current account deficit remained in deficit (ABS 2010c). Regardless of whether Australia has a positive or negative balance of trade, it is likely to always have a current account deficit due to the interest repayments on borrowings from overseas.

During the period of the Rudd government, the minerals and energy export boom continued, with the industry making up about 56 per cent of total exports near the time when Rudd was replaced (ABS 2010b). As usual, the demand for minerals and energy had almost nothing to do with internal policy and much to do with the very strong demand for coal, liquefied natural gas (LNG) and iron ore in China, India and other emerging economies. For example, between 2007–08 and 2009–10, the value of coal exports rose by almost 46 per cent—a combination of increased volume and higher prices (ABARE 2010). The strength in mineral exports undoubtedly helped to temper the effects of the GFC on the Australian economy. The rate of growth in exports slowed significantly in 2007–08, but increased again during the following year, as China began to recover more quickly from the effects of the financial crisis than many analysts expected. Overall, the current account deficit fluctuated wildly—as is common—during the period of the Rudd government, from deficits of about $59 billion in mid-2007 and $73.1 billion in June 2008 to $37.5 billion in June 2009 and a deficit of approximately $56.1 billion in June 2010 (ABS 2010b).

While the demand for mineral exports grew, the growing strength of the Australian dollar during the latter part of Rudd's leadership put downward pressure on export earnings in other sectors of the Australian economy. The rural sector—only just beginning to recover from the severe droughts of the early to mid-2000s—was dealt a major blow by the stronger exchange rates, which significantly reduced income from exports. Australia's relatively high interest rates compared with interest rates in many other countries during the GFC increased the demand for Australian dollars, contributing to a higher exchange rate. As discussed earlier, the commencement of significant amounts of government borrowing by the Rudd government to fund its spending policies put further upward pressure on interest rates. Unlike parts of the mining sector, the rural, manufacturing and services sectors face much competition in international markets and are largely price takers, unable to affect the price received for exports in international markets.

Living standards and income distribution

Labor governments have usually been associated with protecting or promoting the interests of the worse off, in comparison with the Coalition parties. Therefore, it is interesting to compare the term of the Rudd government with that of the Hawke–Keating and Howard governments with respect to income distribution.

Income distribution is usually measured in terms of equivalised disposable household income (Lewis et al. 2010). According to the Australian Bureau of Statistics (ABS), the real average equivalised disposable household income in 2007–08 was $811 a week, which was almost 26 per cent higher than in 2005–06, at $644 a week (ABS 2009). The median, however, says nothing about the distribution of earnings.

Table 10.1 provides some internationally recognised measures of income inequality based on measures of equivalised disposable household income. The P20/P50 ratio is the ratio of the earnings of the lowest quintile of income recipients (the bottom 20 per cent) to median earnings. The ABS classification of 'low incomes' excludes the bottom 10 per cent due to difficulties with unreported income. The P80/P20 ratio is the ratio of the highest 20 per cent of income recipients to that of the lowest 20 per cent of income recipients and so on. The Gini coefficient is a summary measure of inequality, between 0 and 1, and the lower its value, the higher is the degree of inequality.

It appears that there has been no significant change in income inequality from the mid-1990s to 2007–08. This contrasts with the observed earnings inequality arising from labour markets where demand and wages for those with higher skills and training have grown at a faster rate than for those with lower skills (Lewis et al. 2004). The reason for the unchanged distribution of income during the Howard era was the relative generosity of the Howard government with respect to pensions (but not unemployment benefits) and increased payments to families with children, which also benefited low and middle-income earners (Lewis 2006).

The Rudd government significantly increased pensions in 2010 beyond indexation—by $29.20 for singles and $44 for couples (Macklin 2010). A factor affecting the lowest-paid employees was the decision (its last) by the Australian Fair Pay Commission to not increase the minimum wage at all in July 2008. This meant that real wages for this group of workers fell in real terms. Fair Work Australia increased the minimum wage by $20 a week in 2010 but this did not match the rise in the cost of living between 2008 and 2010. Although the relevant statistics are not yet available, it is likely that under Rudd and Gillard, the lowest-paid employed will have been made worse off. The lower pay would have stimulated demand and employment somewhat but would also, given pension increases, have further exacerbated the growth of pensioners rather than growth in the numbers seeking work.

Table 10.1 Selected income distribution indicators: equivalised disposable household income

	1995–96	2005–06	2007–08
Ratio of incomes at top of selected income percentiles (P)			
P20/P50 ratio	0.61	0.60	0.59
P80/P50 ratio	1.57	1.54	1.56
P80/P20 ratio	2.58	2.58	2.63
Percentage share of total income received by persons according to income category			
Low income[a]	11.0	10.4	10.1
Middle income[b]	17.7	17.4	17.0
High income[c]	37.3	39.2	40.5
Gini coefficient	0.296	0.314	0.331

(a) persons in the second and third income deciles

(b) persons in the middle-income quintile

(c) persons in the highest-income quintile

Source: ABS (2009).

Conclusion

The major economic focus on the Rudd government has been on its handling of the economy during the GFC. The second focus was on the taxation of resources and the ETS. The evaluation of the impact of the stimulus package on jobs and growth is unlikely to be settled empirically and, as with many debates in economics, views will, to a large extent, depend on the politics and the economic doctrine adhered to. The GFC certainly caused a revival of Keynesian sentiment throughout the world and Australia was no exception. In all probability the stimulus package did have some short-run effect in preventing unemployment rising more than it otherwise would have, but much of the spending was wasteful and could have damaged long-term economic growth.

The failure of the ETS and the RSPT to be legislated was symptomatic of the Rudd government's very poor performance in delivering economic policy. The contrast with the slow, gradual process by which the GST was introduced by the former Coalition government from its inception to implementation is a lesson other politicians could well learn.

Anne Garnett *is a senior lecturer in economics at Murdoch University and a Research Fellow at the Centre for Labour Market Research.*

Phil Lewis *is Director of the Centre for Labour Market Research and Professor of Economics at the University of Canberra.*

References

Australian Broadcasting Corporation (ABC) 2010a. 'Sales surge slows stimulus success', *ABC News*, 6 May 2010, <www.abc.net.au>

Australian Broadcasting Corporation (ABC) 2010b. 'Labor defends BER consult costs', *ABC News*, 4 August 2010, <www.abc.net.au>

Australian Bureau of Agricultural and Resource Economics (ABARE) 2010. *Australian Commodities*, vol. 17, no. 2 (June quarter), Australian Bureau of Agricultural and Resource Economics, Canberra, <www.abare.gov.au>

Australian Bureau of Statistics (ABS) 2007. *Migration, Australia, 2005-06*, Cat. No. 3412.0, Australian Bureau of Statistics, Canberra.

Australian Bureau of Statistics (ABS) 2009. *Household Income and Income Distribution*, Cat. No. 6523.0, Australian Bureau of Statistics, Canberra.

Australian Bureau of Statistics (ABS) 2010a. 'Australian National Accounts: national income, expenditure and product', *Time Series Workbook*, Cat. No. 5206.0, Australian Bureau of Statistics, Canberra, <www.abs.gov.au>

Australian Bureau of Statistics (ABS) 2010b. *Balance of Payments and International Investment Position, Australia*, Cat. No. 5302.0, Australian Bureau of Statistics, Canberra.

Australian Bureau of Statistics (ABS) 2010c. *International Trade in Goods and Services*, Cat. No. 5368.0, June, Australian Bureau of Statistics, Canberra.

Australian Bureau of Statistics (ABS) 2010d. 'Labour Force, Australia', *Time Series Workbook*, Cat. No. 6202.0, Australian Bureau of Statistics, Canberra, Table 1, <www.abs.gov.au>

Australian Bureau of Statistics (ABS) 2010e. 'Retail Trade, Australia', *Time Series Workbook*, Cat. No. 8501.0, Australian Bureau of Statistics, Canberra, Table 2, <www.abs.gov.au>

Australian Government 2010a. *Building the Education Revolution Implementation Taskforce: Interim report*, Commonwealth of Australia, Canberra.

Australian Government 2010b. *Nation Building—Economic Stimulus Plan*, Commonwealth of Australia, Canberra, <www.economicstimulusplan.gov.au>

Australian Government 2010c. *Statement 10: historical Australian government data*, Budget Paper No. 1: Budget Strategy and Outlook 2010–11, Commonwealth of Australia, Canberra, <www.budget.gov.au/2010-11>

Australian National Audit Office (ANAO) 2010. *Building the Education Revolution: primary schools for the 21st century*, The Auditor General Audit Report No. 33 2009–10 Performance Audit, Australian National Audit Office, Canberra.

Department of Immigration and Citizenship (DIAC) 2009. *Immigration Update July to December 2009*, Department of Immigration and Citizenship, Commonwealth of Australia, Canberra.

Knight, E. 2010. 'Smoke and mirrors trick with resources tax', *Sydney Morning Herald*, 7 July 2010.

Lewis, P. 2006. *Minimum wages and employment*, Research Report 1/06, Australian Fair Pay Commission, Melbourne.

Lewis, P. 2008. *The labour market, skills demand and skills formation*, Research Report No. 6, The Academy of Social Sciences in Australia, Canberra.

Lewis, P., Daly, A. and Fleming, D. 2004. 'Why study economics? The private rate of return to an economics degree', *Economic Papers*, vol. 23, no. 3, pp. 234–43.

Lewis, P., Garnett, A., Treadgold, M. and Hawtrey, K. 2010. *The Australian Economy: Your guide*, (Fifth edition), Pearson Australia, Sydney.

Macklin, J. 2010. 'Pensions to increase on 20 March', *Australian Labor News*, <www.alp.org.au/federal-government/news>

Probyn, A. and Wright, S. 2010. 'Billion-dollar bungle that saved mine deal', *West Australian*, 3 July 2010, p. 1.

Reserve Bank of Australia (RBA) 2010. *Cash Rate Target—Interest rate decisions*, Reserve Bank of Australia, Sydney, <www.rba.gov.au>

Rudd, K. 2009. 'The global financial crisis', *The Monthly*, February, pp. 20–9, <www.themonthly.com.au>

Stevens, G. 2010. Monetary policy and the regions, Address to Foodbowl Unlimited Forum Business Luncheon, Shepparton, Vic., 20 September, <www.rba.gov.au/speeches/2010>

Swan, W. 2010. Budget speech, Budget 2010–11, Commonwealth of Australia, Canberra, <www.budget.gov.au>

The Australian 2010a. '$1bn to fix PM's insulation debacle', *The Australian*, 23 April 2010.

The Australian 2010b. 'School building shapes as bigger debacle than batts', *The Australian*, 1 April 2010.

The Australian Greens 2010. Green Loan Scheme debacle—matter of public importance speech, 3 February, <http://greensmps.org.au>

van Onselen, P. 2010. 'Politics trumps a moral challenge', *The Australian*, 29 April 2010, <www.theaustralian.com.au/news>

11. Climate change

ANDREW MACINTOSH, DEB WILKINSON AND RICHARD DENNISS

The Rudd government's first term in office was tainted by its public failings on climate policy. In the lead-up to the 2007 federal election, Kevin Rudd presented Labor as the party of climate reform, the party that was willing to take climate change seriously and make the bold decisions needed to set the Australian economy on a new course. Expectations were raised to unprecedented heights and there were hopes that Australia might provide an example of an advanced, emissions-intensive economy that was willing to place global interests above short-term national ones. These hopes dissipated over the course of the next three years, culminating in the government's decision in April 2010 to shelve its plans to introduce an emissions trading scheme (ETS).

The abandonment of the ETS sparked a chain of events that ultimately led to Rudd's removal as Prime Minister. It also marked the point where Labor went from unbackable favourites to win a second term in office to a marginal proposition. The precise causes of the downturn in the popularity of the Labor government are hard to determine but climate change was undoubtedly a factor. For some voters, the failure to introduce a carbon price was probably determinative. But possibly of greater significance was the perception created by the decision to walk away from the ETS that Labor stood for nothing—that its 'core beliefs' were merely issues of political convenience. Beyond the ETS, mismanagement of other climate programs—particularly the home insulation and Green Loans programs—also stained the government's reputation. Even during Labor's disastrous 2010 election campaign, climate change continued to dog the government, no more so than when Prime Minister, Julia Gillard, announced that a re-elected Labor government would hold a 'citizens' assembly' to pass judgment on the merits of climate policy proposals. The suggestion quickly became an object of derision from some quarters and, soon after the Gillard government took office after the 2010 election, it appeared to shelve the proposal.

This chapter tells the story of what happened with the Rudd and Gillard governments' climate policies, starting with a brief description of the years leading up to the 2007 federal election.

The Howard government and the 2007 federal election

For much of the Howard government's term in office, climate change wallowed at the edges of mainstream public debate. The government was comfortable with this situation as it diverted attention away from its failure to limit the rise in Australia's greenhouse gas emissions and the obstructionist stance it took in international negotiations (Hamilton 2007; Macintosh 2008; Pearse 2007). In mid to late 2006, however, the government was wrong-footed by a marked shift in public opinion (Baker 2007; Frew 2006; Minchin 2006). A confluence of events—including a prolonged drought in southern Australia, the release of Al Gore's *An Inconvenient Truth* and the publication of the *Stern Review on the Economics of Climate Change*—sparked media interest in and rising levels of public concern about climate change. The inadequacy of the government's greenhouse policy was exposed and there were visible signs of public discontent over the government's response to climate change (Frew 2006; Grattan and Topsfield 2006; Minchin 2006).

Labor under Kim Beazley tried to seize the opportunity provided by the upswing in interest in climate change, announcing plans to ratify the Kyoto Protocol, introduce an ETS and set a target of reducing Australia's emissions by 60 per cent on 2000 levels by 2050 (Crouch 2006; Edwards 2006). Kevin Rudd maintained the stance adopted by Beazley and painted Labor as the pro-climate alternative to the Howard government. In what would become vintage Rudd style, he organised a one-day climate summit at Parliament House in March 2007, where he famously described climate change as the 'great moral challenge of our generation' and promised to 'forge a national consensus on climate change' (Kelly 2007; Koutsoukis 2007). He also announced that a Rudd government would establish a domestic equivalent of the Stern Review—which became the Garnaut Climate Change Review—and establish a Department of Climate Change within the Prime Minister's portfolio.

Although Labor went to great lengths to differentiate itself from the Howard government on climate change, as the election approached, the distance between the parties on substantive policy issues narrowed. Howard established a team within Treasury to look at the design and cost of an ETS, effectively mirroring the work of the Garnaut Review (Colebatch 2007). It also promised to introduce an ETS by 2011–12 and increase the proportion of electricity supplied by low-emission sources to 15 per cent by 2020 (roughly a 5 per cent increase) (Australian Government 2007; Howard 2007). Rudd promised to introduce an ETS by 2010, ratify the Kyoto Protocol, invest $500 million in both renewable energy and clean coal and increase the proportion of electricity supplied by renewable sources to 20 per cent by 2020 (ALP 2007; Rudd 2007; Rudd et al. 2007). Conspicuously absent from the election platforms of both major parties were details on the issue that mattered most: short to medium-term mitigation targets. Both parties claimed they would announce their targets after the election when they had more information on international negotiations and the costs of action (Colebatch 2007; Macintosh 2008).

Bali and the post-election euphoria

Prior to the election, Paul Kelly (2007) wrote that Rudd had 'enshrined climate change as the new moral passion for the Labor Party in a way that recalled Ben Chifley's invocation of the Light on the Hill'. In the early days of the Rudd government, there were signs Kelly was right. The first official act of the Rudd government was to ratify the Kyoto Protocol (Australian Government 2008a). When this news was announced on the first day of the Bali Climate Change Conference on 3 December 2007, it was greeted with a minute-long standing ovation and gushing praise by environmental groups (Porteous 2007; Topsfield et al. 2007). Although Australia shied away from making any firm commitment on mid-term targets at the conference, it agreed to the inclusion of a reference to the conclusion of the Intergovernmental Panel on Climate Change (IPCC) that aggregate developed-country emissions must be between 25 and 40 per cent below 1990 levels by 2020 in order to provide a reasonable chance of keeping warming to 2°C. This was seen by many as a sign of progress and of a willingness on behalf of the Australian government to be a constructive force in the international negotiations. Rudd perpetuated this view, claiming credit for the Bali Road Map and saying that his government was prepared to 'roll up our sleeves and do the hard work' to forge a new international climate regime (Australian Government 2008a; Thompson 2007).

The May 2008 budget was supposed to set the platform for the Rudd government's climate agenda. The three pillars of its climate policy would be: reducing Australia's emissions; promoting adaptation to unavoidable climate change; and 'helping to shape a global solution' (DCC 2008:7). The centrepiece of its emissions reduction strategy would be the ETS, which would be introduced by 2010. This would be complemented by a number of renewable energy, energy efficiency and research, development and demonstration (RD&D) programs, including the following (DCC 2008).

- Renewable Energy Target (RET) scheme: A tradeable certificate scheme that was originally supposed to mandate a 45 000 GW/h increase in renewable electricity generation on 1997 levels by 2020.

- Solar Homes and Communities Plan (SHCP): Provided $8000 rebates to home-owners to support the installation of solar photovoltaic energy systems.

- Green Loans Program (GLP): $300 million over five years for home sustainability assessments and low-interest loans of up to $10 000 to help home-owners to cover the costs of solar, water and energy efficiency products.

- Renewable Energy Fund: $500 million over seven years to accelerate the development, commercialisation and deployment of renewable energy.

- National Clean Coal Fund: $500 million over seven years to support RD&D related to clean-coal technologies.

- Green Car Innovation Fund: $500 million over five years to 'encourage the Australian automotive industry to develop and manufacture low emissions cars' (DCC 2008:26).

The rise and fall of the Carbon Pollution Reduction Scheme

The undertaking to introduce an ETS by 2010 lay at the heart of Rudd's climate agenda. According to the government, the decision to 'move early' on the scheme was the only economically and morally defensible action. In February 2008, the Prime Minister told Parliament that 'the costs of inaction on climate change are much greater than the costs of action' and that 'Australia must...seize the opportunity now to become a leader globally' (Rudd 2008:1147). While time was of the essence, the government promised that a thorough policy development process would be followed, involving the Garnaut Review, a green paper on ETS design issues, Treasury modelling to inform mitigation target decisions and a final white paper, which would be published in December 2008.

Despite the initial signs that the government supported an aggressive mitigation strategy, it was not long before evidence emerged that the rhetoric would not be matched by equally ambitious action. Rudd originally said the Garnaut Review would be the key input into its decisions on mitigation targets and the ETS but it soon became apparent that Professor Ross Garnaut, a Labor insider with close ties to the Prime Minister, was supportive of aggressive mitigation targets and an economically robust ETS. The government's response was to downgrade the review's prominence, making it one of a number of 'inputs' into the policy process (Martin 2008; Porteous and Williams 2008). The Minister for Climate Change, Penny Wong, also moved quickly to hose down expectations of higher targets, saying: 'what we took to the election and to the Australian people...is a reduction of 60 per cent by 2050; that is the approach the government will take' (Porteous 2008).

The review's final report was released in September 2008 and it recommended the establishment of an economically 'pure' ETS with broad sectoral coverage, no free allocation of permits, no price caps, quantitative limits on the use of international offsets and limited transitional assistance to the coal industry (Garnaut 2008a). Garnaut was particularly concerned about the potential for the free allocation of permits to open the door to industry influence, leading to changes in design that undermined the environmental credibility and economic efficiency of the scheme. In a discussion paper, released in March 2008, Garnaut wrote:

> Free allocation would be highly complex, generate high transaction costs, and require value-based judgements...The complexity of the process, and the large amounts of money at stake, encourage pressure on government decision-making processes, and the dissipation of economic value in rent-seeking behaviour. (Garnaut 2008b:33)

The final report stated categorically: 'The Review concludes that there are no identifiable circumstances that would justify the free allocation of permits' (Garnaut 2008a:332).

Garnaut's calls for an economically robust approach fell on deaf ears. Even before the review tabled its final report, the government had started to acquiesce to industry demands. The Green Paper, released on 1 July 2008, indicated that the government was planning to exempt deforestation from the ETS entirely, temporarily exclude agriculture, cut fuel tax on a cent-for-cent basis to offset the impact of the scheme on transport fuels and institute a price cap for the first five years of the scheme to guard against unexpectedly high prices (Australian Government 2008b). The scheme, called the Carbon Pollution Reduction Scheme (CPRS), would also include a generous assistance package for polluters, containing three main elements: first, a 'limited amount of direct assistance' for coal-fired electricity generators to 'ameliorate the risk of adversely affecting the investment environment' (Australian Government 2008b:370). Second, 20 per cent of permits would be given free to emissions-intensive trade-exposed (EITE) industries (rising to 30 per cent if agriculture was included) and this proportion would remain relatively constant over time until other competitor economies imposed an equivalent carbon price, at which time the assistance would be withdrawn. Third, a Climate Change Action Fund (CCAF) would be established to provide financial assistance to businesses and communities adversely affected by the introduction of the CPRS.

Source: David Pope, *The Canberra Times*, 6 September 2008

The government was no doubt concerned that, if it failed to appease key business groups, it would face a fierce industry-led campaign to topple the CPRS in the run-up to an election. The willingness to bend to industry demands was probably also related to the mathematics of the Senate. In order to get the CPRS Bill through Parliament, the government had two options: either it could try to negotiate an outcome with the Greens and two independent senators (Nick Xenophon and Steve Fielding) or it could work with the Coalition, which supported increased industry assistance. The government's preference was for the latter.

The difficulty was that the Coalition was tearing itself apart over carbon pricing. Some Coalition MPs were climate sceptics and opposed carbon pricing under any circumstances; others wanted the ETS to be delayed until other major emitters had introduced similar schemes; and another group was keen to see a carbon price introduced as soon as possible. The issue caused constant headaches for the Liberal leader, Brendan Nelson, until he was replaced by Malcolm Turnbull in September 2008 (Berkovic 2008; McManus 2008; Taylor 2008a). Turnbull was quick to call for delay, saying that 'to start in 2010 is hasty, it's rash, it's rushed' (Butterly 2008). And as the global financial crisis (GFC) took hold in late 2008, the calls for delay intensified, along with the pressure to accede to the demands from industry for additional support.

Facing pressure from the industry lobby, and wanting to attract the support of the Coalition, the government put forward a compromised scheme. The

White Paper declared that the stabilisation of the atmospheric concentration of greenhouse gases at about 450 parts per million (ppm) of carbon dioxide equivalent (CO_2-e) was 'in Australia's interests', but it put forward mitigation targets (5–15 per cent below 2000 levels by 2020) that were inconsistent with this objective (Australian Government 2008c:1–6). The level of industry assistance was also enhanced from the Green Paper; the 'limited amount' of assistance to coal-fired electricity generators morphed into 130.7 million free permits over five years, worth A$3.9–5.4 billion (nominal). To meet the demands of the coalmining industry, whose concerns centred on permit liabilities arising from fugitive emissions, the government allocated A$750 million over five years from the CCAF. Several changes were also made to appease the EITE lobby, increasing the initial allocation of free permits to 25 per cent and bringing the value of the EITE package to $44–82 billion (nominal) over the period 2010–20.[1]

In spite of the government's efforts to appease polluters, many within the business community remained unsatisfied. The GFC was in full swing and the business sector was keen to postpone the commencement of the scheme until the economic downturn had abated. Some industries were also aggrieved by the potential impact of the scheme on their interests and continued to seek special treatment, with coal generators, coalminers, farmers and steel and cement manufacturers amongst the more vocal (Breusch 2008; Chappell 2008; Hart 2008; Paull 2008; Taylor 2008b). Outside the industry lobby, the reaction to the White Paper was arguably even more unenthusiastic. The environmental lobby was outraged at the low targets and extent of the industry handouts (Galacho 2008), and media commentators from across the political spectrum condemned the scheme for being too ambitious, not ambitious enough or because of its economic inefficiency. Typifying the position of many observers, Garnaut (2009a) stated in a senate committee hearing in April 2009 that it would be a 'line-ball call' whether to pass the legislation or 'have another crack at it and do a better one when the time is right'. As the weeks went by, the scheme looked increasingly friendless and, most importantly, there were no signs the Coalition was in a hurry to do a deal.

Initially, the government stood firm against the wave of opposition, claiming it intended to proceed as planned. Minister Wong (2009a) argued that 'it is time now to stop talking and start doing' and, responding to calls to delay commencement, she stated, 'our government's view is that we cannot allow the global financial crisis to weaken our determination to address the very real and long-term threat that climate change poses' (AAP 2009). These and other similar attempts to push back against the scheme's critics failed. The pressure continued to mount for significant changes to be made and there was speculation that the

---

1 The estimate range reflects uncertainties associated with the growth rate of EITE industries, mitigation targets and the carbon price.

CPRS would be the 'first big policy loss for the government' (Kenny 2009). Faced with this reality, on 4 May 2009, the government announced changes to the scheme (DCC 2009a; Wong 2009b).

The CPRS start date was deferred until 1 July 2011 and there would be a fixed price of $10 per permit for the first year of the scheme. Assistance to EITE industries was increased significantly courtesy of a 'Global Recession Buffer', which would raise the assistance rate to eligible entities for five years. An additional $300 million was allocated to the CCAF and new measures were announced to 'assist business and community sector organisations to identify energy efficiency opportunities' (DCC 2009b). To placate the environmental lobby, the government offered two changes. First, it promised to take additional Green Power purchases (a voluntary renewable energy program offered to business and household electricity users) above 2009 levels into account when setting future caps under the scheme. Second, it adjusted its 2020 mitigation pledge, promising to cut emissions by 25 per cent below 2000 levels if certain conditions were satisfied. These conditions were unrealistic, rendering the 25 per cent target little more than a token gesture. Notwithstanding this, three of the country's largest environment groups—the Australian Conservation Foundation (ACF), Worldwide Fund for Nature (WWF) Australia and the Climate Institute— joined forces with the Australian Council of Social Service (ACOSS) and the Australian Council of Trade Unions (ACTU) and campaigned in support of the CPRS (Baer 2010; Climate Institute 2009a, 2009b; Galacho 2009a; Toni 2009).[2]

The response from the main business groups was mixed. Some, such as the Australian Industry Group and the Business Council of Australia, welcomed the design modifications but emphasised that additional changes were needed to protect industry (BCA 2009; Ridout 2009). The Minerals Council of Australia, on the other hand, argued that the scheme was 'fundamentally flawed' and commissioned research to emphasise that it would result in a reduction in employment in the mining industry (MCA 2009).

As was the case with the White Paper, the May 4 changes were unable to bridge the gap between the government and the opposition. The opposition was riddled with internal division, with the Nationals and the right wing of the Liberal Party wanting to vote down the scheme, while the moderate arm of the Liberal Party was looking to compromise. The Leader of the Opposition, Malcolm Turnbull, was amongst those who supported the imposition of a price on carbon but even he was still unimpressed by the revamped CPRS. He immediately called for additional assistance for EITE industries and urged the government to delay a vote on the scheme until after the Copenhagen Climate Conference in December 2009 (Franklin 2009a). The Prime Minister, keen to pass the scheme and exploit

2   The Australian Conservation Foundation later withdrew its support.

the division in the opposition, pressured the Liberal leader, stating at a 4 May press conference, 'it's time to get off the fence Mr Turnbull and it's time to act in the national interest' (Rudd 2009).

In an attempt to deflect criticism and delay voting on the legislation, the Coalition, in conjunction with independent Senator Xenophon, sought additional modelling on the CPRS from consultants Frontier Economics. Released on 10 August, the Frontier Economics report suggested the CPRS would have significant adverse economic impacts that could be avoided if modifications were made to provide greater protection for electricity generators and EITE industries (Frontier Economics 2009). The report was used to justify the Coalition's agreed position to vote against the CPRS legislation. With the Greens and independents also opposed to the scheme, the legislation was doomed and was eventually voted down in the Senate on 13 August 2009.

The demise of the CPRS Bill raised the prospect of a double-dissolution election if the government was to reintroduce the legislation. The government used the threat of a double dissolution to pressure the opposition, with Penny Wong saying that the 'Liberal Party can do this the easy way, or the hard way' (Taylor 2009a). Keen to avoid a double-dissolution election, Turnbull announced that he would negotiate with the government later in the year with a view to reaching an agreed position on the scheme (Taylor 2009b). Quizzed about the level of support for his strategy within the Liberal Party, Turnbull said there was 'very, very strong support for the constructive approach I'm taking to this issue from the party room' (Taylor 2009b). This was untrue. Liberal powerbrokers on the right, including former Howard government Finance Minister, Nick Minchin, were opposed to the introduction of an ETS—at least before other major economies had enacted similar schemes. The opposition's policy up to that point had been to postpone voting on the CPRS until after the Copenhagen Climate Conference and the conservative arm of the Coalition wanted this position to stand. And as the negotiations between the government and Coalition progressed, the divisions within the opposition intensified. In an attempt to quell the discontent within Coalition ranks, Turnbull effectively staked his leadership on his strategy of constructive engagement with the government, declaring publicly that 'to do nothing, to literally be a party with nothing to say, which is what some people are suggesting we should be, a party with no ideas is not the party I am prepared to lead' (Blair 2009).

Turnbull and the opposition spokesman on emissions trading, Ian Macfarlane, framed their negotiating position around the concerns of industry, targeting four particular issues: increasing assistance for EITE industries, lessening the impacts on small and medium-sized businesses, increasing compensation for electricity generators and getting agriculture excluded from the scheme (Gordon 2009). The final deal, announced on 24 November 2009, addressed all four issues

(DCC 2009c; Wong 2009c). The quantum of free permits for coal-fired electricity generators was increased from 130.7 million over five years to 228.7 million over 10 years, bringing the value of the package to $9–12.5 billion. Assistance to coalminers rose to $1.7–2.2 billion over five years, most of which would be in the form of free permits for emissions-intensive mines (48.6 million permits over five years, worth ~$1.4–1.9 billion). The EITE package was enhanced again, raising the total value to $48–83 billion over the period 2011–20. To deal with medium and large business enterprises, a Transitional Electricity Cost Assistance Program was created, worth $1.1 billion over two years. Further, agricultural emissions were permanently excluded from the scheme and farmers would be able to generate offset credits for a number of activities (DCC 2009c:7).

The strategy employed by the government was to appease industry, corner the opposition by meeting the majority of its demands and then push the scheme through Parliament on a tight time frame. The two drivers behind this strategy were that the government wanted to fulfil its election commitment to introduce an ETS (albeit a year later than promised), while simultaneously exploiting the division in the Coalition. Turnbull was more than ready to play his part due to fear of a double-dissolution election and a personal view that it was important to introduce a carbon price. He was also pleased with the deal that he and Macfarlane had brokered, stating that 'we got nearly everything we asked for' and that he thought they had done 'pretty well' (Galacho 2009b). Many within the opposition, however, were not of a same view.

As Turnbull took the package to his party room on 24 November 2009, he was aware the plan to pass the revised legislation would not receive unanimous support. All of the Nationals opposed the legislation, as did a significant number of Liberal members. One unnamed Liberal senator warned: 'if we reject the ETS, on whatever pretext we reject it, at least we will do so as a unified party…if we don't reject it, the party will split' (Franklin 2009b). Another anonymous Liberal source suggested that if Turnbull pushed ahead with his plan, 'it would basically be all over for him' (Franklin 2009b). The warning was prophetic. The party-room meeting triggered an implosion in the Coalition, with bitter infighting and calls for a new leader. After a week of public brawling, Turnbull was deposed as Liberal leader and replaced with Tony Abbott, who only months before had described climate change as 'absolute crap' (Grattan 2009; Peake 2009). Upon taking the leadership, Abbott called a secret party-room ballot in which there was overwhelming support (54–29) for a plan to defer or defeat the legislation (Franklin 2009c). Abbott then announced to the media that the Coalition would oppose the CPRS, labelling it a 'great big new tax on everything' (Franklin 2009d). In the subsequent senate vote, on Wednesday, 2 December, the CPRS Bill was defeated in the Senate—41 votes to 33. Two Liberal senators,

Sue Boyce and Judith Troth, crossed the floor to vote with the government but it was not enough to overcome the opposition of the Greens, two independents and the remaining Coalition senators.

In the aftermath of the vote, the government said it would retain the changes agreed with the Coalition and reintroduce the Bill again in 2010 in order to 'give the Liberal Party one chance to work through and deal with this legislation in the national interest' (Franklin 2009c). The outcome of the Copenhagen Climate Conference, however, stripped climate change of its political potency. Public expectations had been raised to unrealistic levels in the lead-up to the conference and, when these were not met, media and public interest in climate policy waned. In July 2008, polls suggested 55 per cent of people rated climate change as a very important issue. By February 2010, this had fallen to 40 per cent (Newspoll 2010). Senator Wong and her chief of staff met with the Greens on three occasions in early 2010, trying to gauge whether the government could find a way to get the scheme through the Senate. Then, on 27 April 2010, the government unexpectedly announced it was temporarily shelving the CPRS. Citing the obstruction of the Senate and slow progress in the international negotiations, the Prime Minister stated that the introduction of the scheme would be delayed until at least the end of 2012, at which time the government would be in 'a better position to assess the level of global action on climate change prior to the implementation of a CPRS in Australia' (Rudd 2010a).

In October 2009, Ross Garnaut described the policymaking process associated with the CPRS as 'one of the worst…we have seen on major issues in Australia' (Garnaut 2009b). It is certainly difficult to identify many other instances where Australian governments have been willing to make environmental and economic sacrifices on the scale they did in the CPRS process. It is also hard to trump the CPRS for political mismanagement. The Rudd government linked its public standing to climate policy and its ability to introduce an environmentally and economically credible ETS. It then offered a compromised scheme with weak mitigation targets. Over a 22-month period, the scheme progressively became more economically inefficient as the government offered millions of free permits and other handouts to polluters and affected businesses. It also made sport out of the Coalition's internal divisions over carbon pricing—a strategy that contributed to the downfall of Turnbull and the Senate's rejection of the legislation—and refused to engage constructively with the Greens and two independent senators. The price it paid was a loss of public confidence, the demise of a prime minister and a failure to fulfil one of its core election promises.

The energy efficiency, renewable energy and RD&D programs

The downfall of the CPRS was symbolic of the poor policy development processes and substandard administration that plagued the government's other climate programs. Of these, the Home Insulation Program (HIP) proved the most disastrous and politically damaging. It was supposed to provide $2.7 billion to cover the cost of installing free ceiling insulation (up to a prescribed limit) in 2.7 million homes (Hawke 2010; Rudd et al. 2009; SECARC 2010). Launched as part of the National Building and Jobs Plan in February 2009, the HIP was primarily intended to be an economic stimulus measure. By pumping money into the insulation industry, the government hoped to create employment in a low-skilled industry, thereby sheltering vulnerable workers from the effects of the economic downturn. In addition, the program was intended to capture cheap greenhouse gas abatement opportunities in the residential sector that might otherwise not be exploited (Hawke 2010; Rudd et al. 2009; SECARC 2010).

Although it offered numerous theoretical benefits, the HIP faced significant practical obstacles. The inherent dangers associated with the installation of home insulation and lack of pre-existing regulatory and training structures meant that a program of this nature was bound to confront safety problems. In the case of the HIP, the risks were magnified by its size, the speed at which the government sought to roll it out and the fact that it explicitly targeted low-skilled workers. To make matters worse, the government made a number of program design decisions that increased the safety and property risks, including failing to ensure all insulation workers received training and insisting that householders faced no upfront costs, which lowered the incentive to provide proper oversight. Responsibility for the program was also vested in a department (the Department of the Environment, Water, Heritage and the Arts) that lacked the experience and capacity to administer a program of this nature (Hawke 2010; SECARC 2010).

The consequences of the design and administrative flaws were tragic. Four insulation workers—all under the age of twenty-five—died installing insulation under the program. In addition, between October 2009 and June 2010, 174 house fires were linked to HIP installations (SECARC 2010). Owing to the deaths and house fires, the HIP was shut down on 19 February 2010 (Garrett 2010). A subsequent review of the program by Dr Allan Hawke (2010) found there were significant shortcomings in the way it was designed and implemented. The majority of the Senate Environment, Communications and the Arts References Committee made more pointed findings, describing the HIP as 'a breathtaking and disastrous waste of more than a billion dollars of tax-payers' money which has had devastating consequences for many honest and hard-working Australian families' (SECARC 2010:87).

Politically, the HIP was a disaster. The program's problems received extensive media coverage and were used by the government's opponents to illustrate what they saw as widespread incompetence. The Environment Minister, Peter Garrett, and his department were both stripped of their responsibilities for energy efficiency. Penny Wong became the Minister for Climate Change, Energy Efficiency and Water and energy efficiency was added to the remit of the Department of Climate Change. In addition, Greg Combet was given the task of cleaning up the HIP (Rudd 2010b). To perform this task, the government allocated $790 million over three years to 30 June 2012 to cover the cost of home safety inspections and rectifications (Australian Government 2010a). When the costs of the clean-up are included, the final bill for the HIP is likely to be in the order of $2.3 billion (Australian Government 2010a; Hawke 2010; SECARC 2010). At the time of writing, the environmental return on this investment was unclear but rough calculations suggest the HIP will reduce greenhouse gas emissions by about 1.5 Mt of CO_2-e per annum at the end of the program—66 per cent below the initial projection of 4.5 Mt CO_2-e/p.a.

While the HIP and CPRS were unravelling, the Green Loans Program (GLP) was also experiencing major difficulties. As announced in the 2008 budget, the GLP was supposed to consist of $300 million over five years to provide 360 000 home sustainability assessments and up to 200 000 low-interest loans to improve household energy and water efficiency (DEWHA 2008; Garrett 2008). Before it commenced, the program underwent a major restructure. In the 2009 budget, the government reduced the program funding to $175 million and the number of loans was revised downwards to 75 000 (DCC 2009d; DEWHA 2009; Garrett 2009). These and other related changes were supposed to ensure the GLP was 'better focused' but, soon after the program commenced in July 2009, it struck problems (Garrett 2009). The government had underestimated the likely demand for the home sustainability assessments, leading to budget blowouts. The program was also plagued by maladministration. Two external reviews of the GLP in 2010 were scathing of the way it was designed and managed, finding 'repeated and systematic' breaches of the *Financial Management Act 1997* and other probity requirements (Faulkner 2010:2), lack of program oversight, failure to appoint staff with appropriate skills and capacity, 'poor contract management and lack of commercial terms in contracts' (p. 3), budget mismanagement and cost overruns, 'comprehensive failures of risk management' (RCS 2010:16) and poor documentation and record keeping (Faulkner 2010; RCS 2010).

Of all the problems associated with the GLP, the one that caused the greatest political headaches was the mismanagement of the assessor accreditation process.

It was originally envisaged that 2000 trained assessors would be required to carry out the planned sustainability assessments. Expressions of interest were sought from organisations that could accredit assessors but only one came forward: the Association of Building Sustainability Assessors (ABSA) (RCS 2010). The process set up by the ABSA required assessors to undergo training at a cost of between $1500 and $2000, become a member of the ABSA for $650, pay an annual renewal of $400 and obtain public liability insurance for about $1500. The requirement for assessors to become members of the ABSA was a clear conflict of interest, which went unnoticed by the Environment Department. Further, as the number of assessments ballooned beyond expectations in late 2009, so did the number of people seeking accreditation. By early January 2010, the number of contracted assessors had reached 3119, which was 1100 above the planned number, and several thousand more were in the pipeline. The oversupply in accredited assessors meant there was insufficient work and pressure to limit numbers to reduce competition. In response, the ABSA unilaterally decided to stop accepting applications for accreditation on 21 January 2010. The Environment Department was powerless to stop the cessation of accreditation because it had no contractual arrangement with the ABSA (RCS 2010).

By the time the ABSA cut-off date came around, it was estimated that 10 000 people had undergone assessment training (Hudson 2010; RCS 2010). It was clear there would not be sufficient work to sustain these new assessors. As one of the program reviewers noted: 'It is highly unlikely there will be sufficient work for many of these assessors and many will not recoup their training fees and cost of registration' (RCS 2010:10). Not surprisingly, the situation attracted further bad publicity for the government and it initially responded by restructuring the program. On 19 February 2010, in the same press release that announced changes to the HIP, Peter Garrett announced that the loans component of the GLP would be terminated, a cap would be placed on the number of assessors and there would be a weekly cap on the number of assessments that could be undertaken (Garrett 2009). Five months later, the GLP was scrapped and rolled into a new program called Green Start (Wong 2010).

The troubles that beset the government's energy efficiency measures were largely replicated in its renewable energy and RD&D programs. Much like the GLP, the Solar Homes and Communities Plan (SHCP) was prematurely terminated in June 2009 after a massive cost overrun of about $900 million that was caused by the government's inability to manage program demand. And despite costing the taxpayer more than $1 billion, the SHCP will reduce emissions by only ~0.09 Mt CO_2-e/p.a. (0.015 per cent of Australia's 2008 emissions) at an abatement cost in excess of $250/t CO_2-e (ANAO 2010; Macintosh and Wilkinson 2010). The Renewable Energy Target (RET) scheme, which was probably the best of the renewable programs, underwent two major restructures in the space of 12 months as a result of the government's failure to anticipate the impacts of known program design flaws. The RD&D programs were repeatedly restructured and re-badged and, other than in relation to the coal programs, spending was generally significantly below budget forecasts (Macintosh 2010; Smith 2010). The fortunes of the Solar Flagships Program provide a telling example. Announced in the 2009 federal budget, it was supposed to be one of the government's centrepiece renewable energy RD&D measures and originally consisted of a $1.6 billion investment over six years (DCC 2009d; DRET 2009). Due to administrative problems, the program struggled to adhere to its time lines. Some $144 million was allocated to the program in 2009–10, but actual spending was $20 million (Australian Government 2009, 2010b). In the lead-up to the 2010 election, $220 million was stripped out of the program to fund the Clean Car Rebate (or 'cash for clunkers'), which was subject to widespread derision (Metherell 2010; Milne 2010).

Conclusion

In the lead-up to the 2007 election, Labor used climate change as a way of differentiating itself from the Coalition, promising voters that a federal Labor government would chart a new course on climate policy. Expectations were raised that the Rudd government would turn Australia's emissions downward and start the process of transforming the economy. Climate change was to be one of the defining elements of the new era, whereby Rudd would demonstrate that the Labor Party was the champion of progressive reform.

The reality fell well short of expectations and the opportunity for reform was squandered through a combination of incompetence, political myopia and bad luck. The promise to introduce an ETS by 2010 went unfulfilled as a result of the Rudd government's willingness to sacrifice principle and long-term strategic goals for short-term political advantage. It displayed a disinterest in the environmental and economic integrity of the scheme and proved incapable of selling it to the public. Most importantly, it insisted on pushing the scheme through Parliament in late 2009 in order to exploit the political weakness of the opposition leader, Malcolm Turnbull. This hardened the resolve of the Coalition to oppose the scheme and snapped the momentum for reform.

While the demise of the CPRS will undoubtedly be one of the things that is most remembered about the Rudd government, the fortunes of the other climate programs possibly tell us more about how the government functioned. Most of the other programs ran into problems and fell short of their desired objectives. The HIP was a tragedy; the GLP was an embarrassment. Hundreds of millions of dollars were wasted on the SHCP and the RD&D programs were generally mismanaged. The RET was possibly the government's one saving grace but even it confronted difficulties.

In defence of the Rudd government, achieving significant and lasting change on climate policy was never going to be easy. Globally, it has required governments to overcome powerful vested interests and community apathy and ignorance, while navigating a path through complex international negotiations. Where the Rudd government set itself apart was in the extent to which it raised expectations and then failed to match them. This left many wondering whether Labor's interest in climate change was merely political. The maladministration associated with the energy efficiency and renewable energy programs also stained the government's reputation. The challenge for the minority Gillard government will be to erase the memories of the Rudd years and demonstrate that Labor is capable of delivering climate reform in a cost-effective manner.

Andrew Macintosh *is Associate Director, ANU Centre for Climate Law and Policy.*

Deb Wilkinson *is a Research Associate, ANU Centre for Climate Law and Policy.*

Richard Denniss *is the Executive Director of the Australia Institute.*

References

Australian Associated Press (AAP) 2009. 'Delay in action on climate change would cost jobs—Wong', *Australian Associated Press Financial News Wire*, 31 March.

Australian Government 2007. *Australia's Climate Change Policy: Our economy, our environment, our future*, Commonwealth of Australia, Canberra.

Australian Government 2008a. *First 100 Days: Achievements of the Rudd government*, Commonwealth of Australia, Canberra.

Australian Government 2008b. *Carbon Pollution Reduction Scheme: Green Paper*, Commonwealth of Australia, Canberra.

Australian Government 2008c. *Carbon Pollution Reduction Scheme: Australia's Low Pollution Future—White Paper*, Commonwealth of Australia, Canberra.

Australian Government 2009. *Portfolio budget statements 2009–10*, Budget Related Paper No. 1.16, Resources, Energy and Tourism Portfolio, Commonwealth of Australia, Canberra.

Australian Government 2010a. *Portfolio budget statements 2010–11*, Budget Related Paper No. 1.4, Climate Change and Energy Efficiency Portfolio, Commonwealth of Australia, Canberra.

Australian Government 2010b. *Portfolio budget statements 2010–11*, Budget Related Paper No. 1.17, Resources, Energy and Tourism Portfolio, Commonwealth of Australia, Canberra.

Australian Labor Party (ALP) 2007. *Renewable Energy Fund*, Fact sheet, Australian Labor Party, Barton, ACT.

Australian National Audit Office (ANAO) 2010. *Administration of Climate Change Programs—Department of the Environment, Water, Heritage and the Arts, Department of Climate Change and Energy Efficiency, and Department of Resources, Energy and Tourism*, Australian National Audit Office, Canberra.

Baer, H. 2010. The Australian climate movement: a disparate response to climate change and mainstream climate politics in a not so 'lucky country', Presentation to the Democratizing Climate Governance Conference, The Australian National University, Canberra, 15–16 July.

Baker, R. 2007. 'PM feels the heat', *The Age*, 19 February.

Berkovic, N. 2008. '$10bn cuts needed to offset ETS: Turnbull', *The Australian*, 4 August.

Blair, T. 2009. 'Malcolm astutely seizes the muddle ground', *Daily Telegraph*, 3 October.

Breusch, J. 2008. 'Rudd defends cautious climate plan', *Australian Financial Review*, 16 December.

Business Council of Australia (BCA) 2009. Changes to the proposed Carbon Pollution Reduction Scheme, Media release, 4 May, Business Council of Australia, Melbourne.

Butterly, N. 2008. 'Turnbull turns up heat on Rudd ETS timetable', *West Australian*, 2 October.

Chappell, T. 2008. 'Energy business disappointed in emissions trading scheme', *Australian Associated Press Financial News Wire*, 15 December.

Climate Institute 2009a. Time to move on climate action and the low carbon economic recovery, Joint media release with WWF Australia, ACF, ACOSS and the ACTU, 4 May, Climate Institute, Sydney.

Climate Institute 2009b. CPRS better targeted, more transparent and signals investors, Media release, 5 May, Climate Institute, Sydney.

Colebatch, T. 2007. 'Differences slight on climate change', *The Age*, 19 November.

Crouch, B. 2006. 'Beazley vow on climate', *Sunday Mail*, 15 October.

Department of Climate Change (DCC) 2008. *Climate Change Budget Overview 2008–09*, Department of Climate Change, Commonwealth of Australia, Canberra.

Department of Climate Change (DCC) 2009a. *Summary: Key changes to the Carbon Pollution Reduction Scheme legislation*, Department of Climate Change, Commonwealth of Australia, Canberra.

Department of Climate Change (DCC) 2009b. *Preparing Business for a Low Carbon Future*, Department of Climate Change, Commonwealth of Australia, Canberra.

Department of Climate Change (DCC) 2009c. *Details of Proposed CPRS Changes: 24 November 2009*, Department of Climate Change, Commonwealth of Australia, Canberra.

Department of Climate Change (DCC) 2009d. *Climate Change Budget Overview 2009–10*, Department of Climate Change, Commonwealth of Australia, Canberra.

Department of Resources, Energy and Tourism (DRET) 2009. *Clean Energy Initiative*, Department of Resources, Energy and Tourism, Commonwealth of Australia, Canberra.

Department of the Environment, Water, Heritage and the Arts (DEWHA) 2008. *Environment Budget Overview 2008–09*, Department of the Environment, Water, Heritage and the Arts, Commonwealth of Australia, Canberra.

Department of the Environment, Water, Heritage and the Arts (DEWHA) 2009. *Environment Budget Overview 2009–10*, Department of the Environment, Water, Heritage and the Arts, Commonwealth of Australia, Canberra.

Edwards, V. 2006. 'Beazley blueprint to tackle emissions', *The Australian*, 16 October.

Faulkner, P. 2010. *Independent Inquiry—Green Loans Program. Review of procurement processes and contractual arrangements*, Commonwealth of Australia, Canberra.

Franklin, M. 2009a. 'Turnbull still ready to fight Labor scheme', *The Australian*, 5 May.

Franklin, M. 2009b. 'Leader can't let tail wag the dog', *The Australian*, 23 November.

Franklin, M. 2009c. 'Abbott's climate poll dare', *The Australian*, 2 December.

Franklin, M. 2009d. 'Abbott's tax-free carbon plan', *The Australian*, 3 December.

Frew, W. 2006. 'Climate comes in from the cold', *Sydney Morning Herald*, 28 October.

Frontier Economics 2009. *The Economic Impact of the CPRS and Modifications to the CPRS: Report for the Coalition and Senator Xenophon*, Frontier Economics Pty Ltd, Melbourne.

Galacho, O. 2008. 'Business a winner in Rudd scheme', *Herald Sun*, 16 December.

Galacho, O. 2009a. 'PM's green pledge was all hot air', *Herald Sun*, 5 March.

Galacho, O. 2009b. 'Ticks, crosses for ETS revamp', *Herald Sun*, 25 November.

Garnaut, R. 2008a. *The Garnaut Climate Change Review: Final report*, Cambridge University Press, Melbourne.

Garnaut, R. 2008b. *Emissions trading scheme*, Discussion Paper, 20 March, Garnaut Climate Change Review, Canberra.

Garnaut, R. 2009a. Emissions trading and reducing carbon pollution, Transcript of hearings of Senate Select Committee on Climate Policy, *Senate Select Committee on Climate Policy Hansard*, 16 April.

Garnaut, R. 2009b. *Ross Garnaut joins the 7:30 Report*, Transcript, *7:30 Report*, ABC TV, 12 October 2009.

Garrett, P. 2008. Green loans for Aussie homes, Media release, 13 May, Parliament House, Canberra.

Garrett, P. 2009. Australian homes to benefit from Green Loans rollout, Media release, 8 May, Parliament House, Canberra.

Garrett, P. 2010. Significant changes to Commonwealth environmental programs, Media release, 19 February, Parliament House, Canberra.

Gordon, J. 2009. 'Don't cave in to Coalition, climate lobby warns PM', *Sunday Age*, 4 October.

Grattan, M. 2009. 'Turnbull takes on rebel Libs', *The Age*, 3 October.

Grattan, M. and Topsfield, J. 2006. 'Howard told: get serious on warming', *The Age*, 7 November.

Hamilton, C. 2007. *Scorcher: The dirty politics of climate change*, Black Inc. Agenda, Melbourne.

Hart, C. 2008. 'Permit breakthrough for LNG export', *The Australian*, 16 December.

Hawke, A. 2010. *Review of the Administration of the Home Insulation Program*, Commonwealth of Australia, Canberra.

Howard, J. 2007. National clean energy target, Media release, 23 September, Parliament House, Canberra.

Hudson, P. 2010. 'Great concept, but there is not enough interest in green loans', *Herald Sun*, 16 February.

Kelly, P. 2007. 'Green light on the hill is hard to miss', *The Australian*, 4 April.

Kenny, M. 2009. 'Carbon plan taking toll—Rudd's bright star's dimming', *The Advertiser*, 13 March.

Koutsoukis, J. 2007. 'Rudd plans China talks on climate', *Sunday Age*, 1 April.

Macintosh, A. 2008. 'Domestic influences on the Howard government's climate policy: using the past as a guide to the future', *Asia Pacific Journal of Environmental Law*, vol. 11, nos 1–2, pp. 51–84.

Macintosh, A. 2010. 'Beware of climate policy promises', *Crikey*, 22 July.

Macintosh, A. and Wilkinson, D. 2010. *Searching for Public Benefits in Solar Subsidies: A case study on the Australian government's residential photovoltaic rebate program*, The Australia Institute, Canberra.

McManus, G. 2008. 'Nelson gives in on policy', *Herald Sun*, 30 July.

Martin, P. 2008. 'Fair-weather friends greet climate report', *The Canberra Times*, 22 February.

Metherell, M. 2010. 'Gillard's "cash for clunkers" scheme', *Sydney Morning Herald*, 24 July.

Milne, C. 2010. Record investment in solar? Record rate of pulling money out of solar!, Media release, 29 July, The Australian Greens, Canberra.

Minchin, L. 2006. 'Howard blows hot and cold on emissions', *The Age*, 15 November.

Minerals Council of Australia (MCA) 2009. 23 510 jobs lost in the minerals industry by 2020 under emissions scheme, Media release, 22 May, Minerals Council of Australia, Canberra.

Newspoll 2010. 'Importance of federal issues', *Newspoll*, February 2010, <http://www.newspoll.com.au/cgi-bin/polling/display_poll_data.pl>

Paull, N. 2008. 'Carbon trading crushes cement', *The Observer* [Gladstone], 18 December.

Peake, R. 2009. 'Malcolm in the muddle to mayhem', *The Canberra Times*, 28 November.

Pearse, G. 2007. *High and Dry: John Howard, climate change and the selling of Australia's future*, Penguin Group, Melbourne.

Porteous, C. 2007. 'World cheers as Rudd signs Kyoto', *The Courier-Mail*, 4 December.

Porteous, C. 2008. 'Climate change bomb', *The Courier-Mail*, 23 February.

Porteous, C. and Williams, P. 2008. 'Cool wind greets greenhouse call—Labor talks down push for lower emissions', *The Courier-Mail*, 22 February.

Resolution Consulting Services (RCS) 2010. *Review of the Green Loans Program: Final report*, Report to the Department of the Environment, Water, Heritage and the Arts, Commonwealth of Australia, Canberra.

Ridout, H. 2009. 'Most businesses don't understand climate change laws', Transcript, 20 July, Australian Broadcasting Corporation, Sydney.

Rudd, K. 2007. An action agenda for climate change, Annual Fraser Lecture, Belconnen Labor Club, Canberra, 30 May 2007.

Rudd, K. 2008. Climate change, House of Representatives, *Debates*, Thursday, 21 February.

Rudd, K. 2009. Transcript, Press conference, 4 May 2009, Prime Minister's Courtyard, Canberra.

Rudd, K. 2010a. Transcript of doorstop at Nepean Hospital, Penrith, NSW, 27 April 2010.

Rudd, K. 2010b. Prime Minister—ministerial changes, Media release, 26 February, Parliament House, Canberra.

Rudd, K., Evans, C. and Garrett, P. 2007. *New Directions for Australia's Coal Industry: The national clean coal initiative*, Australian Labor Party, Barton, ACT.

Rudd, K., Swan, W. and Garrett, P. 2009. Energy efficient homes—ceiling insulation in 2.7 million homes, Joint media release, 3 February, Parliament House, Canberra.

Senate Environment, Communications and the Arts References Committee (SECARC) 2010. *Inquiry into the Energy Efficient Homes Package*, Commonwealth of Australia, Canberra.

Smith, W. 2010. 'The search for certainty: solar policy in Australia—Part 1', *Solar Progress*, August–September, pp. 3–5.

Taylor, L. 2008a. 'Nelson's new climate shift—shadow cabinet forces leader back to Howard position', *The Australian*, 30 July.

Taylor, L. 2008b. 'Industry revolt on green plan', *The Australian*, 17 December.

Taylor, L. 2009a. 'Coalition ructions aside, ALP must compromise', *The Australian*, 11 August.

Taylor, L. 2009b. 'Turnbull vows to negotiate', *The Australian*, 13 August.

Thompson, T. 2007. 'Climate of agreement—Rudd claims success despite failure to set emission targets', *The Courier-Mail*, 17 December.

Toni, P. 2009. *Regarding WWF's Decision to Support the Carbon Pollution Reduction Scheme*, Worldwide Fund for Nature Australia, Sydney.

Topsfield, J., Forbes, M. and Wilkinson, M. 2007. 'Rudd's first act: yes to climate pact', *The Age*, 4 December.

Wong, P. 2009a. 'ETS is better than tax', *The Australian*, 23 February.

Wong, P. 2009b. New measures for the Carbon Pollution Reduction Scheme, Media release, 4 May, Parliament House, Canberra.

Wong, P. 2009c. A carbon pollution reduction scheme in the national interest, Media release, 24 November, Parliament House, Canberra.

Wong, P. 2010. Green Loans transition to Green Start, Media release, 8 July, Parliament House, Canberra.

12. Sorry, but the Indigenous affairs revolution continues

WILL SANDERS AND JANET HUNT

Introduction

In Indigenous affairs, the Rudd Labor government was bequeathed three major legacies from the 11-and-a-half-year reign of the Howard Coalition government. The first, dating from the recommendations of the 1997 *Bringing Them Home* report of the Human Rights and Equal Opportunity Commission, was John Howard's refusal to apologise for policies up to 1970 that had led to large-scale separation of Aboriginal children from their families and communities on the basis of race. The second, dating from 2004 and early 2005, was the abolition of the Aboriginal and Torres Strait Islander Commission (ATSIC), a national statutory authority and representative body for Indigenous Australians. The third, dating from 2007, was the Howard government's intervention in the Northern Territory, the so-called Northern Territory Emergency Response (NTER), in the wake of a major Aboriginal child protection report. During its two and half years, the Rudd government attempted to address each of these three major legacies, though in different time scales and in very different ways. First, quite quickly and with great fanfare, the Rudd government said 'sorry' to the Stolen Generations. Somewhat more slowly, it reviewed then extended the NTER. More slowly still, the Rudd government moved to re-establish a national representative body for Indigenous Australians. We will examine each of these developments in turn and suggest how they have contributed to the Rudd government's approach to Indigenous affairs. We will also note two other developments in Indigenous affairs during the Rudd years: belated support for the UN Declaration on the Rights of Indigenous Peoples and developments in multilateral intergovernmental agreement making.

Analytically, our chapter is built on the idea of generational revolutions in Australian Indigenous affairs (Sanders 2008). This suggests that, as a difficult cross-cultural policy arena and the moral cause célèbre of Australian nationhood, Indigenous affairs goes through generational cycles. Approaches to Indigenous affairs that are pursued confidently at one point in time become seen, after 30 or

40 years, as having failed to live up to expectations. Established approaches are then abandoned in favour of some newly labelled and conceived approach. Such a generational revolution occurred in the late 1960s and early 1970s, when the key term of Indigenous affairs changed from assimilation to self-determination and the Commonwealth changed from having a regional role in the Northern Territory to having a national role in Indigenous affairs. Another generational revolution appears to have occurred in the early 2000s, with the diagnosed failure and abandonment of both self-determination and ATSIC. Since then the new language and institutional arrangements of Indigenous affairs have emphasised ideas such as responsibility sharing, partnership and a whole-of-government approach. These ideas are not actually as new as claimed, but this is of little moment. They are new enough to disparage what has gone before as a failure and to launch a raft of reforms. Our argument is that the Rudd government has gone along with and continued this generational revolution in Indigenous affairs that developed in the late Howard years. This will be evident in the way in which we write about some of the events of the Rudd years in Indigenous affairs, such as the continuing dominant language of past policy failure. We will return, in our concluding analysis, to the idea of generational revolutions and to one other general aspect of the Rudd government's approach to Indigenous affairs: its emphasis on evidence.

'Sorry' and 'closing the gap'

As Leader of the Opposition, Rudd made clear that, unlike Howard, he was willing to respond to the 1997 *Bringing Them Home* report by sponsoring a governmental and parliamentary apology to the Stolen Generations. Once elected, discussion turned to the timing of the apology and what it would involve. During January 2008, it was decided that the apology would be the first item of business for the new Parliament on 13 February (following the formal opening of Parliament, which would for the first time include an Indigenous welcome to country). Rudd also made clear that the apology would not involve direct monetary compensation for individual members of the Stolen Generations, as had also been recommended by the *Bringing Them Home* report and had recently been implemented in a Tasmanian government scheme (Grattan and Wright 2008; Lennon 2008). Despite this restriction, which caused some adverse comment from Indigenous leaders and others, the apology was both presented and received as a major change in public policy, which clearly and immediately differentiated the Rudd government from its predecessor.

Rudd's address to the Parliament supporting the motion of apology contained some powerful rhetoric. He spoke of nations needing to 'become fully reconciled to their past' in order to 'go forward with confidence', of Australia needing to 'remove a great stain from the nation's soul and, in a sprit of true reconciliation, to open a new chapter' (Parliament of Australia 2008). He recounted the story of one old Aboriginal woman who had been taken from her family near Tennant Creek in 1932 at the age of four. He spoke of this being just 'one story' among 'thousands' that 'cry out to be heard…cry out for an apology', and of 'universal human decency' demanding that the nation 'right an historical wrong'. He spoke of 'our parliaments' being 'ultimately responsible' for enacting laws that 'made the stolen generations possible' and of them needing to bear the 'burdens' of past laws as well as the 'blessings' (Parliament of Australia 2008). The climax of this powerful rhetoric seemed to come in a series of short, simple sentences:

> It is time to reconcile. It is time to recognise the injustices of the past. It is time to say sorry. It is time to move forward together. To the stolen generations, I say the following: as Prime Minister of Australia, I am sorry. On behalf of the government of Australia, I am sorry. On behalf of the Parliament of Australia, I am sorry. I offer you this apology without qualification. (Parliament of Australia 2008)

Rudd went on to propose that if the apology is 'accepted in the spirit of reconciliation in which it is offered', there could 'today' be 'a new beginning for Australia' (Parliament of Australia 2008).

In the final third of his address to Parliament, Rudd moved to a somewhat different tone and focus. He spoke of Australians being 'practical' as well as 'passionate' and of the importance of 'substance' as well as 'symbolism'. He spoke of 'our challenge for the future' being to build a 'bridge based on a real respect' and 'a new partnership between Indigenous and non-Indigenous Australians'. A 'part of that partnership', he noted, would be 'expanded Link-up and other critical services to help the stolen generations to trace their families if at all possible and to provide dignity in their lives' (Parliament of Australia 2008).

The 'core of this partnership', he argued, would, however, be 'closing the gap between Indigenous and non-Indigenous Australians on life expectancy, educational achievement and employment opportunities'. He argued that 'old approaches' to these issues were 'not working' and that the new partnership would allow 'flexible, tailored, local approaches to achieve commonly-agreed national objectives'. He resolved to 'begin with the little children—a fitting place to start on this day of apology for the stolen generations'. Within five years, he aimed to have 'every Indigenous four-year old in a remote Aboriginal community enrolled in and attending a proper early childhood education centre' (Parliament of Australia 2008).

This would, Rudd argued, 'be hard', but not 'impossible'. Achieving it depended on 'clear goals, clear thinking, and placing an absolute premium on respect, cooperation and mutual responsibility as the guiding principles of this new partnership on closing the gap' (Parliament of Australia 2008).

The 'mood of the nation', Rudd argued, was 'calling on' politicians to move beyond 'infantile bickering…point scoring and…mindlessly partisan politics' to 'elevate this one core area of national responsibility to a rare position beyond the partisan divide' (Parliament of Australia 2008). He then proposed a 'joint policy commission' led by himself and the Leader of the Opposition, which would begin by developing 'an effective housing strategy for remote communities over the next five years' before then possibly turning its attention to 'the task of constitutional recognition of the first Australians'. All this, he said, was 'consistent with the longstanding platform commitments of my party', the 'pre-election position of the opposition' and 'the government's policy framework, a new partnership for closing the gap' (Parliament of Australia 2008).

Some of this rhetoric in the last third of Rudd's address was reminiscent of the Howard government, which had also emphasised the 'practical' over the 'symbolic' and the pursuit of equality of outcomes in areas such as education, employment and housing (Sanders 2005). Another element of continuity was the emphasis on past policy failure and the consequent call for significantly changed policy and institutional approaches. Rudd's Minister for Families, Housing, Community Services and Indigenous Affairs, Jenny Macklin, continued this emphasis in an address to the National Press Club in late February 2008. She began by focusing on a West Australian coroner's report into 22 recent Aboriginal deaths in the Kimberley. The coroner, she said: 'paints a picture of a failed community…where…there isn't just a gap between Aboriginal and non-Aboriginal Australians—there is a vast and worsening gulf' (Macklin 2008a).

Macklin used these findings of failure to announce a trial income-management scheme for welfare recipients in 'selected Western Australian communities'. This would 'use existing legislative authority' and 'be part of the national child protection framework'. It would also, Macklin noted, draw in the WA government through requirements for 'appropriate services' and 'an expansion of alcohol restrictions' (Macklin 2008a). What was 'at stake', Macklin argued, was 'a generation of Indigenous children…for whom time is fast running out'. 'Decades of failure', she argued, had 'spawned…another country…the unluckiest of countries…within our borders' (Macklin 2008a). Macklin insisted on finding 'new ways of doing things because the old ways have so comprehensively failed' and on working 'with Indigenous people in a partnership built on respect and mutual responsibility'. All her decisions, she argued, would be guided 'by one single criterion—evidence', which was her 'abiding fixation' (Macklin 2008a).

Macklin went on to talk about 'decent housing' as an 'essential foundation to bridging the gulf' and of how the government would act to overcome 'extreme overcrowding' in Indigenous housing both by promoting home ownership and by building more public housing in remote areas using a 'strategic alliance' approach (Macklin 2008a). The advantages of this approach, she argued, included the 'involvement of each community in how the work is delivered in that community', a 'greater visibility of the cost of risk', 'innovation in design and…logistical solutions' and 'employment and training of local Indigenous people' (Macklin 2008a). Macklin also spoke about encouraging the states to make changes to their land regimes in discrete Indigenous communities in order to 'secure long term [land] tenure' to 'underpin major housing investment', and of the Commonwealth already doing this in the Northern Territory (Macklin 2008a). Her commitment was to increasing the range of housing options or choices available to Indigenous people, particularly those in remote areas. This would take 'years of hard work' and 'determination', but she declared herself 'ready' for this as both a 'realist' and an 'optimist' (Macklin 2008a).

One of us responded to this address by arguing that the focus on past policy failure and a change to new ideas in Indigenous affairs was becoming overdone. It was time to start focusing and building on the strengths and successes of established organisations and approaches, even if limited. It was also noted that new ideas would, by their nature, not have evidence to support them (Hunt 2008). Macklin's rhetoric suggested just how much the Rudd government was going along with the generational revolution in Indigenous affairs established in the late Howard years. Ideas of failure and change were still dominating and so too, through the 'closing the gap' label, were ideas of pursuing socioeconomic equality rather than valuing Indigenous diversity or difference (Altman 2009).

Source: David Pope, *The Canberra Times*, 14 August 2009

Extending the NTER

Unlike the differentiation over the apology to the Stolen Generations, the Rudd opposition's response to the Howard government's launching of the NTER on 21 June 2007 was primarily one of support. Rudd committed, if he won government, to reviewing the NTER after one year's operation, though there were two elements of it that he promised to halt before this review: the abolition of an Indigenous-specific workfare scheme called Community Development Employment Projects (CDEP) and the abolition of permits for access to Aboriginal land in the Northern Territory.[1] In office, Rudd remained true to these commitments. The new government immediately placed a moratorium on further CDEP closures (which by the election had fallen from 8000 to 5000 participants across the Northern Territory), though there was also a commitment to reforming CDEP over coming months. In January 2008, Minister Macklin met with the NTER Taskforce and used the occasion to reiterate the government's support for an 'evidenced-based approach' to the 'excellent job' they were doing in a 'challenging environment' (Macklin 2008b). During that month, she also signed regulations for the introduction of income management to a number of additional declared areas in the Northern Territory, thereby showing support for what was coming to be seen as the most central measure of the NTER. Then in February, Macklin declined to produce regulations that would have ended the need for permits to travel on roads on Aboriginal land in the Northern Territory and also introduced legislation to reinstate a revised version of the permit system in communities (Macklin 2008c).

In early June 2008, Macklin appointed an independent NTER Review Board comprising three members (two of whom were Indigenous) and an 11-member expert support group. She emphasised again the government's commitment to an 'evidenced-based approach to closing the gap between Indigenous and non-Indigenous Australians', as well as directing the Review Board to make an assessment of the impact of each NTER measure (Macklin 2008d). Later in the month, Macklin expressed the view that the NTER was, after one year, 'making important progress' and that the government was 'determined to keep moving forward' (Macklin 2008e).

The NTER Review Board report, published in October 2008, expressed similar sentiments of progress. The board said it had 'observed definite gains' as a result of the NTER and 'had heard widespread, if qualified, community

---

1   The CDEP scheme was introduced on a small scale in remote areas by the Fraser Coalition government from 1977, administered by the Department of Aboriginal Affairs. During the late 1980s and early 1990s, it became a large national program, accounting for one-third of the budget of the Department of Aboriginal Affairs, and later ATSIC, and having up to 35 000 Indigenous participants.

support for many NTER measures'. It argued that the 'situation in remote communities and town camps was—and remains—sufficiently acute to be described as a national emergency' and that the NTER 'should continue' (Yu et al. 2008:10). The board also argued, however, that the NTER had 'diminished its own effectiveness through its failure to engage constructively with the Aboriginal people it was intended to help' and that the 'positive potential' of particular NTER measures had been 'dampened and delayed by the manner in which they were imposed' (Yu et al. 2008:9–10). Accordingly, two of the board's three overarching recommendations aimed to improve the way in which the NTER was being pursued. One recommended that the NT and Commonwealth governments 'reset their relationship with Aboriginal people based on genuine consultation, engagement and partnership' and the other that government 'actions affecting Aboriginal communities' be made to 'conform with the *Racial Discrimination Act 1975*' and thereby 'respect Australia's human rights obligations' (Yu et al. 2008:12).[2]

On specific NTER measures, the Review Board noted that income management was 'the most widely recognised measure' and that 'competing views' of its application to more than 13 000 Aboriginal people by June 2008 were 'expressed with considerable passion' (Yu et al. 2008:20). The Review Board recommended that 'the blanket application of compulsory income management' in declared areas of the Northern Territory should 'cease', but that compulsory income management based on 'relevant behavioural triggers' should be introduced across the whole Northern Territory for more limited numbers of people, as well as 'voluntary' income management for others who wanted it (Yu et al. 2008:23). Most other specific NTER measures—in areas such as policing, alcohol management, education, families, health, child protection and land—were similarly supported by the board, albeit often with modification.

The Rudd government's response to this independent Review Board report was swift and clear. Compulsory income management would continue as a 'comprehensive' measure applying to large numbers of Aboriginal people in the Northern Territory because of its 'demonstrated benefits for women and children' (Macklin 2008f:1). The government accepted the three overarching recommendations of the report and would, as a consequence, work towards 'greater emphasis on community development and engagement' in the NTER, and would over the next year 'design a compulsory income management policy' that was not built on the suspension of the *Racial Discrimination Act*. But the government was 'not prepared to disrupt current beneficial measures or place them at risk of legal challenge', so in the short-term comprehensive,

2   The original NTER legislation, passed in August 2007, had suspended the application of the *Racial Discrimination Act* to its various measures.

compulsory income management in declared areas would continue unchanged (Macklin 2008f:3). This response was both an endorsement and a repudiation of the Review Board's work. It made very clear that the Rudd government was committed to supporting and extending the NTER, not only in the large-scale application of the key income-management measure, but more generally as well.

The Rudd government then took more than a year to develop a policy statement about how it would reinstate the *Racial Discrimination Act* while continuing to pursue large-scale, compulsory income management and other measures within the NTER (Australian Government 2009a; Macklin 2009a). Along the way it passed legislation that brought the Indigenous-specific CDEP workfare scheme closer to the social security system, moving participants from being part-time employees of participating organisations to more clearly being welfare recipients who may be subject to income management. The government also in this period held widespread consultations with Aboriginal people in the Northern Territory, though with the clear intention of maintaining and extending income management and other measures within the NTER (Australian Government 2009b, 2009c). This led to some concerted criticism (Nicholson et al. 2009). At the end of this year-long process, the Rudd government's proposal was to introduce compulsory income management across the whole Northern Territory during the second half of 2010 for about 20 000 people divided into four categories: those aged under twenty-five who had been in receipt of an unemployment-related benefit for more than three months, those aged over twenty-five who had been in receipt of an unemployment- related benefit for more than a year, people judged by a social security delegate to be vulnerable to issues such as 'financial crisis, domestic violence or economic abuse' and those referred by child protection authorities (Australian Government 2009a:9). There would also be the option of voluntary income management, with some minor additional payment incentives, for those who wanted it. Evaluation of this proposed new, non-discriminatory income-management scheme in the Northern Territory during 2011–12, as well as of the trials already under way in Western Australia and Queensland, would then inform the implementation of income management in other areas of 'disadvantage in Australia' (Australian Government 2009a:10).

These proposals for compulsory income management, which would cover large numbers of people across the Northern Territory from late 2010, and also in time extend to other people and areas, provoked considerable public debate during the early months of 2010. The former chief minister of the Northern Territory and now chief executive of the Australian Council of Social Services, Clare Martin, strongly opposed large-scale, compulsory income management and so too did most welfare organisations. A few welfare interests were, however, more supportive and once the Coalition opposition had declared its support in late March 2010, the proposed legislation seemed destined to pass. By coincidence, it was on 21 June 2010, the third anniversary of the launching of the NTER, that the Senate finally passed the social security amendment bill that provided for this new scheme of income management not relying on the suspension of the *Racial Discrimination Act* (Macklin 2010a, 2010b). This extension of a key measure within the NTER would be one of the last legislative acts of the Rudd government, before Julia Gillard became Prime Minister on 24 June.

A new national indigenous representative body

The abolition of ATSIC in 2004 and 2005 had led to Indigenous-specific programs being reallocated to commonwealth departments and there no longer being a broad-based, national Indigenous representative body. The Howard government's replacement advisory body, the National Indigenous Council, was a small group of government-appointed individuals and, within a month of coming to office, Macklin faced the decision of whether their terms should be extended beyond December 2007. Her decision to disband the National Indigenous Council inevitably led to the issue of what approach to a national Indigenous representative body the Rudd government would now be taking. Macklin spoke of the government undertaking 'discussions with Indigenous people' in an attempt to 'strengthen links' with 'urban, regional and remote Indigenous communities'. The aim would be to have a new national Indigenous representative body in place by the end of the parliamentary term. But whatever the new body might look like, the Rudd government would 'not be establishing a new ATSIC' (Macklin 2008g).

During 2008, it was the Aboriginal and Torres Strait Islander Social Justice Commissioner within the Australian Human Rights Commission, Tom Calma, who took the running on this issue. As a five-year statutory appointee chosen by the Howard government in late 2004, Calma had a useful degree of independence from the Rudd government. In July, he released a research paper that discussed past Australian and overseas experience of Indigenous representative bodies and identified issues for discussion (ATSISJC 2008a). Calma then started addressing conferences and seminars identifying six foundational principles for a new national Indigenous representative body: legitimacy and credibility with both governments and Indigenous people, two-way accountability, transparency, representation of the diverse range of Indigenous peoples, links to Indigenous bodies at state/territory and regional levels and independent and robust advocacy and analysis (ATSISJC 2008b).

In December 2008, the Rudd government asked Calma to convene an independent steering committee to progress the representative body issue. In March 2009, Calma and the steering committee organised a three-day workshop of 50 Indigenous men and 50 Indigenous women from 'all age groups' and geographic areas, selected from 263 applicants, to 'lay the groundwork for a new national Indigenous representative body' (AHRC 2009a). Minister Macklin addressed the workshop and asked for its 'advice about the best way forward', while also anticipating that there would be 'a great diversity of views about the role of the new national representative body and who should be on it' (Macklin 2009b). Macklin hoped, however, that Calma and the steering committee would report to her by July and that the new body might be established by the end of 2009.

The March 2009 workshop actually identified considerable common ground among Indigenous people on a national representative body. There was a push for equal representation of women and men, led by former ATSIC chairwoman Lowitja O'Donoghue. There was agreement that the new body should not deliver programs and services, but rather should have a strong advocacy and monitoring role. It was also agreed that members of the new body should not be appointed by government, but rather should be selected on the basis of merit by Aboriginal and Torres Strait Islander people—though whether by election or delegation was still to be worked out. Also there was agreement that the national body needed to build up from local and regional levels to ensure the representation of the diversity of Aboriginal and Torres Strait Islander communities. One final point of agreement was rejection of the term 'Indigenous' in the body's name in favour of either 'First Nations' or 'First Peoples' (AHRC 2009b).

Calma and the steering committee disseminated a model for the new national Indigenous representative body in August 2009. It comprised a National Congress of 128 members, eight of whom would form a National Executive, with the other 120 drawn from three different 40-member chambers: a National Peak Bodies Chamber, a Sectoral Peak Bodies Chamber and an individual Merit Selection Chamber. The national body would also have an Ethics Council, to conduct the merit selection process and to develop and maintain ethical standards. Further, it would be a company limited by guarantee, rather than a statutory authority, in order to be more independent of Parliament and to attract 'corporate and philanthropic support', though it was also suggested that the government should fund the establishment phase and the first five years of operation. The approach being adopted was described as developmental and the tasks listed in August 2009 for achievement by the end of 2010 were to establish a company and office and to convene the first National Congress (AHRC 2009c).

On 22 November 2009, Minister Macklin announced that the Rudd government supported this model and would fund the establishment of the new representative body with $6 million (Macklin 2009c). The new body was to be called the National Congress of Australia's First Peoples and, on 2 May 2010, the inaugural, full-time male and female co-chairs of the company were announced as Sam Jeffries and Kerry Arabena, along with six other directors (AHRC 2010a). Calma was, by then, no longer the Aboriginal and Torres Strait Islander Social Justice Commissioner, but his successor, Mick Gooda, remained heavily involved in the inauguration of the new representative body (AHRC 2010b).[3] More than five years since the abolition of ATSIC, Australia now had the beginnings of a new national Indigenous representative body, supported, but not quite so directly created, by the Commonwealth Parliament and government. The Rudd government could claim to have delivered on a longstanding Labor commitment.

Declaration on the Rights of Indigenous Peoples

One other event during the last days of the Howard government to which Rudd needed to respond was the passing of the Declaration on the Rights of Indigenous Peoples by the UN General Assembly on 13 September 2007. This declaration had been more than 20 years in the making and there were times when Australia was a strong supporter of it. In the last years of its development, however, and in the final vote in the General Assembly, Australia and three other British-majority settler countries—Canada, New Zealand and the United States—were the only four countries that opposed the declaration. This ensured that the Rudd government would come under considerable pressure to change Australia's stance.

Tom Calma had already been critical of the reasoning behind the Howard government's impending opposition to the declaration in his 2006 *Social Justice Report* and it was to him, again, that the Rudd government turned in 2008 for counsel on how to change course. Between April and August 2008, Calma sought and received 'a great deal of feedback' on the declaration

---

3   Calma became an inaugural member of the Ethics Council of the new representative body in January 2010—about the time he was finishing his term as Aboriginal and Torres Strait Islander Social Justice Commissioner within the Australian Human Rights Commission.

from Indigenous organisations and individuals (AHRC 2008). Others too were expressing strong views to the Rudd government during 2008 about changing Australia's stance (HRLRC and ILC 2008). After some criticism for not acting earlier, the Rudd government indicated in March 2009 that it would be making a statement belatedly giving Australia's support to the declaration.

Minister Macklin's speech at Parliament House in Canberra on 3 April 2009 described Australia's change of position to 'support' the declaration as 'another important step in re-setting the relationship between Indigenous and non-Indigenous Australians' (Macklin 2009d:1). She emphasised that under Article 1 of the declaration, Indigenous peoples 'as a collective or as individuals' enjoy 'all human rights and fundamental freedoms as recognised in international law'. She also noted 'with solemn reflection on our history and the failed policies of the past' that Article 8 indicated the right of Indigenous peoples 'not to be subject to forced assimilation or destruction of their culture' and that Article 10 said they were 'not to be forcibly removed from their lands or territories' (Macklin 2009d:2). Macklin emphasised that the declaration needed to be considered in its totality and that the right to self-determination of Indigenous peoples in Article 3 should be read in conjunction with Article 46, which stated that nothing in the declaration should impair the 'territorial integrity or political unity' of states such as Australia (Macklin 2009d:3). She also noted Article 7, identifying the right of Indigenous peoples 'to lives that are safe, secure and free from intimidation and violence', and Article 22, focusing on the rights of Indigenous 'elders, women, youth, children and people with disability'. Macklin saw these groups as 'vulnerable people' who needed particular attention and who also drew rights from more longstanding UN conventions (Macklin 2009d:4). Macklin was, quite explicitly here, defending the Rudd government's support for aspects of the NTER that were, at the time, the subject of a complaint before the UN Committee on the Elimination of Racial Discrimination and were, more generally, subject to strong criticism (Nicholson et al. 2009). Macklin noted and welcomed an impending visit of the UN Special Rapporteur for Indigenous Peoples, James Anaya, who would examine the NTER and other matters, and she also reiterated the Rudd government's intention to pass legislation that would 'lift the suspension of the *Racial Discrimination Act* in the Northern Territory' (Macklin 2009d:3–4). The minister was clearly keen to rebut any idea of inconsistency between the Rudd government's support for the Declaration on the Rights of Indigenous Peoples and what it was doing in the Northern Territory. The NTER was, as she saw it, pursuing Indigenous rights, even if it required some reform in how it was doing so.[4]

---

4   Anaya's report in February 2010 was of the view that the NTER, as then constituted, was contrary to the declaration and other human rights instruments (Anaya 2010).

Multilateral intergovernmental agreement making

One final aspect of the Rudd government's approach to Indigenous affairs, which emerged during its term rather than being clear at the outset, was development in multilateral intergovernmental agreement making. Rudd's proposed bipartisan 'joint policy commission' struggled to become a reality in the year after his apology address in February 2008, and perhaps multilateral intergovernmental agreement making emerged as an alternative way to project an image of national unity and concerted commitment in Indigenous affairs.

After a Council of Australian Governments (COAG) meeting in November 2008, it was announced that state and territory governments were joining with the Commonwealth in major reforms of their financial relations. A new Intergovernmental Agreement on Federal Financial Relations was being finalised, which would reduce 90 previous Specific Purpose Payments from the Commonwealth to the states and territories to just five (COAG 2008a). These five national agreements, with dollars attached, would be in the areas of health care, education, skills and workforce development, disability services and affordable housing. But there would also be a sixth, crosscutting intergovernmental agreement called the National Indigenous Reform Agreement. This sixth agreement focused on six 'close-the-gap' targets that had already been agreed to at other COAG meetings earlier in the year and it aimed to articulate a framework for achieving these targets (COAG 2008b). Although this agreement would not itself have dollars attached, it identified subsidiary Indigenous-specific national partnership agreements that would. Five of these were already identified and more were anticipated. One such national partnership agreement, signed in December 2008, focused on remote Indigenous housing and identified almost $5 billion that would be available to the states and territories over the next 10 years (COAG 2008c). Another, focusing on remote service delivery, adopted a more modest approach in identifying $188 million of commonwealth money to be combined with $104 million of state and territory funding over just a one-year period. The latter also identified that 'initial investment' would be concentrated in 26 remote locations: 15 in the Northern Territory, four in Queensland, three in Western Australia, two in South Australia and two in New South Wales (COAG 2008d).

Multilateral intergovernmental agreement making is not entirely new in Australian Indigenous affairs. In 1992, in the flurry of collaborative federalism initiated by the late Hawke and early Keating governments, a general multilateral agreement had been signed: the *National Commitment to Improved Outcomes in the Delivery of Programs and Services for Aboriginal Peoples and Torres Strait Islanders* (COAG 1992). Since that time, however, intergovernmental agreements in Indigenous affairs had been bilateral—between the Commonwealth and particular states and territories—rather than multilateral. The return to multilateralism, involving quite specific expenditure figures and conditions, marked an interesting development in Indigenous affairs in which the Commonwealth was possibly becoming more directive and even possibly setting up competition between the states and territories. The latter seemed to be demonstrated at the end of 2009 in the remote Indigenous housing partnership, when some states and territories were having trouble delivering results. After a COAG meeting one year on from the original signing, the Prime Minister announced that the National Partnership Agreement on Remote Indigenous Housing was undergoing 'renegotiation' to 'enable a more competitive process for allocation of funding by the Commonwealth' from financial year 2010–11 (Rudd 2009). In July 2010, Macklin announced that Western Australia had 'demonstrated its capacity to deliver additional capital works' and would receive an extra $4 million in 2010–11, while Queensland and South Australia would together be penalised this amount (Macklin 2010c). Multilateral agreement making was thus also turning into a form of competitive, centralised funding allocation and direction.

Another interesting aspect of this multilateralism was the appointment by the Rudd government in 2009 of a Coordinator-General for Remote Indigenous Services. This statutory officer would 'drive the implementation of major reforms in housing, infrastructure and employment in remote Indigenous communities' and 'report directly to the Minister for Indigenous Affairs'. Along with a requirement for a formal report twice a year to 'provide information to Commonwealth, state and territory agencies on obstacles within their areas of responsibility and advise the Minister for Indigenous Affairs and COAG on the need for any necessary changes', the Coordinator-General would be 'given the authority to coordinate across agencies, to cut through bureaucratic blockages and red tape, and to make sure services are delivered effectively' (Macklin 2009e). If this public management language is to be believed, Indigenous affairs was about to be transformed. Multilateral agreement making and the Coordinator-General were going to form the panacea and, unlike all the failed policies before them, would finally find the magic formula for Australian Indigenous affairs. But perhaps, like so much else in Indigenous affairs, there was more aspiration and moral indignation in this managerial language than strategy or capacity.

Evidence, competing principles and generational revolutions

The Rudd government's preferred frame for Indigenous affairs is the idea of an evidenced-based approach, which is said to transcend ideology. One of us has already critiqued this frame as an analytical approach and suggested instead the idea of three competing principles in Indigenous affairs: equality, choice and guardianship (Sanders 2009). Figure 12.1 arranges these principles in a triangular policy space. It also allows for three different interpretations of the equality principle and for relating the choice and guardianship principles to positive and negative views of Indigenous difference and diversity. These competing principles and their alternative interpretations make Indigenous affairs a complex policy arena, which can be drawn in quite different directions over time, through generational revolutions and the rebalancing principles.

Figure 12.2 suggests how dominant debates in Australian Indigenous affairs have moved since the 1930s. The generational revolution of the late 1960s and early 1970s reflected a move away from the principles of legal equality and guardianship on the right of this analytical schema towards the principles of socioeconomic equality and choice on the left. The more recent generational revolution in Indigenous affairs since the year 2000 would seem, at one level, to be a move back to the right towards the principle of guardianship. At another level, however, Indigenous affairs is, at all times, balancing the three interpretations of the equality principle and the choice and guardianship principles. Noel Pearson suggests that the 'quest' is for a 'radical centre' in Australian Indigenous policy in which 'policy positions' are 'much closer and more carefully calibrated than most people imagine'. He also suggests that this will involve continuing 'dialectical tension' between 'opposing principles', rather than a clear resolution of policy in favour of any one principle (Pearson 2007). This schema and Pearson's idea of the radical centre do not see evidence as either so significant or neutral as in the Rudd Labor perspective. Evidence always needs to be interpreted and contextualised and, in so being, is inevitably drawn into the balancing of competing principles. Good Indigenous affairs public policy—if Australia is ever to achieve it— will be based on a self-conscious awareness of competing principles and of the tendency towards generational revolutions in this difficult cross-cultural and highly morally charged policy arena. Simple notions of evidence-based policy are inadequate as a central idea for either understanding or judging Australian Indigenous affairs.

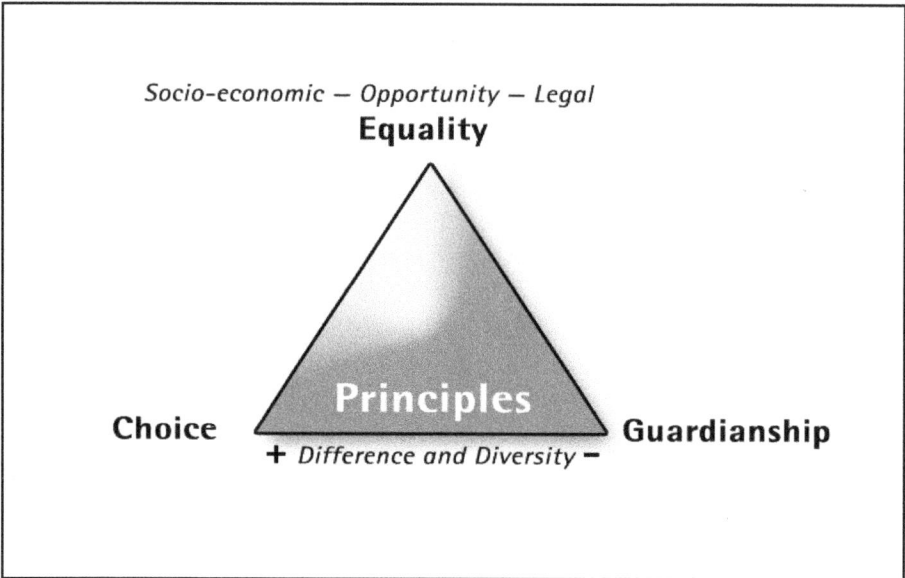

Figure 12.1 Competing principles in Indigenous affairs

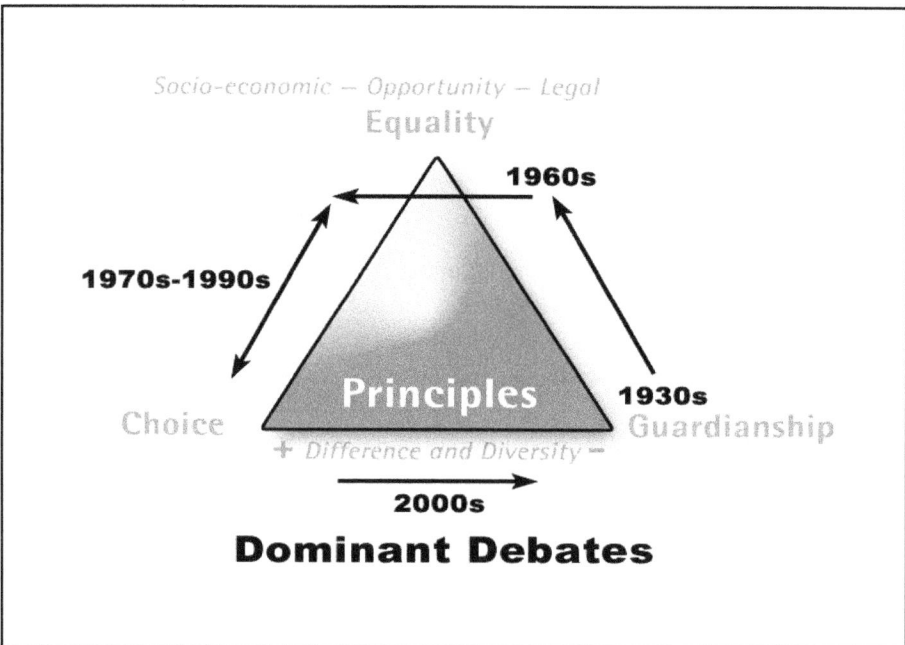

Figure 12.2 Dominant debates in Indigenous affairs

Will Sanders *is Senior Fellow and Deputy Director at the Centre for Aboriginal Economic Policy Research, Research School of Social Science, The Australian National University.*

Janet Hunt *is a Fellow in the Centre for Aboriginal Economic Policy Research, Research School of Social Sciences, The Australian National University.*

References

Aboriginal and Torres Strait Islander Social Justice Commissioner (ATSISJC) 2008a. *Building a Sustainable National Indigenous Representative Body— Issues for consideration*, Human Rights and Equal Opportunity Commission, Sydney.

Aboriginal and Torres Strait Islander Social Justice Commissioner (ATSISJC) 2008b. Speech for the Australian Institute of Aboriginal and Torres Strait Islander Studies Seminar Series, 4 August.

Altman, J. 2009. *Beyond closing the gap: valuing diversity in Indigenous Australia*, Working Paper 54, Centre for Aboriginal Economic Policy Research, The Australian National University, Canberra.

Anaya, J. 2010. Observations on the Northern Territory Emergency Response in Australia, Advance version, February, United Nations Special Rapporteur on Indigenous People, Office of the United Nations High Commissioner for Human Rights, Geneva, <http://www.hrlrc.org.au/files/Special-Rapporteur-Report-NTER.pdf>

Australian Government 2009a. Landmark reform to the welfare system, reinstatement of the *Racial Discrimination Act* and strengthening of the Northern Territory Emergency Response, Policy statement, Commonwealth of Australia, Canberra.

Australian Government 2009b. *Future directions for the Northern Territory Emergency Response*, Discussion Paper, 21 May, Commonwealth of Australia, Canberra.

Australian Government 2009c. *Report on the Northern Territory Emergency Response Redesign Consultations*, Commonwealth of Australia, Canberra.

Australian Human Rights Commission (AHRC) 2008. *Australia's Support for the Declaration on the Rights of Indigenous Peoples*, Australian Human Rights Commission, Sydney, <http://www.hreoc.gov.au/social_justice/declaration/comments.html>

Australian Human Rights Commission (AHRC) 2009a. National Indigenous workshop kicks off in Adelaide next week, Media release, 6 March, Australian Human Rights Commission, Sydney.

Australian Human Rights Commission (AHRC) 2009b. *Getting it Right— Progress towards a new national representative body: a community guide*, May, Australian Human Rights Commission, Sydney.

Australian Human Rights Commission (AHRC) 2009c. *Our Future in Our Hands— Creating a sustainable national Indigenous representative body: a community guide*, August, Australian Human Rights Commission, Sydney.

Australian Human Rights Commission (AHRC) 2010a. New congress to represent Aboriginal and Torres Strait Islanders, Media release, 2 May, Australian Human Rights Commission, Sydney.

Australian Human Rights Commission (AHRC) 2010b. First national executive is a milestone moment for Indigenous Australians, Media release, 2 May, Australian Human Rights Commission, Sydney.

Council of Australian Governments (COAG) 1992. *National Commitment to Improved Outcomes in the Delivery of Programs and Services for Aboriginal Peoples and Torres Strait Islanders*, Endorsed 7 December, Council of Australian Governments, Perth.

Council of Australian Governments (COAG) 2008a. *Communiqué*, 29 November, Council of Australian Governments, Canberra.

Council of Australian Governments (COAG) 2008b. *National Indigenous Reform Agreement*, November, Council of Australian Governments, Canberra.

Council of Australian Governments (COAG) 2008c. *National Partnership Agreement on Remote Indigenous Housing*, December, Council of Australian Governments, Canberra.

Council of Australian Governments (COAG) 2008d. *National Partnership Agreement on Remote Service Delivery*, December, Council of Australian Governments, Canberra.

Grattan, M. and Wright, T. 2008. 'Rudd rules out compensation', *The Age*, 2 February.

Human Rights Law Resource Centre and Indigenous Law Centre (HRLRC and ILC) 2008. UN Declaration on the Rights of Indigenous Peoples, Letter to the Hon. Kevin Rudd MP, Prime Minister, 16 May, Human Rights Law Resource Centre and Indigenous Law Centre.

Hunt, J. 2008. *Failure, evidence and new ideas*, Topical Issue Paper No. 1, Centre for Aboriginal Economic Policy Research, The Australian National University, Canberra.

Lennon, P. 2008. 'Cash is a mere gesture', *The Australian*, 29 January.

Macklin, J. 2008a. Closing the gap—building an Indigenous future, Address to the National Press Club, Canberra, 27 February.

Macklin, J. 2008b. Macklin meets Northern Territory Emergency Taskforce, Media release, 17 January, Parliament House, Canberra.

Macklin, J. 2008c. Permit system on Aboriginal land in NT, Media release, 17 February, Parliament House, Canberra.

Macklin, J. 2008d. NT Emergency Response Review Board, Media release, 6 June, Parliament House, Canberra.

Macklin, J. 2008e. Northern Territory Emergency Response—one year on, Media release, 20 June, Parliament House, Canberra.

Macklin, J. 2008f. Compulsory income management to continue as key NTER measure, Media release, 23 October, Parliament House, Canberra.

Macklin, J. 2008g. National Indigenous Council, Media release, 15 January, Parliament House, Canberra.

Macklin, J. 2009a. Strengthening the Northern Territory Emergency Response, Media release, 25 November, Parliament House, Canberra.

Macklin, J. 2009b. Speech, National Indigenous Representative Body Workshop, 11 March.

Macklin, J. 2009c. Australian Government response to 'Our Future in Our Hands', Media release, 22 November, Parliament House, Canberra.

Macklin, J. 2009d. Statement on the United Nations Declaration on the Rights of Indigenous Peoples, Speech, Parliament House, Canberra, 3 April.

Macklin, J. 2009e. Office of Coordinator-General of Remote Indigenous Services, Media release, 27 May, Parliament House, Canberra.

Macklin, J. 2010a. Major welfare reforms to support vulnerable Australians, Media release, 22 June, Parliament House, Canberra.

Macklin, J. 2010b. *Racial Discrimination Act* to be restored in the Northern Territory, Media release, 22 June, Parliament House, Canberra.

Macklin, J. 2010c. Remote Indigenous housing progress, Media release, 15 July, Parliament House, Canberra.

Nicholson, A., Behrendt, L., Vivian, A., Watson, N. and Harris, M. 2009. *Will They Be Heard?—A response to the NTER consultations June to August 2009*, Jumbunna Indigenous House of Learning, University of Technology, Sydney.

Parliament of Australia 2008. House of Representatives, *Debates*, 13 February, Parliament of Australia, Canberra.

Pearson, N. 2007. 'White guilt, victimhood and the quest for a radical centre', *Griffith Review*, vol. 16, pp. 13–58.

Rudd, K. 2009. Renegotiation of the National Partnership Agreement on Remote Indigenous Housing, Media release, 7 December, Brisbane.

Sanders, W. 2005. 'Never even adequate: Indigenous affairs and reconciliation', in C. Aulich and R. Wettenhall (eds), *Howard's Second and Third Governments: Australian Commonwealth Administration 1998–2004*, UNSW Press, Sydney.

Sanders, W. 2008. 'In the name of failure: a generational revolution in Indigenous affairs', in C. Aulich and R. Wettenhall (eds), *Howard's Fourth Government: Australian Commonwealth Administration 2004–2007*, UNSW Press, Sydney.

Sanders, W. 2009. *Ideology, evidence and competing principles: from Brough to Rudd via Pearson and the NTER*, Discussion Paper 289, Centre for Aboriginal Economic Policy Research, The Australian National University, Canberra.

Yu, P., Ella Duncan, M. and Gray, B. 2008. *Northern Territory Emergency Response: Report of the NTER Review Board*, October, Commonwealth of Australia, Canberra.

13. Foreign policy

ANDREW CARR AND CHRIS ROBERTS

In 2007, when Kevin Rudd was sworn in as Prime Minister, he was widely expected to be a strong leader of Australian foreign policy (Manne 2008). While most analysts believed that a strong alliance with the United States would be maintained, it was also anticipated that Rudd would reassert a traditional Labor preference for stronger engagement with Asia. For those concerned that the previous Howard government had drifted too far into the orbit of US influence, Rudd also provided the hope that Australia would return to a more independent middle-power activism with action on issues such as nuclear non-proliferation and climate change. Finally, Rudd's experience in China—first as a student and later as a diplomat—also suggested an opportunity to solidify Australia's relationship with China, its largest non-allied trading partner. Many of these perceptions, however, were not fully realised by the conclusion of Rudd's prime ministership and problematic episodes in foreign policy were, at times, compounded by the Prime Minister's chaotic and overcentralised leadership style. While his personal activism did lead to a number of foreign policy successes, including the elevation of the G-20 as the world's primary economic forum, on balance, Rudd's single term in office did not live up to expectations.

DFAT, defence and new directions in Australian foreign policy

Following the election of the Labor Party, Rudd quickly sought to make his mark in the management of Australia's foreign affairs. While commentators have noted the general centralisation of government in the Prime Minister's office (Kelly 2005:1), Rudd expanded this practice considerably and quickly sought to centralise the flow of information within the government as well as making key appointments. For example, Duncan Lewis—formerly from the Defence Signals Directorate—was appointed as the first National Security Advisor; his duties included the creation of the *National Security Statement* as well as the Counter-Terrorism White Paper and the Defence White Paper. Rudd also appointed personal envoys to report on challenging issues: Richard Woolcott in connection with the Asia-Pacific Community (APC) proposal and Ross Garnaut in relation to climate change. While this approach enabled him to closely scrutinise government policies, Rudd was criticised for a lack of consultation and the practice also resulted in delayed policy implementation (Stuart 2010:150).

Rudd selected Robert McClelland to be Australia's Foreign Minister, but this appointment did not survive Labor's transition into government. McClelland's primary faux pas occurred three weeks before the election when, in the midst of Indonesian hearings concerning the death penalty for the Bali Bombers, he criticised the use of the death penalty in Indonesia. Consequently, Rudd was forced to replace McClelland with Stephen Smith. As Smith had no prior experience in foreign policy, a major power imbalance emerged and Rudd further exacerbated this through his centralisation of strategic analysis into the Department of the Prime Minister and Cabinet and/or his own office (Stuart 2010:viii). As Graeme Dobell (2009a) subsequently argued, 'Kevin Rudd [was] his own über Foreign Minister'.

Given Rudd's early career work for the Department of Foreign Affairs and Trade (DFAT)—at one point being groomed as a future department secretary (Macklin 2007:88)—he was relatively well positioned to adopt the *über* role. Despite this, relations between Rudd and DFAT remained awkward, with some DFAT officials complaining that he was an overly demanding taskmaster who interfered in the day-to-day running of the department (Flitton 2009:5). Because of these tendencies, some DFAT officials complained that they had been reduced to little more than a 'visa-processing offshoot of the prime minister's office' (Stuart 2010:130). Consequently, after Rudd was removed from the prime ministership, Stephen Smith, as Foreign Minister, deemed it necessary to declare that DFAT needed to 'return itself entirely to the centre of policy deliberations in the national capital and to make sure that we were contesting advice and contesting views' (Grattan 2010:4). Further—and despite his criticism of the previous Howard government for reducing the budget of DFAT—Rudd similarly reduced the department's budget in 2008 (DFAT 2008) with only small budgetary increases in 2009 and 2010. Problematically, he also increased the department's responsibilities and this led to reduced morale (Weisser 2008). Thus, under the leadership of Australia's first *diplomat-in-chief*, Australia continued to maintain one of the smallest international diplomatic presences of any Organisation for Economic Cooperation and Development (OECD) country (Lowy Institute 2009).

Rudd also broke with a century of Labor Party tradition by demanding (and receiving) the right to choose his own cabinet (Donald 2007). His choice for the Defence Minister, Joel Fitzgibbon, however, was never able to develop a sound working relationship with the department. Notably, 16 months into the term, officials from defence were accused of leaking a 'dirt file' detailing a potentially inappropriate relationship between Fitzgibbon and a Chinese businesswoman with connections to the Chinese Communist Party (CCP) (Baker et al. 2009:1). This development—combined with accusations that Fitzgibbon's brother (the director of the private health insurance company NIB) had been provided inappropriate access to government officials—led to the first and only ministerial resignation from the Rudd government. Fitzgibbon was replaced with John Faulkner (Coorey 2010:1).

Rudd's managerial style also led to delays with the delivery of the Defence White Paper (Walters 2008b:2). Nonetheless, it provided a bold reassessment of Australian military strategy (White 2009) and, in line with the budgetary trends of the Howard government, recommended annual 3 per cent increases to the defence budget. The final report was, however, also notable for simultaneously demonstrating the strengths and weaknesses of Rudd's prime ministership with some sections being highly lucid in their analysis but with inadequate deliberation of the implications of other sections (Hugh White, Interview with authors, Canberra, 2010). For example, the paper openly discussed the implications of both a rising China and a potential decline of US interest in the Asia-Pacific but, as discussed later, its 'muddled' language needlessly strained relations with China (Garnaut et al. 2009). Critics also doubted whether the $20 billion in budgetary savings proposed by the White Paper were feasible (White 2009).

In the context of public perception, the Rudd government successfully obtained the confidence of the Australian public in its handling of international affairs (Crikey 2010). Such confidence was, in part, aided by disunity and change in the opposition as they experimented with three different shadow foreign ministers—Andrew Robb, Helen Coonan and Julie Bishop—during the Rudd period. These three ministers were relatively ineffective in their attempts to question the Rudd government's foreign policy and, in terms of public opinion, made some serious errors in judgment. Julie Bishop, for example, suggested that Australia should acquiesce to Chinese demands and not grant a visa to Rebiya Kadeer, a Uighur dissident and documentary filmmaker. Bishop also 'blundered badly' (Stuart 2010:159) when she likely abused her privileged access to classified material by publicly asserting that Australian intelligence services forged foreign passports. Meanwhile, some analysts were critical of the lack of attention by the opposition to the formation of creditable alternative polices for defence and foreign affairs—at least beyond some strong but shallow rhetoric concerning asylum-seekers (Ungerer 2010).

Middle-power activism: more bark than bite?

Beyond the administration of DFAT and the Department of Defence, Rudd was also determined to return Australia to an activist middle-power role. His middle-power vision for Australia was first outlined in a 2006 article in *The Monthly* magazine entitled 'Faith in politics'. Rudd described his vision as

> one which seeks to take Chifley's vision of a 'light on the hill' into an uncertain century. This is an enlarging vision that sees Australia taking the lead on global climate change...on the Millennium Development Goals...This is an Australia that becomes a leader, not a follower, in the redesign of the rules of the international order that we helped craft in 1945, to render future genocides both intolerable under international law and impossible through international resolve. (Rudd 2006)

While in office, Rudd reaffirmed this ambition in his 2008 *National Security Statement*. After reiterating his support for both the ANZUS alliance and multilateral institutions, he declared that his government would 'promote an international environment, particularly in the Asia-Pacific region, that is stable, peaceful and prosperous, together with a global rules-based order which enhances Australia's national interests' (Rudd 2008a:2). Rudd envisaged an Australia that would be a leader in the spread of global ideas and the promotion of multilateralism and international law. He also envisioned an Australia that would be at the forefront of tackling climate change and that would lead a charge against both nuclear non-proliferation and whaling.

Thanks to the work of the Hawke and Keating governments and, to a lesser extent, the Howard government, Australia is widely seen as a 'global champion of non-proliferation' (Lantis 2008:1). Such perceptions have been reinforced by Australia's hesitancy to fully utilise and profit from the possession of the world's largest uranium deposits. Rudd built on these perceptions by founding the International Commission on Nuclear Non-Proliferation and Disarmament (ICNND) in early 2008. The commission, which was co-chaired by two former foreign ministers—one from Australia (Gareth Evans), the other from Japan (Yoriko Kawaguchi)—was established to provide policy recommendations concerning practical short, medium and long-term steps to control proliferation and, eventually, complete nuclear disarmament. The commission was supported by the United States following the election of President Barack Obama, as nuclear disarmament has been a priority for the President (Davies 2009:10). Obama also recognised Australia's potential middle-power role and invited Rudd to speak at the 2010 Nuclear Security Summit—the largest gathering of world leaders since the founding of the United Nations. The summit could have been one of the highlights of the Prime Minister's term as it would have demonstrated the importance of Australia in US foreign policy and provided Australia with a unique opportunity to influence international policies about a key global challenge. Because of Rudd's overcentralisation, however, the Prime Minister became distracted with the details of health reform and, following a new wave of criticism caricaturing him as 'Kevin 747', he cancelled his attendance (Stuart 2010:130).

Throughout Rudd's prime ministership, he pressured Japan to agree to a complete prohibition of whaling. His strategy evolved from increasing monitoring and public denunciation in 2008 to seeking recourse from the International Court of Justice (ICJ) by 2010. This activism, however, risked a relationship with a key strategic ally in terms of trade and the promotion of other goals such as nuclear non-proliferation or new forms of regional multilateralism. Nevertheless, Rudd's attempt to influence the standards of appropriate behaviour in Japan was reminiscent of the Keating government and its concept of 'good international citizenship'; however, his diplomacy did not seem to apply the lessons from that period. Gareth Evans, the foreign minister most clearly identified with the concept, set up four criteria for successful middle-power activism: 'careful identification of opportunities for action, sufficient physical capacity to follow issues through, including the energy and stamina to ensure that good ideas did not fall by the wayside, intellectual imagination and creativity, and credibility through independence and consistency' (Scott 1999:234). Australia was unable to influence Japan on the issue, inter alia, and the June 2010 negotiations through the International Whaling Commission subsequently collapsed.

The preceding analysis indicates that while Rudd possessed intellectual imagination and creativity, his record demonstrated a limited capacity to follow through with the implementation of ideas and policies. For example, his pre-election pledge that he would seek to prosecute Iranian President, Mahmoud Ahmadinejad, at the ICJ for 'inciting genocide' was later dropped when it received significant criticism (Shanahan 2007:1). Rudd also indicated his strong opposition to the use of the death penalty anywhere in the world, but, following the earlier mentioned statement by Robert McClelland, Rudd dropped the subject.

Rudd's focus on action probably came at the expense of exploring more 'niche' opportunities where Australia's contribution as a so-called middle power would be greater. Thus, foreign policy analysts, such as former DFAT secretary Stuart Harris (Interview with authors, Canberra, 2010), have noted that a feature of prime minister-centred governance has been a focus on short-term initiatives with little preparation or follow through. Further, the chaotic and overly centralised leadership style of the Prime Minister probably impacted on his attempts to utilise multilateral forums to promote Australia's interests and/or influence interstate behaviour.

Source: David Pope, *The Canberra Times*, 8 January 2009

Multilateralism in Australia's international relations: a mixed record?

Rudd was well aware of how difficult it is for middle powers, such as Australia, to effectively contribute to the evolution of international policy concerning international security and economic issues. In order to overcome these disadvantages, Rudd fervently believed in the utility of multilateral organisations (such as the United Nations) as a means for middle powers to exercise a voice. On this issue, he appeared to identify with Herbert 'Doc' Evatt and his significant contributions to that organisation. In 2002, he suggested to Parliament that 'Evatt grasped this single and central fact: for small powers, the multilateral system offers the only chance; for middle powers, it offers the best chance' (Rudd 2002:4329).The similarities between Rudd and Evatt are worth noting. Both were passionate about foreign policy but even after taking over the leadership of their party they remained relative outsiders in their own parties. Both were very demanding taskmasters, and neither was well liked by his colleagues. While Evatt was allowed to contest and lose three elections as ALP opposition leader in the 1950s, Rudd is the only prime minister to have been deposed in his first term. Rudd maintained this perspective through to his election as Prime Minister, adding, in 2008, that there is 'a brittleness in a foreign policy based only on bilateral relations' (Rudd 2008a:5). In this vein,

Rudd promoted the G-20, launched a bid for a seat at the UN Security Council and, more controversially, attempted to create a new multilateral security organisation for the Asia-Pacific. Of these three initiatives, however, the Prime Minister's most successful and important contribution to international order and Australian foreign policy occurred when he helped to secure the G-20 as the premier financial forum for world leaders (Fullilove 2010).

During the Asian financial crisis in 1998, Australia supported an initiative by US President Bill Clinton to establish the G-20, as it would cover two-thirds of the world's population or 90 per cent of the global economy (Costello and Coleman 2008:183). Despite the 'nurturing and building work' that then Treasurer, Peter Costello, put into the forum (Dobell 2010), the G-7 (later G-8) remained the premier economic summit. In 2008, however, Rudd utilised the global financial crisis to successfully lobby to increase the significance of the G-20. Australia's diplomacy commenced with the United States, where Rudd convinced Obama to support replacing the G-8 with the G-20. According to US Assistant Secretary of State, Kurt Campbell, Rudd 'was relentless in his making of the case, he persuaded key players, made the case with a number of players who were a bit reluctant' (Sheridan 2009:13). Some foreign policy analysts interpreted Rudd's role in the G-20 as his most 'redeeming international achievement' (Medcalf 2010). Other analysts went as far as to suggest that Rudd's contribution to the G-20 would 'alone' ensure a positive appraisal of his foreign policy record (Dobell 2010). For Rudd, the benefits of the G-20 were clear: 'before the G20, global economic decision-making was dominated by the G8—a small group of major economies mostly in Europe and North America. Australia was left out in the cold, cut off from the major economic decisions of our time' (Dobell 2009b:5).

Rudd also sought an influential position for Australia in the world's top security forum—a UN Security Council seat in 2013. This initiative was symbolically important given the previous Howard government's scepticism of the United Nations (Sheridan 2004). While Australia's bid came several years after Finland's and Luxembourg's, Australia quickly gained momentum by dedicating $13.1 million to the task (Fullilove 2009:2). Nonetheless, the Liberal–National opposition described the bid as a 'quixotic pursuit...[a] wild goose chase' whose real purpose was an 'ego-driven tool to promote [Rudd] internationally' (Dorling 2009:5). They further argued that the bid would more likely cost $1.5 billion when any associated aid and development funding was included (Milne 2009:10). While the Prime Minister's efforts were successful in the context of the G-20, and the jury is still out concerning Australia's bid for a Security Council seat, Rudd soon found his vision to establish a multilateral security organisation in the Asia-Pacific far more difficult.

Since the late 1960s, rather than being satisfied with merely 'engaging' the Asia-Pacific, successive Australian governments have demonstrated a desire to build and expand regional institutions to facilitate goals such as trade liberalisation. Bob Hawke was the first to succeed when he created the Asia-Pacific Economic Cooperation (APEC) group in 1989 through a combination of good timing and skilful diplomacy (Dobell 2000:18). His successor, Paul Keating, had hoped that it could eventually be developed in a manner that would be closer to the model of the European Union but key regional policy makers believed that such an institutionalised and legally binding approach would be unworkable in the context of East Asia. Further, some of the South-East Asian states were concerned that APEC could threaten the central role of the Association of South-East Asian Nations (ASEAN) in regional institutions for dialogue and cooperation. Given this concern, ASEAN lobbied to maintain ASEAN's modus operandi, including 'consensus-based decision-making', in APEC (Stubbs 2008:464). Nonetheless, Rudd returned to 'treading a well-worn path' (Heseltine 2009:2) when he announced (without forewarning) his vision to establish an Asia-Pacific Community (APC) by 2020. In a 4 June 2008 speech, he argued:

> We need to have a vision for an Asia Pacific Community...A regional institution which spans the entire Asia-Pacific region—including the United States, Japan, China, India, Indonesia and the other states of the region. A regional institution which is able to engage in the full spectrum of dialogue, cooperation and action on economic and political matters and future challenges related to security. The purpose is to encourage the development of a genuine and comprehensive sense of community whose habitual operating principle is cooperation. (Rudd 2008b:6)

Rudd's proposal for the APC was initially well received in Australia, where Paul Kelly (2008:16), for example, declared it 'one of Australia's most ambitious foreign policy initiatives for some years'. Rudd subsequently appointed Richard Woolcott—a former DFAT head who had undertaken a similar role for Hawke vis-a-vis APEC—as a special envoy to travel to and consult with senior policy makers throughout Asia. The ability of Woolcott to promote the Rudd initiative was, however, undermined from the outset because many of his former government contacts had left office. Further, the impetuousness of much of Rudd's foreign policy was also evident in the lack of planning behind the proposal as Woolcott was given only a few hours' notice before his appointment was announced (Thayer 2009:4).

A further problem with the APC concerned confusion about its intended purpose and institutional design. While the Prime Minister stated that he wanted to 'begin the regional debate' (Rudd 2008b:7), his references to the European Union were interpreted by many as evidence of Australia pushing for a specific design (Frost 2009:8). Regardless of whether this was true, both critics and supporters were united in their call for more information (Flitton 2008:6; Heseltine 2009:2). Meanwhile, after visiting 21 countries and meeting more than

300 officials and experts, Woolcott reported that while there was 'interest' in the APC proposal, there was a lack of firm support for its implementation in the near future. Further, many policy makers raised concerns that the implementation of a new regional body would result in further strains on regional governments as the members of ASEAN, for example, are already attending close to 700 meetings each year. While the key powers—China and the United States—expressed 'interest', they were also not willing to make a firm commitment; their ambivalence was a critical obstacle to the APC as the ability to manage political and economic challenges in the evolving US–China relationship was a key motive behind the proposal (Thayer 2009:4).

While other countries, such as South Korea, Japan, New Zealand and Vietnam, also indicated a 'polite' interest, Singapore emerged as the main opponent of the idea. The potency of Singapore's opposition was such that it gained a voice in the (limited) Australian media coverage (see Koh 2009:14) and was even accused of attempting to publicly embarrass Rudd (Hartcher 2009:11). Given perceptions of Singapore's 'Western-friendly' identity, its opposition was indicative of the level of difficulty the APC faced. Not all commentary in Singapore, however, was negative as Rudd was praised—a likely face-saving gesture—for having forced a regional discussion about future multilateralism including reforms to the current security institutions of the Asia-Pacific. Likewise, there was little trace of hostility towards Rudd for his proposal with Australia's 'odd-man-in' status (Higgott and Nossal 2008:624) historically serving to exempt it from some of the more 'face'-bound regional norms (Dobell 2000:46–7). Still, the combination of 1) a lack of consultation, 2) a related perception that the proposal would undermine ASEAN centrality, 3) the problem of limited 'inclusiveness' in terms of membership, and 4) the inability of Australia to garner strong support from the more powerful members of the proposed organisation, meant that Rudd's APC proposal was—as Singapore's Ambassador, Barry Desker, described—'dead in the water' from the outset (Walters 2008a).

In view of the reception of the APC, Rudd offered a mea culpa during a May 2009 speech at Singapore's Shangri-la Dialogue, where he 'lavishly' praised ASEAN (Thayer 2009:5). Further, he reframed his proposal to be more ASEAN friendly including a suggestion (to the consternation of some) that the APEC leaders meeting should be downgraded in order to support a regional commitment for his APC proposal (Shanahan 2010). Despite these belated attempts to resurrect the proposal, Rudd was forced to publicly acknowledge that the APC was finished a few months later (Callick 2010:9). Rather than being a surprise, this acknowledgment was inevitable as, under the best of circumstances, Rudd's proposal was unlikely to compete with the growing web of multilateral economic and security organisations throughout the Asia-Pacific. This web included the recent emergence of the East Asia Summit (EAS) in addition to

ASEAN, the ASEAN Regional Forum, the ASEAN+3 (APT), APEC, the South Asian Association for Regional Cooperation (SAARC) and the Shanghai Cooperation Organisation (SCO). A more successful approach could have been to focus on modifying or even merging some of these regional arrangements—a task Australian prime ministers have usually set aside in favour of bold new proposals (Griffiths and Wesley 2010:21).

Nonetheless, Rudd's diplomacy did reinvigorate a debate about the future of the EAS and, in June 2010, ASEAN expanded the forum from 16 to 18 members including the United States and Russia. Thus, at the cost of the Prime Minister's time, a little reputation and a $1.4 million conference in December 2009, Rudd's activism did have some impact (JSCFADT 2010). Other aspects of Australian multilateral relations remained strong. On 27 February 2009, Australia and New Zealand signed a free-trade agreement (FTA) with ASEAN— the Australia–ASEAN–New Zealand Free Trade Agreement (AANZFTA)—the 'most comprehensive trade agreement that ASEAN has ever negotiated' (Dobell 2009b:142). Meanwhile, Australia was also invited by ASEAN to join with the Asian block in the Asia–Europe Meeting (ASEM)—a symbolically important invitation given Australia's longstanding identity as a European outpost.

From bilateral relations to the entry of Julia Gillard as Prime Minister

While Rudd's proposals for an APC and efforts against whaling impacted on Australia's relationship with Singapore and Japan respectively, these policies generated little sustained damage. The same cannot be said in the case of India, where Rudd's multilateral instincts led him to cancel a former Howard government agreement to sell uranium to India that would be outside the Non-Proliferation Treaty (NPT) framework. Despite Rudd's reservations concerning the former bilateral arrangement, some analysts believe that the NPT is unworkable and inappropriate in the context of India and that Australia should, therefore, make an exception (Ungerer 2010). Nonetheless, Australia's termination of the agreement strained India–Australia relations (Mayer and Jain 2010:140), which were further exacerbated by a series of assaults on Indian students in Melbourne during 2009. The frequency of these assaults incited strong condemnation from Indian officials and the adverse media coverage was serious enough to warrant the dispatch to India of Deputy Prime Minister, Julia Gillard. Relations with Indonesia, in contrast, proved to be more resilient despite potential strains over the number of asylum-seekers passing through Indonesian waters. For example, the extent to which Australia–Indonesia relations have improved was evident when, in March 2010, Susilo Bambang Yudhoyono became the first Indonesian President to address a joint sitting of Australia's Parliament.

In the context of US relations, while the Howard government had established a very strong partnership with former President George W. Bush (Sheridan 2006), the Rudd government did not maintain the same level of bilateral affinity due to various ideological differences and the pledge by the Australian Labor Party (ALP) to withdraw Australian troops from Iraq. When Obama became President, however, an ideological reconvergence occurred. In a 2010 interview with the ABC, President Obama praised Rudd as 'somebody who I probably share as much of a world view as any world leader out there, I find him smart but humble, he works wonderfully well in multilateral settings, he's always constructive, incisive' (ABC 2010). While Obama's election rendered it easier to withdraw Australian troops from Iraq, Obama's focus on Afghanistan validated Rudd's argument that Afghanistan should be the cornerstone of the war on terrorism and this, in turn, meant that the Australian government needed to back its words with a tangible military commitment (Dart 2008). Consequently, pressure from Obama, combined with the departure of other countries from Afghanistan, led to a 40 per cent increase in Australia's military deployment (Pearlman 2009:2). Meanwhile, two postponed trips to Australia and Asia were interpreted by some as a sign of the President's lack of interest in the region (Noonan 2010:15; Norington 2010:17). Nonetheless, on balance, the US–Australia relationship remained one of Australia's most robust and easily maintained bilateral relationships.

Positive relations with China, in contrast, were not so easily maintained despite Rudd's previous in-country experience. For example, a bold lecture on human rights at a Chinese university in 2008 was not well received by the CCP and marked the beginning of a temporary decline in relations. While his statements provided an early indication that the Rudd government would be less willing to compromise its moral authority for material gain, later actions undermined this principled stand. As noted earlier, the release of Australia's Defence White Paper also contributed to a decline in relations with China. Crucially, the document contained an explicit discussion of defence concerns about Chinese military modernisation (Tubilewicz 2010:152). The White Paper's strategic concerns were followed by a recommendation that Australia needed to substantially strengthen its military forces, with the strong implication that Australia needed to be operationally ready and prepared for a future conflict with China—a strategy that was immediately criticised by former Prime Minister Keating (2009:8).

The Chinese Government indicated that it was 'amazed' and 'displeased' with the White Paper and denied that its military modernisation program posed any strategic threat to Australia or the Asia-Pacific more broadly (Tubilewicz 2010:153). Further, some former Chinese officials went as far as to characterise the White Paper as little more than a 'crazy', 'stupid' and 'dangerous' document that 'risked inciting an arms race across the region' (Garnaut et al. 2009:2). Meanwhile, tension in Australia–China relations was compounded when the board of the Rio Tinto mining company withdrew from an agreement worth $19.5 billion that would have enabled Chinalco—a Chinese 'state-owned enterprise' (SOE)—to acquire a majority stake in the company. Soon after, Stern Hu, an Australian employee of Rio Tinto, was arrested on charges of accepting bribes and stealing commercial state secrets and certain analysts interpreted these actions to be retribution for Rio Tinto's withdrawal from negotiations with Chinalco (Sainsbury 2010:26). Despite a domestic outcry, the Rudd government made no significant protest against Hu's imprisonment and merely sought a transparent trial, which, in the end, was not granted.

While Australia's relations with China began to improve by late 2009, Rudd never managed to forge the closeness that many expected. Nonetheless, via the Defence White Paper, Rudd did manage to ensure that Australia thought seriously about the long-term strategic implications of a rising China (White, Interview with authors, Canberra, 2010). Despite this, Rudd also faced criticism that in the pursuit of economic opportunities he was overly acquiescent to a foreign authoritarian government (Middleton 2009). Hugh White (Interview with authors, Canberra, 2010) suggests that, given the difficulties Rudd faced with China, together with some of his multilateral diplomacy, he should have focused on more niche diplomacy for the purpose of elevating Australia's international status by, for example, helping to mediate relations between the United States and a rising China. Such diplomacy, if conducted in a benign and subtle fashion, might be better received internationally and, in turn, would more effectively employ a potential 'middle-power' role.

Conclusion

In the context of foreign affairs, the Rudd government came to office with great potential and its early displays of administrative confidence and vision added to this perception. While maintaining the main pillars of Australian foreign policy—such as the ANZUS Treaty—Rudd envisioned a more activist middle-power role for Australia. This was most clearly evident through activism on nuclear non-proliferation, climate change, whaling and the pursuit of a more binding and institutionalised security organisation in the Asia-Pacific. In the case of the last, the proposal was poorly timed and under-prepared with the result that it received little more than polite interest. The APC proposal was, however, motivated by the need for both local stakeholders and major powers to come together and constructively address some of the fundamental security issues and disputes that continue to afflict the Asia-Pacific region. The proposal was also motivated by a general recognition by Australia, and several other countries in the Asia-Pacific, of the necessity of ensuring that the United States remains engaged in the region in both the economic and the security spheres. Nonetheless, these goals have begun to take form in the context of the EAS and its expanded membership. History might not provide Rudd with significant credit for this shift but, nonetheless, he did make an important contribution to the debate.

Beyond the APC, Rudd also sought an enhanced role in other multilateral institutions including a UN Security Council seat and a seat for Australia in the upgraded G-20. While his two and a half years in office were not without foreign policy achievements, the abrupt termination of his prime ministership initially left any analysis of his foreign policy with a lingering sense of 'what if?' A second term could have witnessed the development of a more delegated work style and policy flow that could have provided a formidable base to an activist prime minister. A second term could have seen him fully consolidate his extensive experience in the diplomatic corps in a way that could be better utilised at the prime ministerial level. While Rudd's own centralising tendencies and short period in office have ensured that 'a great deal of sound and fury ha[s] ended up signifying nothing' (Stuart 2010:154), his new appointment as foreign minister means that he has an additional opportunity to modify (if not rewrite) his foreign policy record. Thus, history could have recorded the Rudd government's foreign policy as one that over-promised but under-delivered, but the final verdict now has to wait until the current Gillard government concludes its period in office.

Andrew Carr *is a PhD student at the University of Canberra.*

Chris Roberts *is an Assistant Professor in the Faculty of Business and Government, University of Canberra.*

References

Australian Broadcasting Corporation (ABC) 2010. 'Face to face with Obama', *7.30 Report*, ABC TV, 14 April.

Baker, R., Dorling, P. and McKenzie, N. 2009. 'Defence leaks dirt file on own minister', *Sydney Morning Herald*, 26 March, p. 1.

Callick, R. 2010. 'Kevin Rudd's Asia vision quietly buried', *The Australian*, 21 June, p. 9.

Coorey, P. 2010. 'Labor's Minister for Integrity calls time', *Brisbane Times*, 8 July, p. 1.

Costello, P. and Coleman, P. 2008. *The Costello Memoirs*, Melbourne University Press, Carlton, Vic.

Dart, J. 2008. 'Rudd congratulates Obama but rejects Afghanistan troop boost', *The Age*, 7 November.

Davies, A. 2009. 'Biden to take up Rudd's nuclear arms push', *Sydney Morning Herald*, 16 February, p. 10.

Department of Foreign Affairs and Trade (DFAT) 2008. *Department of Foreign Affairs and Trade Budget Savings*, Department of Foreign Affairs and Trade, Commonwealth of Australia, Canberra.

Dobell, G. 2000. *Australia Finds Home: The choices and chances of an Asia Pacific journey*, ABC Books, Sydney.

Dobell, G. 2009a. 'The Prime Minister's Foreign Minister', *The Interpreter*, 22 June, The Lowy Institute, Sydney.

Dobell, G. 2009b. 'Australia–East Asia/US relations: Australia adjusts to new realities', *Comparative Connections: A Quarterly E-Journal on East Asian Bilateral Relations*, vol. 11, no. 3, pp. 135–52.

Dobell, G. 2010. 'The Kevin's foreign affairs pass mark', *The Interpreter*, 20 January, The Lowy Institute, Sydney.

Donald, P. 2007. 'Rudd breaks tradition to select own federal cabinet', *ABC Local Radio* [Sydney], 26 November.

Dorling, P. 2009. 'Fixing DFAT will take a long time: Smith', *The Canberra Times*, 19 March, p. 5.

Crikey 2010. 'Essential report', *Crikey*, 12 April.

Flitton, D. 2008. 'Experts offer mixed reviews of ambitious forum plan', *The Age*, 6 June, p. 6.

Flitton, D. 2009. 'PM blocks diplomatic posting', *The Age*, 25 May, p. 5.

Frost, F. 2009. *Australia's Proposal for an 'Asia Pacific Community': Issues and prospects*, Parliamentary Library, Commonwealth of Australia, Canberra.

Fullilove, M. 2009. *The Case for Australia's UN Security Council Bid*, The Lowy Institute, Sydney.

Fullilove, M. 2010. 'Gillard has different global view', *Australian Financial Review*, 1 July, p. 67.

Garnaut, J., Grattan, M. and Davies, A. 2009. 'Military build-up "risks new Asian arms race"', *The Age*, 4 May, p. 2.

Grattan, M. 2010. 'Bigger role for DFAT after Rudd, says Smith', *The Age*, 5 June, p. 4.

Griffiths, M. and Wesley, M. 2010. 'Taking Asia seriously', *Australian Journal of Political Science*, vol. 45, no. 1, pp. 13–28.

Hartcher, P. 2009. 'Rudd puts lesson in rat cunning to use', *Sydney Morning Herald*, 8 December, p. 11.

Heseltine, C. 2009. 'Asia-Pacific community: reinventing the wheel?', *The Asialink Essays*, 7 September, University of Melbourne, Carlton, Vic.

Higgott, R. and Nossal, K. R. 2008. 'Odd man in, odd man out: Australia's liminal position in Asia revisited—a reply to Ann Capling', *The Pacific Review*, vol. 21, no. 5, pp. 623–34.

Joint Standing Committee on Foreign Affairs, Defence and Trade (JSCFADT) 2010. Answers to questions on notice from Department of Foreign Affairs and Trade, Additional estimates 2009–2010, February 2010, Joint Standing Committee on Foreign Affairs, Defence and Trade, Commonwealth of Australia, Canberra.

Keating, P. 2009. Australia and Asia and the new world order after the financial crisis, John Curtin Prime Ministerial Library Anniversary Lecture, Perth, 2 July.

Kelly, P. 2005. *Re-Thinking Australian Governance—The Howard legacy*, Academy of the Social Sciences in Australia, Canberra.

Kelly, P. 2008. 'Shape of the future', *The Australian*, 20 December, p. 16.

Koh, T. 2009. 'Rudd's reckless regional rush', *The Australian*, 18 December, p. 14.

Lantis, J. S. 2008. 'Elections and enduring realities: Australia's nuclear debate', *Arms Control Today*, vol. 38, no. 3.

Lowy Institute 2009. *Australia's Diplomatic Deficit: Reinvesting in our instruments of international policies*, The Lowy Institute, Sydney.

Macklin, R. 2007. *Kevin Rudd: The biography*, Penguin Group, Melbourne.

Manne, R. 2008. 'What is Rudd's agenda?', *The Monthly*, vol. 40.

Mayer, P. and Jain, P. 2010. 'Beyond cricket: Australia–India evolving relations', *Australian Journal of Political Science*, vol. 45, no. 1, pp. 133–48.

Medcalf, R. 2010. 'Rudd: bewildering in Asia', *The Interpreter*, 25 June, The Lowy Institute, Sydney.

Middleton, K. 2009. 'Risk in Rudd's China advocacy', *The Canberra Times*, 28 March.

Milne, G. 2009. 'Stern Hu forgotten in Kevin Rudd's hopeless UN quest', *The Australian*, 20 July, p. 10.

Noonan, P. 2010. 'Now for the slaughter', *Wall Street Journal*, 20 March, p. A15.

Norington, B. 2010. 'Now we know we're off Barack Obama's radar', *The Australian*, 20 March, p. 17.

Pearlman, J. 2009. 'Rudd backs Obama push in Afghanistan', *Sydney Morning Herald*, 3 December, p. 2.

Rudd, K. 2002. Second Reading Speech on International Criminal Court Bill 2002, House of Representatives, *Debates*, pp. 4329–34.

Rudd, K. 2006. 'Faith in politics', *The Monthly*, vol. 17.

Rudd, K. 2008a. *National Security Statement*, Commonwealth of Australia, Canberra.

Rudd, K. 2008b. It's time to build an Asian Pacific community, Address to the Asia Society AustralAsia Centre, Sydney.

Sainsbury, M. 2010. 'Jailing of two Chinese steel executives ends Rio Tinto's bribery saga', *The Australian*, 9 August, p. 26.

Scott, K. 1999. *Gareth Evans*, Allen & Unwin, Sydney.

Shanahan, D. 2007. 'Rudd would charge Iran's leader', *The Australian*, 3 October, p. 1.

Shanahan, D. 2010. 'Downgrade APEC, says Rudd', *The Australian*, 20 May, p. 2.

Sheridan, G. 2004. 'Howard abandons his push for UN Security Council seat', *The Australian*, 29 January, p. 4.

Sheridan, G. 2006. *The Partnership: The inside story of the US–Australian alliance under Bush and Howard*, UNSW Press, Sydney.

Sheridan, G. 2009. 'Kevin Rudd is a global player', *The Australian*, 13 November, p. 13.

Stuart, N. 2010. *Rudd's Way: November 2007–June 2010*, Scribe, Melbourne.

Stubbs, R. 2008. 'The ASEAN alternative? Ideas, institutions and the challenge to "global" governance', *The Pacific Review*, vol. 21, no. 4, pp. 451–68.

Thayer, C. 2009. Kevin Rudd's Asia-Pacific community initiative: suggestions and insights for the future process of East Asian regional cooperation, Presentation to International Conference on East Asia and South Pacific in Regional Cooperation, The Shanghai Institute of International Affairs, People's Republic of China.

Tubilewicz, C. 2010. 'The 2009 Defence White Paper and the Rudd government's response to China's rise', *Australian Journal of Political Science*, vol. 45, no. 1, pp. 149–57.

Ungerer, C. 2010. 'Foreign policy debate is missing', *The Canberra Times*, 12 April, p. 9.

Walters, P. 2008a. 'Kevin Rudd Asian plan "dead in the water"', *The Australian*, 4 June.

Walters, P. 2008b. 'Defence caves in on white paper', *The Australian*, 15 November, p. 2.

Weisser, R. 2008. 'Rudd slashes old department's budget', *The Australian*, 15 January.

White, H. 2009. 'Muddled report leaves gaps in our defence', *The Australian*, 4 May.

Part IV. Rudd as Prime Minister

14. The rise and fall of the magic kingdom: understanding Kevin Rudd's domestic statecraft

MARK EVANS

> There is nothing more difficult to take in hand, more perilous to conduct, or more uncertain in its success, than to take the lead in the introduction of a new order of things. (Niccolo Machiavelli, *The Prince*, Chapter 6, para 5)

> Clearly politics has its own momentum but you have to keep one eye on the rear-vision mirror. That's where the lessons of history are to be found and by any measure the election of 2007 was political history. (Jones 2008:ix)

If 2007 was considered a progressive landmark in Australian political history, 2010 would prove to be one of its low points. The collapse in the support for the Australian Labor Party (ALP) at the August election demonstrated the damage the party has done to itself in the eyes of many voters by allowing factional ambition to undermine representative and responsible government and to determine that the firing of prime ministers should rest with the party rather than the public.

Most assessments of Kevin Rudd's demise as the twenty-sixth Prime Minister of Australia after two years and 204 days in power have tended to focus on the role of his 'troublesome' personality in undermining his power base and ultimately his legacy. He has variously been accused of being 'a man of words, but little else' (Nethercote 2010), governing 'as a state premier' (Crabb 2010), of being 'a fraudulent facsimile of the real thing' (Penberthy 2009), a 'control freak' (Kelly 2010), and being 'a politician with rage at his core' (Marr 2010a:4). This last characterisation was expressed in David Marr's essay 'Power Trip: The political journey of Kevin Rudd', when he also observed:

> Leaders aren't there to be liked. Being an arsehole is no bar to high office. They always disappoint. The public understands this. And people know the climb to power can be bloody. Such things are forgiven if it all proves worthwhile. But of Rudd it has to be said that there is a large number of people who, having worked with him as a diplomat, public servant, shadow minister, leader of the opposition or lately as prime minister, loathe the man. Between the verdicts of the public and those who come to know him face to face, there is a curiously wide gulf…[There is a] fundamental question about Rudd that remains unanswered: who is he?

This essay could well represent the tipping point in Rudd's political fortunes as it gave rise to concerted internal party opposition to his leadership. Marr's devastating critique concludes that 'Kevin Rudd remains hidden in full view'. In evaluating the making of Kevin Rudd as a force in Australian politics back in 2007, Simon Mann was asked to reflect on his operating style in the inner sanctum of the reformist government under the then Queensland Labor Premier, Wayne Goss, and came up with a similar conclusion to Marr's:

> Methodical, process-driven and naturally conservative, Rudd was to many people the proverbial man on a mission. Many found his style abrasive and uncompromising, and Goss himself has conceded that Rudd was at times during those torrid years in Queensland a bit of a bastard, 'because sometimes you have to be if you want to make a difference'. (Mann 2008:14)

While there can be no doubt that personality is an important resource of prime ministerial power and, by implication, is a liability if it is absent, it needs to be understood within the broader set of powers and constraints that operate in and on the core executive in the 'OzMinster' system.'OzMinster' is a term used by Ken Matthews AO, retiring Chief Executive of the National Water Commission, in his valedictory address, 6 October 2010, at Old Parliament House. He went on to argue: 'In my view we should be proud of our uniquely Australian model of public administration. For me the fact that it has evolved so far from its Westminster origins is thoroughly positive.' This chapter offers a simple corrective in this regard. It argues that our traditional understanding of prime ministerial power as exercised through cabinet government tends to oversimplify relationships within complex decision-making centres. Indeed, the Rudd debacle clearly demonstrates that sustainable prime ministerial power rests on the incumbent's recognition that their powerbase is determined by a broad set of resource dependencies. Resource dependence theory in this context refers to those resources that a prime minister needs to govern effectively and legitimately. In combination, they provide the key source of prime ministerial power or impotence which in the Australian context includes at least four dimensions: the core executive territory, media relations, the citizenry and the Prime Minister's party itself. In short, as soon as Rudd lost sight of the importance of these resource dependencies, he started to lose his grip on power.

This argument is developed in two parts. Part one begins by situating the study within the context of debates about prime ministerial power. It highlights the importance of understanding power relations in the core executive territory as the product of the interactive relationship between structure (social, institutional and political) and agency (politics) and argues that resource dependency provides the critical variable for understanding this relationship. It then identifies the ingredients of effective and, by implication, ineffective statecraft in order to understand the fall of Kevin Rudd. Part two then applies this framework to the Rudd administration. The constraints of space make it impossible to examine each dimension of statecraft with the detail of scrutiny and analysis that it deserves. What follows is therefore an intentionally simple, selective and critical guide to the Rudd government.

On statecraft and resource dependency

> What is statecraft? The crude answer is that it is the art of winning elections and achieving some necessary degree of governing competence in office. (Bulpitt 1986a:19–39)

Traditionally, the study of prime ministerial power has centred on the prime ministerial government (Crossman 1963; Hennessy 1986, 2000) versus the cabinet government theses (Rhodes et al. 2009:83). The prime ministerial government thesis views executive government as the exertion of the Prime Minister's powers or what has also been referred to as 'monocratic government'. On what empirical basis is this claim justified? Usually, reference is made to the Prime Minister's significant powers of patronage and his/her capacity to shape the political complexion of government and set the policy agenda; access to superior knowledge resources; the ability to shape the Public Service; political visibility; and party leadership. Paul Keating, for example, has often been cited as the personification of this style of government: 'a domineering prime minister with little interest in the process of government' (Rhodes et al. 2009:83).

Conversely, the cabinet government thesis focuses on the two key powers of the Prime Minister—patronage and his/her control of the agenda—and argues that these powers are severely constrained. In Australia, prime ministerial dominance has been a key feature of executive government since World War I (Weller 2007). Crucially, however, the key source of their powers emanates from cabinet itself. As Rhodes et al. (2009:82–3) observe in their magisterial comparison of executive government in Westminster-style democracies, '[f]ew would deny that a centralisation of government occurred under John Howard…Howard was a traditionalist who did not bypass cabinet or the regular "party room" meetings… [but h]is prime ministerial dominance was based on cabinet'.

As Kelly (2005:3) notes, 'good prime ministers must be good team leaders', and he cites Malcolm Fraser (1975–83), Bob Hawke (1983–91) and John Howard (1996–2007) as the exemplars in this regard. Weller (1992:5, 27) observes that 'executive government is collective in its form and its expectations' and 'the development of cabinet government to a higher level of activity and authority has…been a crucial factor in extending the prime minister's authority and span of control'. Thus, Rhodes et al. (2009:83) conclude that 'despite different styles of leadership, Australia continues to produce cabinet government under its various prime ministers'.

There are four key problems with this debate: it is irresolvable (every example of monocratic government can be trumped with an example of cabinet government); it assumes power is a zero-sum game that either the Prime Minister or the cabinet possesses; it simplifies relationships within complex decision-making centres and suggests that the Prime Minister has the capacity to govern solely through the Department of the Prime Minister and Cabinet (PM&C); it ignores broader institutional, political and economic factors including federalism; and it overemphasises issues of personality. So, is there an alternative framework of analysis?

The more compelling work on the core executive focuses on different conceptions of dependency. David Marr's (2010a) account of the Rudd government, for example, develops a form of prime ministerial clique thesis focusing on policy making by cabal or an 'inner' or 'kitchen' cabinet of Kevin Rudd, Julia Gillard, Wayne Swan and Lindsay Tanner. An alternative would be to apply a segmented decision model of executive government (Rose 2001). This approach recognises that the Prime Minister and members of cabinet operate in different policy arenas. Ministers operate below interdepartmental level, while the Prime Minister operates primarily in the areas of strategic development, defence, foreign affairs, and the economy. Hence, power-dependency relationships exist between the Prime Minister and his colleagues in these areas and across the other portfolios of government. This approach stresses the complex nature of contemporary decision making in the core executive, arguing that it is simply not possible for a prime minister to adopt a presidential-style of leadership and stay on top of the job. Or at least, they would do so at their peril!

Martin Smith's (1994) alternative model of prime ministerial power follows a similar cue and formulates a dependency thesis following Rhodes (1995) and Dunleavy and Rhodes (1990) that centres on the contingent power of the Prime Minister. Smith contends that prime ministerial/cabinet relations operate within an institutional and political context underpinned by resource dependencies (see Figure 14.1). By implication, the relative powers of prime minister and cabinet are contingent on the institutional and political context. In certain periods, prime ministers will enjoy enhanced autonomy (in the aftermath of a successful election campaign, for instance) and might even exhibit presidential characteristics; however, their long-term survival rests on the development of strong working relationships with their ministerial colleagues, the Public Service and their party. Smith's characterisation of executive government recognises the importance of resource dependency to the art of governing, or what Jim Bulpitt (1986a, 1986b) has termed 'statecraft'. Now this is an important argumentative turn in this chapter. Smith's analysis takes us only so far in developing a model of prime ministerial power. We also require an insight into the ingredients of effective and, by implication, ineffective statecraft in order to understand the fall of Kevin Rudd, and the concept of resource dependency provides only part of the answer.

So what does statecraft involve? The approach was originally developed by the British political scientist Jim Bulpitt in 1986 and has subsequently been applied by others (see Buller 2000). It emerged in response to a number of authors who stressed the importance of the 'new right' ideological project as an understanding of the emergence and development of Thatcherism in the United Kingdom (see Hall and Jacques 1983). Bulpitt disagreed with writers such as Hall and Jacques that the new-right project provided the grand design of the Thatcher project and shaped the nature of the policy agenda. He argued that ideas themselves were never that important. Instead, he emphasised the importance of what he termed statecraft or the 'politics of governing'.

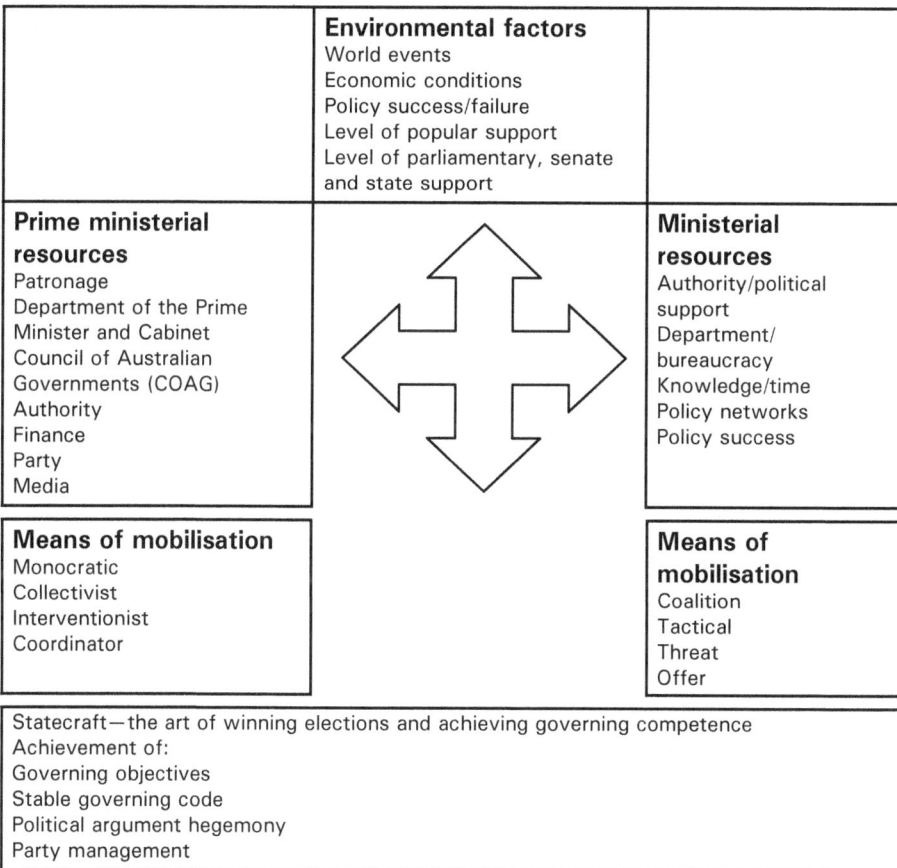

	Environmental factors World events Economic conditions Policy success/failure Level of popular support Level of parliamentary, senate and state support	
Prime ministerial resources Patronage Department of the Prime Minister and Cabinet Council of Australian Governments (COAG) Authority Finance Party Media		**Ministerial resources** Authority/political support Department/ bureaucracy Knowledge/time Policy networks Policy success
Means of mobilisation Monocratic Collectivist Interventionist Coordinator		**Means of mobilisation** Coalition Tactical Threat Offer
Statecraft—the art of winning elections and achieving governing competence Achievement of: Governing objectives Stable governing code Political argument hegemony Party management		

Figure 14.1 A resource-dependency model of prime ministerial power

Note: This is an interactive model in the sense that these sets of variables do not exist in a vacuum; *they interact in complex and often unexpected ways.*

Source: Developed from Smith (1994) and Bulpitt (1986a).

Statecraft crystallises around the study of a core political elite, which Bulpitt (1986a, 1986b, 1995) refers to as 'the centre' or 'the court', composed of party leaders and senior public servants and policy advisers. He argues that this group has its own interests, which are distinct from the rest of society's, and they can often successfully pursue these interests, even in the face of opposition from other actors. In other words, the statecraft approach represents an elite theory of public policy making.

According to Bulpitt, there are three conditions of successful statecraft (see Figure 14.2). First, the centre/court needs to establish a set of governing objectives with the aim of winning elections and retaining office by achieving an image of governing competence. Second, in order to achieve these objectives, it has to develop a governing code—a set of principles, beliefs and practices. This involves the preservation and promotion of domestic autonomy over what Bulpitt calls 'high politics', and the devolution of delivery responsibility to 'low politics'. In practical terms, high politics refers to all those policy issues that the centre considers to be vital to its chances of winning elections and achieving an image of governing competence, so that autonomy over high politics is crucial to the achievement of governing competence. Low politics is a residual category. It refers to all the other matters perceived by the centre to be too mundane, difficult or time consuming to handle. Third, in trying to win elections and achieve some semblance of governing competence, the centre/court will employ a set of 'political support mechanisms' to assist the governing code. These mechanisms refer to the functions of party management and the achievement of political argument hegemony. As Bulpitt (1986a:22) puts it, this refers to 'a winning rhetoric in a variety of locations, winning because either the framework of the party's arguments becomes generally acceptable, or because its solutions to a particularly important political problem seem more plausible than its opponents".

In short, then, statecraft is about the politics of governing. It involves short-term tactical manoeuvring—qualities that are essential to every successful electoral strategy. It is also concerned with longer-term strategic calculation and action. For Bulpitt, governments can think strategically and alter institutions and structures to help them achieve their political goals more easily. The most high-profile illustrations of the application of the statecraft approach in a Westminster-style democracy can be found under Margaret Thatcher in the United Kingdom (1979–90) and the long period of Coalition rule under John Howard in Australia (1996–2007).Bulpitt applied this theory to British 'historical politics' across the twentieth century, identifying three statecraft regimes (1922–61, 1960s–78 and 1979–91) and sets of governing codes and political support mechanisms that delivered successful statecraft (see Bulpitt 1986a, 1986b, 1995). Both projects achieved dominance in high politics, combined with a necessary degree of governing competence thereby ensuring electoral dominance. Both projects were driven largely by pragmatism—owing more to the need to maintain electoral success than to appeal to a particular ideology. Although the statecraft approach remains theoretically underdeveloped, it does provide the contours for an elite theory of domestic statecraft that emphasises the role of the party political elite in forwarding a strategy for winning the war of political ideas and maintaining electoral success. A comprehensive theory would, however, involve a detailed operational exposition of the concepts of political argument hegemony, governing competence, polity management and strategy. Moreover, it can be argued that the statecraft characterisation has particular traction in an 'OzMinster' system where there is a three-year electoral cycle, the window of opportunity for policy change is rarely open for more than two years at a time and the next election campaign is always on the horizon.

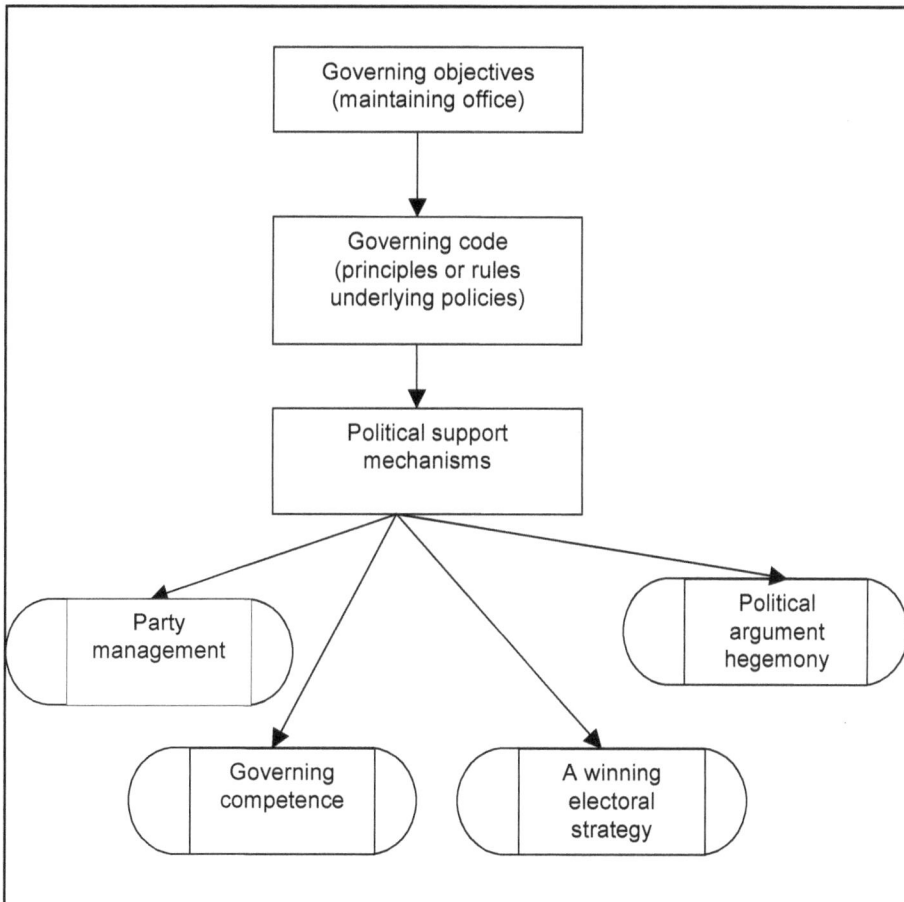

Figure 14.2 The statecraft approach

The following evaluation of Kevin Rudd's domestic statecraft will be organised around the four key dimensions of the statecraft approach: the achievement of governing objectives; the establishment of a stable governing code; political argument hegemony; and party management. It is argued that these dimensions of prime ministerial power are sustainable in contemporary government only if underpinned by the concept of resource dependency.

Kevin07: Rudd ascendant — governing objectives

> We're here to serve the government of the day regardless of its politics; but we couldn't help feeling excited at the prospects of a Rudd government after such a long period of Howard rule. (Author interview with former senior public servant)

Successful statecraft requires the achievement of governing objectives: the ability to win and maintain power through demonstrating governing competence. In his resignation speech, Rudd summarised his perception of the government's major achievements (see Box 14.1). The list is notable for the number of early successes and in terms of the large-scale reforms for delivery failure. Moreover, certain of these early wins would later suffer severe setbacks. The early successes included: signing the Kyoto Protocol to limit greenhouse gas emissions (3 December 2007); the welcome to country from local Aboriginal people at the opening of Australia's forty-second Parliament (13 February 2008); a parliamentary apology led by the Prime Minister for the effect of past government policies on Indigenous people (14 February 2008). In his resignation speech, he stated that he was 'most proud' of this achievement, noting that 'the apology was unfinished business for our nation. It is the beginning of new business for our nation.' Nonetheless, in the main, these policies symbolised a clear break with the Howard years, as Judith Brett (2008:6) puts it, 'from age to youth, from fear to hope, from private to public'. They also provided a strong early signal that this was a prime minister intent on achieving governing objectives. At the same time, it should be noted that of the 23 'achievements' listed in Box 14.1, only 12 were actually completed at the time of the speech. The remainder were works in progress, or, at worst, announcements of future endeavours.

What is also significant about the list is the number of activities in the area of economic management. As George Megalogenis (2008:47) has put it, however, 'economic management is of course the oxymoron of modern politics. The notion that federal governments manage the economy in the same way that a chief executive would run a business is, frankly, delusional.' Nevertheless, creating the image of sound economic management remains, for the most part, the key ingredient of electoral success. Indeed, the 2010 election result would undermine the old shibboleth for understanding voting behaviour—'it's the economy, stupid!'—clearly illustrating that these have been exceptional times. The Rudd government does deserve credit for avoiding recession, which allowed Rudd and Swan to engender the rhetoric of sound economic management at every available opportunity: 'we've set a new benchmark for responsible economic management…better than any other major advanced economy' (McLennan and Cronin 2010:4). In sum, favourable economic circumstances harnessed through prompt economic management provided the Rudd government with the best possible conditions for affecting successful statecraft.

A stable governing code

> Before too long it became evident that the only time we were able to really move things on was when the Prime Minister was out of the country and Julia was in charge. (Former senior public servant, Interview with author)

Successful statecraft, in the main, requires the establishment of a stable governing code throughout the core executive—clear and consistent messages—which can be easily transferred into policy and provide the court with a source of cohesiveness and purpose. It should also provide the essential glue for resource dependency to work as the first principle of governing. The Rudd government fell short of the mark in three main respects in this regard: its failure to govern through cabinet; its inability to develop a strong working relationship with the Public Service at the heart of the core executive; and the absence of a coherent governing code or reform agenda.

First, Rudd failed to empower his cabinet to implement the governing code. As David Marr reflects:

> Well as I understand it, Cabinet doesn't really work any longer…there are Cabinet meetings, but Cabinet is for the most part presented with the decisions that have been taken by what's now commonly called the 'Gang of Four', which is Rudd, Gillard, Swan and Tanner…It has become more and more concentrated power and the administration of the country, more and more concentrated in Rudd's own hands and in the hands of people very close to him. (Marr 2010b:1)

As Trinca et al. (2010:2) observed in the aftermath of Rudd's fall, a senior bureaucrat informed them that 'Rudd was so determined to handle everything himself that his office became a giant black hole'. He was accused of 'failing to move the paper', of asking staff to engage in resource-intensive work 'with no apparent purpose', of treating staff 'as if diseased'. In his own words, the Prime Minister failed to affect 'a new paradigm in Australian governance'. Indeed, the use of the very un-Australian word 'paradigm' would become a metaphor for the failure of his style of leadership within the senior echelons of the Public Service.

Box 14.1 Rudd on Rudd

We kept Australia out of recession. Had we not, half a million people would have been out of work.

We got rid of WorkChoices and restored decency to the work place.

We started to build the nation's infrastructure including the National Broadband Network, which will transform the economy in ways we have yet to conceive.

We began the education revolution—300,000 extra computers in classrooms.

We now have trade centres built to service every one of the nation's secondary schools.

New school libraries are springing up across the country, often in schools that have never had one.

We now have nationwide early childhood education.

We now have a national curriculum.

We now have 50,000 more university places and have invested so much more in our universities, in our research.

We have reformed the health system; a national health and hospitals network…[the new funding arrangements will be seen as a] very, very deep reform.

We are building 20 regional cancer centres right across our country.

We now have a National Organ Transplant Authority.

We have restored decency to the aged pension. The $100 extra is the biggest increase ever.

We now have paid parental leave.

We are on track to halve homelessness in the country.

We are adding 20,000 additional units of social housing.

We signed the Kyoto Protocol.

We boosted the renewable energy target to 20 per cent.

We tried three times to get an emissions trading system through parliament.

We now have a Murray Basin Authority and for the first time in our history have a basin-wide plan and a basin-wide cap on water.

On the global stage Australia is now at the table of the G20. We lobbied hard and long for that. It is a good achievement for Australia for the future.

We are closing the gap between indigenous and non-indigenous Australians.

We greeted the Stolen Generations.

Source: *The Australian*, 24 June 2010, <http://www.theaustralian.com.au/full-transcript-of-kevin-rudds-farewell-speech/story-fn5vfgwx-1225883796571>

Second, Rudd's ill-conceived decision in May 2008 to declare war on the Public Service in response to a cabinet leak exposed to public view what had hitherto been the subject only of Canberra gossip: the Prime Minister's limited interpersonal skills (see, for example, ABC 2008; Fraser and Hannon 2008; Lewis and Rehn 2008; McDonnell 2008). Rudd attacked the Public Service for its lack of work ethic, demanding a '24/7' commitment and stating that 'the public demands it!'. During the episode, Rudd noted that one of his staff had commented recently that one year with him was akin to a 'dog year'—equal to seven 'human years'. The fact that Rudd viewed this to be a compliment is cause for concern. It is unsurprising therefore that the Department of the Prime Minister and Cabinet (PM&C) had a 53 per cent turnover in staff in less than a year, leading one policy advisor to note that 'PM&C was once the place to be; now it's the place not to be' (Former senior public servant, Interview with author). For Rudd, 'it was a storm in a teacup', but for many senior public servants it was an affront to their professionalism and integrity that would not be forgiven or forgotten. He had created an enemy within.

Third, one of Rudd's most glaring weaknesses was his inability to remain focused on the candle of seeing reforms through by dealing with a few significant reforms at a time before moving on. Moreover, his reluctance to empower colleagues to get on with the job was a recipe for created confusion; witness the problems with climate change and home insulation. Within months of Labor winning power, the Prime Minister was instead busy declaring war on everything and everybody: drugs, unemployment, doping in sport, bankers' salaries, whalers, climate change, inflation, water management, housing, free trade with China, the US alliance, cooperative federalism—all became 'priority issues'. Indeed, Rudd's attempts to crystallise these exhaustive and exhausting reform efforts into a stable governing code became increasingly over-intellectualised and desperate, culminating in his highly publicised essay in The Monthly in which he declared that 'the great neo-liberal experiment of the past 30 years has failed' and 'the challenge for social democrats today is to recast the role of the state'. That he would choose a 7000-word treatise in a literary magazine to win hearts and minds is indicative of his increasing detachment from the body politic.

Political argument hegemony

> Certainly, Kevin Rudd has big rhetoric, but, looking closely at his policy initiatives, not yet a huge amount to back it up. Policy for policy, the government still resembles the one which was elected in 2007. The big ticket items have either failed to emerge (the national broadband network) or have been dramatically watered down or delayed such as the government's emissions trading scheme. (Berg 2010:1)

As Chris Berg (2010:1) argues, a further weakness in the statecraft of Kevin Rudd can be identified with his attempts to maintain political argument hegemony after his initial honeymoon period. This was reflected in the disparity between Rudd's rhetoric and his record of delivery. Although Berg overstates his case—as there have been no shortages of policy initiatives under Rudd—he is right to highlight the Prime Minister's inability to see the major policy items through to implementation. Rudd alienated the electorate and, most significantly, radicalised opposition within his own party as a consequence of seven policy debacles in a relatively short period.

- Emissions Trading Scheme: Rudd declared it the 'great moral issue of our time' and then deferred the legislation until 2012.
- Refugees: Rudd stopped the processing of applications from Sri Lankans and Afghans who arrived by boat.
- Home insulation: Rudd announced that 2.2 million Australian homes would get free ceiling insulation, revamped the scheme following deaths and fires, and then scrapped the program in April 2010.
- Building the Education Revolution: The primary school building program costing $16.2 billion for 8000 schools was heavily criticised by an Australian National Audit Office (ANAO) report for a range of inefficiencies.
- Child care: Rudd quietly dumped his election pledge to build 260 childcare centres on school grounds to end 'the double drop-off' for parents.
- Northern Territory Intervention: Rudd continued a Howard policy that some claimed institutionalised apartheid in Australia.
- Mining Super Profits Tax: Rudd was unable to see the tax through in the face of mounting industry and media pressure and problems of internal party management.

Source: David Pope, *The Canberra Times*, 28 April 2010.

All of these debacles were characterised by a common error of judgment: Rudd raised expectations for progressive change and failed to deliver. Moreover, even in those areas where progress was made in the short term—for example, the apology to the 'Stolen Generations' or the emissions trading scheme—Rudd did not have the courage to see the policy through. For example, despite Rudd's apology on behalf of the Parliament to Australia's Stolen Generations for past government policies and practices of forcible removal, the Labor government is yet to deliver practical policy and funding initiatives to support reconciliation initiatives and other reparations for the Stolen Generations. Further, despite declaring the treatment of carbon emissions as the 'great moral issue of our time', he deferred the legislation until 2012 without a whisper of regret.

In sum, the failure to maintain political argument hegemony and thus the momentum of reform was a key failing of Rudd's statecraft. This required courageous leadership. As Tony Blair reflects in his autobiography:

> The lesson is also instructive: if you think a change is right, go with it. The opposition is inevitable, but rarely is it unbeatable. There will be many silent supporters as well as the many vocal detractors. And leadership is all about the decisions that change. If you can't handle that, don't become a leader. And the lesson goes wider: it is about rising above the fray, learning how to speak above the din and clatter, and about always, always, keeping focused on the big picture. (Blair 2010:94)

Party management

We cannot be sure of course, but available evidence appears to suggest that most members of cabinet were ignorant that a coup against Rudd was afoot. Not only does this reveal the illegitimate nature of the process of leadership renewal in so far as it was forced through in the most brutal way by a handful of conspirators, it also shows that their—Victorian Lower House MP Bill Shorten, Victorian Senator David Feeney and NSW Senator and former NSW State Secretary Mark Arbib—judgment on the hiring and firing of a prime minister was sovereign. I will leave others to consider the constitutional implications of this development, but it has more in common with a feudal regime than a representative liberal democracy.

It is evident, however, that Rudd's landslide victory in 2007 created a 'Magic Kingdom' effect at the heart of Australian government in the sense that it lulled Rudd into a false sense of security and masked the fact that his relationship with the party caucus was built on continued electoral success. Christine Jackman traces Rudd's fall from the publication of 'Power Trip: The political journey of Kevin Rudd':

Months earlier…Marr could scarcely have anticipated the political tinderbox into which he would eventually drop his crackling conclusion that the Australian prime minister was 'a politician with rage at his core'. But by midyear Rudd's remarkable personal approval ratings had collapsed, dragging down Labor's lead in the polls, and the mood in the caucus was febrile. Marr's rage thesis gave the mob, fearful for its political life, a rhetorical rallying point around which it could muster and finally canvass openly its angst—and worse—about its once untouchable leader. (Jackman 2010:1)

By the end of that month, Rudd would be gone.

Parting shots: the sorcerer's apprentice

In politics, what a leader does in achieving positive social and economic outcomes for the citizenry should be the basis on which their legacy is assessed rather than issues of personality. Unfortunately, this is rarely the case in practice. Perceptions are everything in politics. History will look more kindly on the Rudd legacy if the Gillard government is able to complete the reformation 'from age to youth, from fear to hope, from private to public' (Brett 2008:6), but it will fail to understand why the momentum for progressive change was lost so quickly after Rudd created so much political capital in his honeymoon period.

This cursory evaluation of the fall of the Rudd government has clearly demonstrated the value of the statecraft approach in exposing the ingredients of sustainable prime ministerial power anchored in the concept of resource dependency: the achievement of governing objectives; the establishment of a stable governing code; political argument hegemony; and party management. Kevin Rudd was not brought down by external events. Indeed, his government's handling of the global financial crisis (GFC), the signing of the Kyoto Protocol and the elevation of Australia to the G-20 are signature themes of his brief tenure as prime minister. Nor did he fall on the wrong side of the ideological battlelines in his party, for it remains a confection of strange bedfellows. Moreover, it would be ludicrous to claim that Tony Abbott's rejuvenation of the Coalition did anything more than make a dent in Rudd's fortunes as Prime Minister. So where does the preponderance of evidence lie? If Rudd as Minister for Foreign Affairs is not to repeat the mistakes of Rudd as Prime Minister, what lessons must he learn? First, he must not lose sight of the importance of his resource dependency on his party where he was always an outsider and will continue to be so. Second, he must not lose sight of his resource dependency on his cabinet colleagues and the advice and goodwill of his public servants and operate in a silo when progressive reform requires a whole-of-government approach and broad ownership. Third, he must not lose sight of his resource dependency on the Australian public, who welcomed him to power as if a prodigal son in 2007. Fourth, he must have the courage of his convictions and engage in courageous leadership. Rudd will always be known as the Prime Minister who failed to deliver on three of his big ideas: the carbon pollution reduction scheme, the emissions trading scheme and the mining super profits tax.

As the consequences of his inaction gained momentum, Kevin Rudd became the sorcerer's apprentice in Walt Disney's *Fantasia*, desperately trying to stem the tide of opposition. Rudd's Magic Kingdom became disconnected from party, politics and ultimately the core executive itself. It was born from electoral success and died due to fatal conceit.

Mark Evans *is Director of the ANZSOG Institute for Governance at the University of Canberra.*

References

Australian Broadcasting Corporation (ABC) 2008. 'Rudd tones down public servant blast', *The World Today*, ABC Online, 30 May.

Berg, C. 2010. 'Keeping up with Kevin: Kevin Rudd's testosterone technocracy', *IPA Review*, <www.ipa.org.au/publications/1661/keeping-up-with-kevin-kevin-rudd%27s-testosterone-technocracy>

Blair, T. 2010. *The Journey*, Random House, London.

Brett, J. 2008. 'The turning tide', in T. Jones (ed.), *The Best Australian Political Writing*, Melbourne University Press, Carlton, Vic., pp. 6–12.

Buller, J. 2000. *National Statecraft and European Integration*, Pinter, London.

Bulpitt, J. 1986a. 'The discipline of the new democracy: Mrs Thatcher's domestic statecraft', *Political Studies*, vol. 34, pp. 19–39.

Bulpitt, J. 1986b. 'Continuity, autonomy and peripheralisation: the anatomy of the centre's statecraft in England', in Z. Layton-Henry and P. Rich (eds), *Race, Government and Politics in Britain*, Macmillan, London.

Bulpitt, J. 1995. 'Historical politics: macro, in-time, governing regime analysis', in J. Lovenduski and J. Stanyer (eds), *Contemporary Political Studies 1995. Volume Two*, PSA, Exeter, UK, pp. 510–20.

Crabb, A. 2010. *Rise of the Ruddbot: Observations from the gallery*, Black Inc., Melbourne.

Crossman, R. 1963. 'Introduction', in W. Bagehot, *The English Constitution*, Collins, London.

Dunleavy, P. and Rhodes, R. A. W. 1990. 'Core executive studies in Britain', *Public Administration*, vol. 68, no. 1, pp. 3–28.

Fraser, A. and Hannon, K. 2008. 'Now it's Rudd's war on the PS', *The Canberra Times*, 30 May.

Hall, S. and Jacques, M. 1983. *The Politics of Thatcherism*, Blackwell, Cambridge.

Hennessy, P. 1986. *The Cabinet*, Blackwell, Oxford.

Hennessy, P. 2000. *The Prime Ministers*, Penguin, London.

Jackman, C. 2010. 'Why we still need to talk about Kevin', *The Australian*, 4 August, <www.theaustralian.com.au/news/arts/why-we-still-need-to-talk-about-kevin/story-e6frg8nf-1225900075141>

Jones, T. (ed.) 2008. *The Best Australian Political Writing*, Melbourne University Press, Carlton, Vic.

Kelly, P. 2005. *Rethinking Australian governance—the Howard legacy*, Occasional Paper Series No. 4, Academy of the Social Sciences in Australia, Canberra.

Kelly, P. 2010a. *The March of the Patriots*, Melbourne University Press, Carlton, Vic.

Lewis, S. and Rehn, A. 2008. 'Kevin Rudd: working for me's a dog year', *Daily Telegraph*, 2 June.

McDonnell, J. 2008. 'Public service in revolt', *The Australian*, 2 June.

McLennan, D. and Cronin, D. 2010. 'Calculating an election win', *The Canberra Times*, 15 May.

Mann, S. 2008. 'The making of Kevin Rudd'. In T. Jones (ed.), *The Best Australian Political Writing*, Melbourne University Press, Carlton, Vic., pp. 13–25.

Marr, D. 2010a. 'Power Trip: The political journey of Kevin Rudd', *Quarterly Essay*, June, Black Inc., Melbourne.

Marr, D. 2010b. 'Marr discusses Rudd's "angry heart"', *7.30 Report*, ABC TV, 7 June, <www.abc.net.au/7.30/content/2010/s2920783.htm>

Megalogenis, G. 2008. 'The small picture men', in T. Jones (ed.), *The Best Australian Political Writing*, Melbourne University Press, Carlton, Vic., pp. 47–50.

Nethercote, J. 2010. 'A man of words, but little else', *The Public Sector Informant*, August.

Penberthy, D. 2009. 'Will the real Kevin Rudd please stand up', *The Punch*, 22 September.

Rhodes, R. A. W. 1995. 'From Prime Ministerial power to core executive', in R. A. W. Rhodes and P. Dunleavy (eds), *Prime Minister, Cabinet and Core Executive*, Macmillan, London.

Rhodes, R., Wanna, J. and Weller, P. 2009. *Westminster Compared*, Oxford University Press, Oxford.

Rose, R. 2001. *The Prime Minister in a Shrinking World*, Polity Press, Cambridge.

Smith, M. 1994. 'The core executive and the resignation of Mrs Thatcher', *Public Administration*, vol. 72, no. 3, pp. 341–63.

Trinca, H., Clegg, B., Dusevic, T., Elliott, G., Gluyas, R., Hepworth, A., Kerr, C., Korporaal, G., Megalogenis, G. and McKenna, M. 2010. 'The enemy within', *The Weekend Australian*, 3–4 July.

Weller, P. 1992. *Menzies to Keating: The development of the Australian prime ministership*, Hurst, London.

Weller, P. 2007. *Cabinet Government in Australia, 1901–2006*, UNSW Press, Sydney.

www.ingramcontent.com/pod-product-compliance
Lightning Source LLC
Chambersburg PA
CBHW061243270326
41928CB00041B/3390